THE IMMIGRANT
AND
THE DRUG ADDICT

THE IMMIGRANT
AND
THE DRUG ADDICT

GUY SORMAN

VIKAS PUBLISHING HOUSE PVT LTD

VIKAS PUBLISHING HOUSE PVT LTD
576 Masjid Road, Jangpura, New Delhi 110014

COPYRIGHT © GUY SORMAN, 1993

ISBN 0-7069-6867-0

Translated from the French by
Asha Puri

Typeset by Alfa Computer Centre, Vikas Marg, Delhi - 92.

Printed at Ramprintograph, Delhi.

PREFACE

THE JUDGE, THE IMMIGRANT AND THE ADDICT

Ozeye sits slumped on his chair in the dock. He is
oblivious to his surroundings; curious spectators stare,
lawyers bustle about and judges take their time
coming. Is his real name Ozeye? That is the name he
has given to the police, but with a Ghanian you can
never tell. Besides, he speaks no French. The proceedings
begin. Ozeye's lawyer has again failed to appear. 'This
is the third time in a row,' notes the judge, ' we'll
just have to do without him.' The judge, in fine fettle,
has many clever things to say, all at Ozeye's expense.
It seems he is trying to impress the public prosecutor,
a blue-eyed blond, who makes a show of appreciating
his wit. Policemen grin knowingly at each other; the
verdict is a foregone conclusion: the prosecutor will
be asking for a six year term and that is what Ozeye
will get.

A year ago, Ozeye had been caught selling six
grams of heroin at the Guy Moquet metro station. At
least this much is clear. The state-appointed defense
counsel has taken a cursory look at the case. Forgetful
of her client, she begins with an attack on the police

force as a whole. She then turns her ire against the policeman who trapped Ozeye by posing as a client. What makes things worse is that Ozeye is an illegal immigrant; he has been living in France without papers.

On the benches reserved for the public are a group of schoolchildren who have come to see republican justice at work. Three black teenagers demonstrate their support for Ozeye. The guards get nervous. The judge, weary of his own facetiousness, gets down to business. 'Ozeye, stand up, the Court sentences you to six years imprisonment and subsequent deportation from France.' Ozeye hasn't understood a word. The clerk runs out to find an interpreter. Another life has gone astray. Such scenes are being enacted every day in French courts, or for that matter, in the courts of any bourgeois society.

For months on end, Ozeye's trial pressed into service a host of police inspectors - to arrest and guard him - judges, prosecutors, clerks, lawyers and wardens. Couldn't all this time and public money have been used instead to bring bigger crime to book? Ozeye is after all a mere pawn in the drug and counterfeit trade and must have been replaced almost immediately by another like him . His case throws up a series of questions: are we to assume that today immigrants and opium have become public enemy number one? Or perhaps the colour of Ozeye's skin had something to do with the sentence? How did the judge connect Ozeye's origins with drugs in his mind? Do these two threaten Western culture? Where does the threat come from- the immigration of an alien culture, the ingestion of a foreign substance, or both? Ozeye and drugs are alien - both spell the disruption of bourgeois order. And for many a Frenchman have come to mean barbarism in its latest avatar. 'Each calls barbaric,' wrote Montaigne,'what he is not accustomed to.'

Why is the law so hard on Ozeye when bigger crimes go relatively unpunished? Because his difference is twofold? Because he is a threat to society? Because repression is the only answer an ailing State has to immigration and drugs? Or because the State is using the fight against barbarism to confer fresh legitimacy upon itself? And if all this is true, why does public opinion support the State in its double repression? Do the French really live in fear of immigrants and addicts, or do they need an enemy, a scapegoat? What do liberals, till now quiet, have to say? My contribution to this debate is the present study in which both bourgeois and barbarian views have been reflected. Those who are fed up with political commentaries may read it as a travelogue. We shall be going to Chicago, Peking, Rabat, Amsterdam, Berlin, Tokyo, London, all those cities where modernity is being confronted by the two faces -real or mythical - of barbarism: immigration and drug addiction. Those who will not trouble to read the book will feign surprise or nod their heads reprovingly at my having dealt with drug addicts and immigrants in a single volume. The following pages will clearly bring out that though these are two distinct groups both illustrate how difficult it is for the barbarian and the bourgeois to live with each other. I shall attempt to explain what makes them different and foreign. And if, by some strange quirk, the immigrant and the drug addict get lumped in the same social bracket, it is through no fault of their own, but because both are forced to live the life of an exile.

The people and events that figure in this book are true; in a few cases, names and places have been changed in order to protect the identity of my interlocutors. This journey, which must have begun somewhere in November 1990, ended in June 1992. Let us make the most of the jet age as long as planes fly and borders are open; it is not going to last for ever. In the meanwhile, it would be indecent to stay at home.

CONTENTS

1

THE BLACK DUTCH

At the point where the Prinsengracht and Leliegracht canals meet in Amsterdam stands the unpretentious statue of a childlike figure, a memorial to the martyrdom of Anne Frank. To some it may seem surprising that our journey begins in Holland, a country that does not traditionally find a place in the accounts of French travellers. A mistake I seek to redress! For I have not chosen Holland inadvertently: this was the land that gave birth to free thought, political liberalism and the market economy. Here the State is of moderate dimensions, authority suspect and tolerance de rigueur. The Dutch take neither their land nor their affluence for granted, for every day they have to contend with the seas and the skies. So Anne Frank had been deported, like most Dutch Jews, even though no other European people had resisted the onslaught of Nazism with such resoluteness. But did they do enough? For over fifty years, Anne Frank has been a cult figure, as the Dutch seem incapable of shaking off their remorse.

Never again are they going to allow even a hint of racial discrimination on their soil. So much so that even their speech has been purged of discriminatory terms. In Holland, you don't call immigrants immigrants: they are part of a cultural minority. Every town has its State financed 'anti-racism office', whose job is to take action against any instance of discrimination, whether related to accommodation, jobs or attitudes in general. In schools, multiculturalism is the norm: even if only seven students of a particular minority ask for a special course, Arabic for example, then it is taught. The law allows all religious communities to run their own schools. What held good for Protestant, Catholic and Jewish schools also applies to the Muslim schools. The State foots the bills and leaves the minorities free to run them as they please. Similarly, Turks and Moroccans have been given equal slots on radio and television.

Any immigrant who has lived in the country for five years can vote and stand for elections to the town hall and local bodies in all the major cities. In 1992, Amsterdam had five Moroccan councillors and fifty immigrants sat on representative bodies all over the country. It so happens that most of them are Socialists. In this way, a fourth pillar, Islam, has been added to the three traditional pillars of Dutch society, namely Catholicism, Protestantism and Liberalism. It is this 'pillar' based social organisation which has allowed competing nations and religions to coexist on so small a territory till now. Tolerance, rather the quest for tolerance, is today the officially accepted 'Manifest Destiny' of the Dutch people, a model that has worked uninterruptedly and reasonably well from the seventeenth century till the 1950's. In 1948, just after the decolonisation of Indonesia, some three hundred thousand odd Europeans, 'Euroindonesians' and Javanese

Indonesians poured in to the metropolis and had little difficulty in integrating. In the space of one generation, the Indonesians, despite their slightly darker skins, became almost perfect Dutch citizens. The fact that they knew Dutch, were well educated and came for the most part from the colonial civil or armed services certainly helped. It is also worthwhile noting that the Government had wisely scattered the Indonesian population all over the country; each village school had its Javanese student.

Unfortunately after the Javanese experience, this wonderful system, founded on tolerance, respect for other cultures and integration, suddenly found itself out of gear, inundated by successive waves of immigrants from Surinam, Turkey and Morocco. Amsterdam and Utrecht have yet to experience the baptism of ethnic riots of the kind seen in Brussels, Paris or London, but everyone in Holland is expecting them, as one out of two immigrants - sorry that should read member of a cultural minority - is currently unemployed. Of the four hundred thousand unemployed in the country, twenty percent are 'allochthonous' (the politically correct antonym of 'autochtonous'). 80% of Amsterdam's crimes are committed by the minorities. One prison cell in two houses an 'allochtonous' person, whereas they only constitute five percent of the total population. Figures so embarrassing that Amsterdam's police chief only agreed to tell me all this in the strictest confidence, admitting he would never make such information public. And immigration which had never been an issue in the past has now become one, much to the consternation of the Dutch. Since the early eighties, a xenophobic party (the Zentrum) has managed to catch a few votes and get a representative elected to

Parliament. Extremism is still marginal and Le Pen without a Dutch counterpart, but quite obviously, tolerance alone does not seem to be enough. Then what has gone wrong? In Holland, it is not the xenophobic parties who make the most noise about immigration, as in the rest of Europe, but the immigrants themselves, or rather their representatives. We shall be meeting those who are spearheading the anti-racist campaign. What they are questioning is not immigration but the Dutch, whose 'covert racism' is supposedly the source of all tension.

CAN TOLERANCE BE REPRESSIVE?

Henry Dors enjoys a peaceful middle-class existence in one of the southern suburbs of Amsterdam, in the company of tulips, his books, his blond wife and mixed children. In spite of being born in Surinam fifty years ago and his black skin, he considers himself to be fully Dutch. Any televised debate on immigration without Dors is incomplete. A former teacher who went on to get elected on Amsterdam's municipal council, he is living proof of the fact that one can be 'completely black and completely integrated'. No one in the Netherlands would dare deny him his Dutch-ness, which is why he can forever admonish his fellow citizens for their covert racism. 'Dutch tolerance', Dors informs me,'is "repressive tolerance".' The Dutch, haunted by a sense of guilt, are in fact disturbed to hear this black teacher telling them in perfect Dutch that they are not above suspicion and that their 'repressive tolerance' is leading to the marginalisation of 'cultural minorities'.

Dors would like us to believe that the educational system explains why the cultural minorities lag behind the rest of Holland. As Amsterdam's and Rotterdam's suburban public schools are packed with minority children, the whites send their children to private schools, leading to a dual system of education. Isolated at school itself, the minorities have a hard time adjusting in later life to Dutch society. What does Henry Dors suggest? 'We must recognise that tolerance alone is not enough to put an end to discrimination.' The Dutch government should actively pursue a policy of integration both in schools and the workplace. Dors favours the American system with its clearly defined quotas which compel schools, companies and government offices to take in minorities. In order to ensure a fair ethnic and cultural representation in every school, the Americans have come up with busing, that is taking children by bus beyond their neighbourhood schools for the purposes of desegregation. Dors would like to see busing being introduced in Holland. In actual fact, busing is being hotly contested in the U.S. and quotas are more the exception than the rule. But as it suits their cause, Dutch anti-racist campaigners choose to interpret American style racial integration as a positive experience. Dors' ultimate goal is to produce good, well-integrated Dutch citizens - 'Black Dutch like me! I am,' declares Dors who is certainly not modest,'a living example for my community.'

Philomena Essed, also of Surinam origin, does not share Henry Dors desire for racial integration. She is even more forthright than Dors: nothing could be worse than racism which is not recognised as such. 'The unspoken racism of the Dutch is more insidious than overt racism; not easy to pinpoint it makes dissent very difficult.' The Dutch shy away from dissent, something a firebrand like Philomena Essed finds hard to take. Philomena Essed is a researcher at the Centre for Racial and Ethnic Studies in Amsterdam and is being paid by the very State she denounces. This is just as it should be in a tolerant, democratic society, perhaps its most distinctive feature. Dissidence doesn't cost much in Holland; it is subsidised. Philomena Essed won public acclaim for her remarkable study on racial discrimination, published in 1990. 'Scientific research', she calls it. While analysing the poor work prospects for minorities — the minority unemployment rate is four times higher - she found that lack of education or insufficient command over the language were fifty percent of the reason why they earn less and lag behind professionally as compared to Whites. The other non objective causes cannot be explained, unless viewed in terms of racial discrimination. Dutch employers can discriminate with an easy conscience. As unemployment allowances are generous, they know that the minorities will be able to survive under the benevolent protection of the State. The daily pinpricks do not make life any easier for the minorities. Dutch society is built on small, closed communities of which the minorities can never be a part. Churches, clubs, associations and family are so many cocoons that exclude Surinamians, Moroccans and Turks; pushed back into a twilight zone, they are neither here nor there.

Philomena Essed does not think that integration is any solution. 'Minorities', she storms, 'do not have to integrate. When you talk of integration, it means you have accepted the superiority of Dutch culture over minority culture. On what basis? Minorities don't have to integrate, it's the Dutch who have to do some soul searching. They ought to take a hard look at their own culture, come to terms with their own racism and recognise minority culture has something to offer. Monoculture is a defunct concept that belongs to the nineteenth century. The Dutch are wrong in clinging on to it. In a truly modern society, the objective alliance of the State with the dominant culture must be broken and replaced by the "neutral State and multicultural society." So how does one go about it? First, by destroying archaic educational models. Dutch school children ought to learn that 'mathematics originated in India, that Africans invented philosophy in Egypt and that Christopher Columbus committed genocide'. After which she launches into the usual diatribe against Western society which is 'destroying the environment, imposing its phallicism and annihilating the Third World'. Her tirade is not entirely off the mark, but this enumeration of Western turpitude is so hackneyed that I stop taking notes. This upsets Philomena Essed who asks for a transcript to be sent to her before the book is published. I categorically refuse to do so. Our interview stops there. In any case, there is nothing more to be said.

ON MULTICULTURALISM

Now for a few words on multiculturalism. Somewhere between the votaries of multiculturalism and the staunch upholders of the Dutch, or French or for that matter Western 'identity', we are, to my mind, far more multicultural than we are usually led to believe. First and foremost, because we would be hard pressed to clearly define the culture in which we live. Cultural discourse, like normative discourse, thrives because of its ambiguousness. The most vociferous champions of traditional values would probably tear each other apart were they asked to define or list these. Moreover, culture *per se* is not static but a constant, spontaneous flux. Culture is that which changes. Even if they were to speak the same language, today's secular Westerners would have little in common with the believers of the forties. Finally,   immigration has had a considerable impact on Western norms. Take music, for instance. As teenagers, all Westerners listen to rock and jazz, thereby imbibing Afro-American culture . This music brings about changes in behaviour, gestures, dance and sexuality which owe more to the 'savage' culture of Africa than to the Judeo-Christian model of the Western world. The West may well have colonised Africa, but does it realise to what extent it in turn has been colonised by Afro-American behaviour? It is not for me to say whether this is good or bad; it is enough for the moment to acknowledge the fact and bring the theoretical debate on multiculturalism back to more manageable proportions.

EUROPEAN STATUS FOR IMMIGRANTS

From Amsterdam, let us now move to Utrecht. In Holland, one simply glides across from one city to the next; the country is nothing but a series of interlacing highways, there is no countryside left and windmills seem mere caricatures. Mohammed Rabbae runs a Centre for foreigners in Utrecht. Once again the battle against the State is being financed by the State. Rabbae, the best known spokesman of the Moroccan community in Holland, asks even more of his host country than Philomena Essed. All Philomena Essed wants is multiculturalism, whereas Mohammed Rabbae is asking the Netherlands, the whole of Europe in fact, to become a multinational society. Immigrants should be allowed to retain not only their cultural identity but also their nationality as well as being granted Dutch citizenship. Rabbae concedes however that minorities have more rights in the Netherlands than anywhere else in Europe. Minorities enjoy all the benefits granted to religious communities: state financed Islamic schools, television and radio slots on national networks, teaching Arabic and minority cultures in public schools and the right to vote and stand for local elections. Why then is the minority turnout so low at the time of voting? And more importantly, why are over fifty percent of the immigrants unemployed?

Whatever the law might say, the facts present a different picture altogether. Democracy and the market need to be redefined as in their current form they are not enough to guarantee immigrants full economic and political citizenship. Clearly, for Rabbae, the labour market is unable to absorb immigrants even when the economy is doing well. He concludes that jobs must be reserved for minorities in the administration and companies. Moreover, all immigrants should acquire Dutch citizenship after five years of legal residence in the country, preferably without their having to ask for it; it should be an automatic 'non humiliating' procedure. Along with their newly acquired Dutch citizenship, immigrants must be allowed to retain their original nationality. The Dutch government does not seem averse to such a suggestion. In any case, according to Sherif law one cannot lose one's Moroccan nationality. Going one step further, Rabbae would have the multinationality principle extended to the fifteen million immigrants who are currently living in the European Community. 'For how long can you go on marginalising them and refuse to grant them the same status as other Europeans? Wouldn't it be better to acknowledge that Europe is a geographical entity in which many cultures and nations reside and coexist and that one of these is the Islamic community?' Should we accept Rabbae's argument, then Europe should move from multiculturalism to multinationalism, with no community or nation being able to claim precedence or pre-eminence. What he is suggesting in fact is one big hotel of nations where all can come and go freely without having to integrate or assimilate.

Farfetched?   Not really. For the same demand is being made by Turks in Germany, Indians in England and Latin American communities in California. Today, immigrants are questioning the very principle of the nation-state.

PLEASE DON'T HESITATE TO DENOUNCE THE BOSS

Anti-racism in Holland is not confined to rhetoric alone; it is a policy that is actually put into practice. In every city, Centres for the fight against racism are on the watch. These comfortable government financed institutions employ a large qualified staff, often recruited from among the minorities. What better job could young graduates wanting to reduce 'repressive tolerance' ask for. In Utrecht, the Centre's office is located in a charming building of the old city which also houses an assortment of feminist associations, Third World activists and ecologists. Complainants can either ring up or go over personally. Any complaint of racism gets an attentive hearing. Most complaints, I am told, are job related: working people come and report racist remarks made against them by their bosses or colleagues. In politically correct parlance this is known as ethnic harassment. Another common grievance is that promotions or increments are refused on racial grounds.

The unemployed - the Centre's most frequent visitors - complain that companies refuse to take them on; sometimes their applications are not even considered. How is the veracity of their claims to be ascertained? That is the purpose of an interview with the anti-racist brigade at the Utrecht Centre. It is not as if the minorities are perennially complaining, quite the reverse in fact. The Utrecht Centre is languishing for want of victims. To remedy the situation, the Centre has to go scouting; it approaches doctors, lawyers and the police and tells them how to identify and report back cases of discrimination. They do not stop at racial discrimination, women and homsexuals too are welcomed at the Centre.

Once presented with an open-and-shut case of discrimination, what does the Centre do? It agitates. For example, it will write to the employer demanding- and always getting - an interview. 'Can we discuss the matter?' is the line normally used by anti-racist activists with companies, making it hard for them to say no. At the very worst, the Centre will prompt the victim to file a complaint against his boss or landlord; in which case, it will pay for the lawyer and the legal proceedings. But things rarely reach such a point, as even in a country like Holland overburdened courts give the lowest priority to such cases. To the extent possible, the anti-racist brigade of Utrecht tries to prevent rather than aggravate conflicts. The Centre has to this end drawn up a code of good conduct intended for employers likely to discriminate inadvertently. The first code, published in 1991, was sent to temporary employment agencies in the habit of 'forgetting' to forward the names of 'minority' employees. The Javanese lady in charge of the Centre constantly reminds me that the employer is not an enemy but a partner. Everything is very civilized. The place looks more like a boardroom than a radical commando type hideout.

What are the achievements of these anti-racist centres? 'When they were first set up in 1985,' I am informed,'even mentioning the word discrimination was taboo. Now at least people are talking about it. We have made some progress.'

IN PRAISE OF NATIONAL IDENTITY

So far we have been listening to what the votaries of anti-racism and multiculturalism have to say, for they are the dominant voice. But is there anyone willing to espouse the cause of national identity? Yes, even though such people are a dying breed. At the Erasmus University of Rotterdam, the sociologist Mart-Jan De Jong is considered a crank and shunned because he is perhaps the only one in the Dutch University establishment to defend cultural assimilation. 'All sociological study on immigration and national culture has come to a grinding halt, as my colleagues insist on appearing progressive and politically correct.' De Jong had invited me to lunch, but so as not to run into his fellow researchers at the cafeteria, all we had was a sandwich in his office.

Mart-Jan De Jong holds that multiculturalism is mystification twice over. The minorities mystify the Dutch and themselves. 'What they don't seem to realise is the extent to which they have been assimilated by the simple fact of living in Dutch society.' The Indonesians have merged completely; it will take a little longer for the Anatolion Turks and the Moroccans who didn't speak the language when they came, but they will pick it up soon enough. That means that in Holland as in France it would take about three generations for a Surinamian or a Moroccan to become a full fledged Dutch citizen, even if he is as black as Henry Dors. Besides, says Mart-Jan De Jong, multiculturalism does not exist anywhere. A society cannot function unless it has a common core of values around which each can gravitate in a halo of tolerance. For De Jong this is elementary sociology. Unfortunately no one seems to share this view in Holland for fear of being branded racist. De Jong concludes that racism is not the main reason for the marginalisation of coloured minorities: 'racial conflicts have objective causes which only time can mitigate'.

So far, so good. Integration over three generations is something we understand. However Moroccans settled in Holland do not want to become Dutch. And even if, through a kind of osmosis, they are finally assimilated in spite of themselves, what should one do in the meantime? Just waiting and watching - which may well be the case - could lead to violence. That brings the Dutch back to square one: why is fifty percent of the minority population unemployed? Is this dangerous? Chan Choenni, a young sociologist from the University of Utrecht, has a concrete answer even though it may not be politically correct. He can afford not to be politically correct - he is not white.

WHY WORK WHEN YOU DON'T HAVE TO?

Choenni too comes from Surinam, but he is of Indian origin. Surinamians do not, according to Choenni, share the Dutch work ethic. In Surinam, work is functional. One only looks for a job if one really has to, never for moral or social reasons. Now, very often there is no need to work in Holland, Europe's most providential state. About one million Dutch - 'unable to work' - are getting a State allowance equal to seventy percent of the last pay drawn. This amount is paid by the State till the age of retirement, even if the beneficiary is on long holiday out of the country. The grounds on which such premature retirement benefits are usually granted are backache, fatigue and depression. In 1991, the Prime Minister, after a vain attempt at reform, threatened to resign if the number of beneficiaries crossed the million mark. The unemployed have it just as easy: after the age of eighteen everyone is entitled to an allowance, calculated on the basis of 'objective' criteria such as needs and marital status. This allowance is slightly lower than the minimum legal wage, which increases with age. Chan Cheonni feels that the effect of welfare aid is twofold on employment or to be specific on minority unemployment. Employers can with an easy conscience decide not to engage or retrench as they know that no one is going to starve; as for employees, they are not supposed to be enthusiastic about work.

Now if what Chan Cheonni says is true, then the only way to bring down minority unemployment is to reduce welfare and make sure there is a substantial difference between the minimum wage and the unemployment allowance. Some Dutch economists have also been advocating the return to a genuine labour market, but they have to tread softly in a nation imbued with ideas of welfare democracy; for the moment, the debate on the welfare-state is purely a theoretical one. Suppose we do accept that curtailing welfare allowances for minorities would compel them to integrate into the work force, wouldn't such liberal ideas lead to social unrest? No one in Western Europe has ever tried to dismantle the welfare state, not even Margaret Thatcher in her time. The Dutch government, based as it is on an all party consensus, is hardly likely to try it out.

THE POSITIVE ACTION PLAN

The national plan to end 'allochthonous' unemployment, if such a thing is possible, is called positive action. Its aim is to integrate minorities into the labour market through negotiations - negotiating being a Dutch mania - involving the State, companies, trade unions and the private sector. This formula has been suggested by Han Entzinger, a sociologist from the University of Utrecht. He has rejected the American model, drawing his inspiration instead from the Canadian experience. In the U.S., administrations and companies which get government contracts are required to recruit minorities in proportion to their numerical strength, especially Blacks and Hispanics. Such 'affirmative action' is monitored by a judge and aims to ensure real equality between the Blacks and the others. 'In actual fact', observes Entzinger, 'affirmative action confines the Blacks and Hispanics to government jobs and causes resentment amongst the Whites'. Whereas in Canada, positive action is based on the willingness of companies to take on minorities, which publish their ethnic balance sheets. Government pressure and public opinion help to promote integration through employment. We will take a closer look at these models later, but for the moment let us just see how the Dutch view them. Han Entzinger feels anti-racist opinion is so strong in his country that merely making public minority employment statistics will compel companies to take them on. However, this leads to an interesting paradox: how can employers be forced to furnish an ethnic breakdown of their employees, as is the practice in the United States and Canada, in an anti-racist country? In any case, what constitutes a minority and for how many generations does it remain one? The position of the Dutch government on the subject is as follows: Holland recognises its moral responsibility towards the peoples it had colonised - Surinamians, West Indians, Indonesians- as well as towards those it had called in the seventies, namely the Turks and Moroccans. In effect, this means that positive action is limited to only these groups, as the Dutch government feels it has no responsibility towards anyone else.

Before going in for positive action on a national scale, the authorities decided to try it out on an experimental basis, pragmatism being Holland's national 'ideology'. After the 1991 agreement between unions and managements, the latter undertook to reserve sixty thousand jobs over a period of five years for cultural minorities. The first company which volunteered to experiment with positive action was the Albert Heijn chain of stores. Actually, the company had little choice in the matter for it was finding it difficult to get native Dutch shop assistants. So the only way out was to take on minorities; furthermore, such a move was in its own interest as a sizable number of its clients in the big cities belonged to minority groups. Albert Heijn's managers had committed themselves in public to recruit allochthonous employees in proportion to their strength in a given area - 20% in Amsterdam - and then promote them to executive posts in the same ratio: in a nutshell, voluntary quotas. In July

1991, six months after he announced the scheme, Peter Jansen, the personnel manager, had to admit relative failure: he had been unable to meet his minority quota, because the number of applicants was too low. Hugo Fernandes Mendes, the man in charge of the minority policy at the Home Ministry, warns, 'If positive action does yield results, we will have to resort to compulsory quotas as in the United States.'

GHETTOS OR QUOTAS?

What are we to infer from this failure, however temporary, of 'voluntary quotas' in the Netherlands? Three conclusions are possible. First, that the cultural minorities, young Moroccans in particular, do not want to work. Second, that over generous welfare allowances are leading them astray. Third, that the jobs offered are not attractive enough. Professor Frank Bovenkerk from the University of Utrecht tends to subscribe to the third point of view. Bovenkerk too happens to be a sociologist. Influential and omniscient, their tribe has taken over from theologians in Dutch society. Instead of tinkering with the soul, the new engineer tinkers with society; comfortable research centres have replaced faculties of theology.

According to Bovenkerk, immigrants refuse work because they feel they are being offered poorly paid dead end jobs. If the starting salary offered to unskilled Morrocans is about the same as the unemployment allowance, then they would be perfectly justified in turning it down, especially as they are likely to remain in the same bracket for a long time. Does this mean that the unemployment allowance ought to be scaled down or done away with? Of course not, says Frank Bovenkerk, as scaling it down would lead to poverty, social turmoil and urban violence, without creating a single new job. He feels the problem has to be tackled from the other end: the pressure must be kept up on the employer and not the unemployed.

What Bovenkerk favours is American style 'affirmative action'. In the U.S., any company contracting business with the government and all public employers have to reserve jobs for minorities depending on their numerical strength in the community. Such companies and administrations are also required to guarantee the promotion of their minority employees at all levels under legal supervision. Now if such a policy were to be applied in the Netherlands, then affirmative action would compel employers to recruit minorities across the board and give them proper training so as to ensure their career prospects in the company. Bovenkerk feels that this will enable the emergence of a Moroccan or Surinamian elite comparable to the new black middle-class in the U.S. Obviously, this elite cannot absorb the entire minority population, but it can well provide a role model for them.

The immediate objection to American style affirmative action is that underqualified minorities will be engaged and standards will vary, depending on the colour of one's skin. Bovenkerk has two answers. First, it is the government's responsibility to train young immigrants so that their qualifications match company requirements. Ten years ago, an experiment of this kind had been successfully carried out in the case of young Moluccans who came as immigrants to the Netherlands. Employers reserved three thousand jobs for the members of this turbulent community. In return, the government paid for special vocational training programmes for them. Today, not a word is said about the Moluccans. Second, it is better to run the risk of employing underqualified executives than to allow the formation of a sub-class of unemployed youth of the same community. In other words, 'quotas are better than ghettos'. The special effort that companies are being asked to make is the price that has to be paid for maintaining social peace, even if it means slowing down the country's economic growth.

Without such voluntarist policies, Bovenkerk feels Dutch cities will witness the same kind of violence and destruction that are coming to characterise the urban landscape of America, France and England. Wouldn't affirmative action lead to a white backlash, as qualifications being equal, a White would lose out to a Black, like in the United States? Bovenkerk does not deny the possibility, but given the present situation, it is clearly the lesser evil. Currently what is upsetting Whites in Holland is that minorities are enjoying the same social benefits without having to work for them. If quotas can get immigrants to work then there will be much less reason for xenophobia.

Nonetheless, it seems strange a white sociologist and not someone from the minorities is making out such a strong case for quotas. In the U.S., affirmative action was the culmination of a long struggle by the Blacks for their rights. In Holland, the initiative is coming from the top - perhaps the native Dutch are more concerned with preserving their own peace of mind.

Bovenkerk doesn't deny this. Quotas are a means to achieve not only social justice but also social stability; they are the price the Whites will have to pay to avoid being swamped by Black ghettos.

2

WHO IS GERMAN?

Whatever happened to the Berlin Wall? Where did it stand, over here or there? The Berliners don't quite seem to remember. I can see that on this side the facades are brighter; over there they are crumbling and Trabants still run. But the old border has disappeared beneath the tarmac and the grass. If the writer Peter Schneider is to be believed, only the police dogs of the former Federal Republic of Germany recollect it perfectly. 'Let them loose, and as if on an invisible leash, they will sniff their way along the old line of demarcation'. Though former West Berliners don't really miss the border, they still look back on it with a touch of nostalgia. Before the reunification, those who crossed the wall were given a hero's welcome, perhaps because they were few and far apart. When the wall was up, everyone stayed on their side. Today, the 'Ossies' (East Germans) are flocking in and so are the East Europeans, who are swooping down from the Volga and the Danube. Hordes of people, previously held back by Communism, are now marching across the porous eastern border.

GASTARBEITER, THE PERMANENT GUEST

The story of German immigration began in Berlin in 1962. Previously, the manpower needs of Federal Germany and West Berlin were met by the exodus of East Germans, the 'Ubersiedler', to the West. When the Wall was built, this source dried up. The Bonn government then hit upon the idea of the 'Gastarbeiter', the guest worker, preferably Turkish. Turkey, a traditional ally of Germany, was in a position to provide unlimited supplies of young, conscientious workers. On paper, the Gastarbeiter formula seemed flawless; the Germans boasted about it while the rest of Europe looked on in envy. German Government and industry had imagined that the Turks would come, work for three or four years and return home once they made their nest-egg. That is what the Italians and the Yugoslavs had done before them.

But the Turks had other ideas. They stayed on! When they first came, they used to stash away the goodies they were going to take back in a little store room; in time, the store room became the children's room. The Gastarbeiter turned out to be a permanent guest who let it be known that he was happy in Germany, his children even more so and he had no intention of leaving. The desire to stay was strengthened quite inadvertently by the German government when it decided to seal its borders in 1973. The day the government curbed immigration, Turkish immigrants already in Germany just refused to budge for fear of being denied re-entry. They sent for their wives and children, and in this they were encouraged by the Government, partly on humanitarian grounds and partly to 'stabilise' the labour force. Now this proved to be a tactical error. Be it France or Germany, there is nothing like closing the borders to transform a migratory movement into a permanent settlement. The number of Turks went up from two million in 1973 to five million in 1992.

In Berlin, the Turks organised themselves into a mini Turkey with the Kreuzberg quarters as their capital. Before the war, this maze of unhealthy buildings and checkered courtyards housed traders and artisans. Spared the devastation of the 1945 bombardment, no one bothered to restore them. Today they are overcrowded with Anatolian peasants whose great grand children have in the space of three generations become true Berliners - neither German, nor Turkish, unless you could call them both! The Government won't give them German citizenship is the constant refrain of the German left-wing - often echoed by the French left - which accuses the right of being selfish if not downright racist. But first the Turks must ask for naturalization, something most of them have not done so far. Ertekin Ozcan, one of the leaders of Berlin's Turkish community, informs me that they do not want to choose. A teacher in Turkey, he has for the last twenty years been living in Germany as an immigrant and is the founder of the Turkish Parents Association. Its aim is to preserve the tenuous links between the second generation of German born Turks and the culture of their forefathers. Ertekin Ozcan knows that the children will never go back to Turkey, they have even forgotten their own language. It seems like the Turks spend more time quarreling among themselves than with their German hosts - a case of generational conflict rather than ethnic discord. Paradoxically, Ozcan is banking on German Government aid to preserve what little remains of Turkish culture in Germany, through the recruitment of teachers in Turkey to teach Turkish in German schools. Had education been multicultural as in Holland, Ozcan feels that Turkish children would achieve better results in German schools. They would be able to integrate more easily and still remain Turkish. Once again, the demand for multiculturalism is being raised. The more the children get to know about their origins, the better they can integrate into the host community. Ertekin Ozcan tells us what he thinks would be the ideal status of a Turkish immigrant in Germany: the right to dual nationality and to vote in local elections for all legal residents, even those not naturalized like in Holland, and a pluralistic education 'as in Sweden'. He has the same ideas for German Turks as Mohammed Rabbae has for Dutch Moroccans. This then is the blueprint for a transnational society as drawn up by foreign communities, especially the Muslims, so they can become 'European immigrants'.

CITIZENS WHEN AT WORK

'When we opened our plastic factory in Berlin which runs day and night, only the Turks came forward to work in eight hour shifts'. Udo Reinhold, Ford's personnel manager still can't get over the fact that not a single German was willing to work at his factory. On the other hand, he is full of praise for 'his' Turks. They are so attached to the company that they 'urge their teenage children to join Ford training centres'. They are 'loyal, conscientious and have team spirit'; a Turkish workshop immediately stands out for its discipline.

Ford is not an isolated example. German employers set great store by their Gastarbeiter, often have them called over and want them to keep coming, in sharp contrast with the official German policy of putting a brake on immigration. Reinhold explains that the Turks have adapted very well and act like true citizens when in the company. Economic citizenship is based on the sound principles of co-management and apprenticeship, the hallmark of German industry. Co-management gives Turkish employees an opportunity to participate at all levels of decision making. Apprenticeship - through which most training and recruitment is done - creates family feeling, bringing employer and employees together. Employers invest in apprenticeship (about 5% of the total wage bill) because in the long run this guarantees them a steady supply of qualified manpower. For the immigrant workers children, apprenticeship means that as soon as they come of age, there is an employer waiting to exercise his claim on them. Apprenticeship is a vital link in the process of integrating the problematic second generation which, as it is well known, has the hardest time in the industrial world.

Obviously the economic integration of the Turks is far from being perfect. One out of every five young Turks in Germany is jobless. This figure may seem low when compared to other immigrant communities in Europe, but in Germany it is felt to be on the high side. Even more worrying is the fact that young Turks, due to inadequate training, hold temporary menial jobs which they could well lose after they cross their forties. Another matter for concern is the low level of education amongst young girls, which is likely to hinder their social adaptation. Parents take them out of school as soon as they reach their teens to keep them in family, as is the custom. It must however be said to the credit of the Turkish community - even those without a job - that they are fiercely motivated, have a solid work ethic and are determined to succeed in German society. How can the Turks, especially the second generation, be made to acquire the same professional skills as the Germans? Unlike in Holland, Great Britain or France, in Germany no one thinks of discrimination in terms of exclusion, no one is suggesting quotas for immigrants. As for 'positive action', it can come only through education. On this subject, there are no two opinions: better professional skills and training are the best way to facilitate Turkish integration. Whenever the Turks do not get equal training opportunities, 'bridge courses' are offered so they can catch up. This is the purpose of Brückkurs.

THE COLOGNE INTEGRATION MODEL

Cologne, the city with the second largest Turkish population after Berlin, has since 1988 started a pilot project for integration through training: Brükkers. The initiative comes neither from the Federal authorities nor the local bodies but from the private sector. It was the Cologne Chambers of Commerce and Trade - in Germany these institutions are responsible for professional training and apprenticeship - which organised the Brückkers, in collaboration with the Labour Office, the German counterpart of the French ANPE (the French national employment exchange). Here integration works as it is not confined to rhetoric alone.

There is nothing fancy about the courses offered. German, mathematics, electrical and metallurgic work are taught in unused industrial sheds. The instructors, who have been initiated into Turkish and Yugoslav cultures, inform me that punctuality and discipline are the two things they insist on. As for young girls, similar initiatives have been launched by Catholic associations, notably Caritas. For forty hours a week, Turkish girls learn German plus the traditional cooking and sewing so as not to frighten away parents. Most of the girls who come to the Caritas training centre wear the Islamic veil. The German instructors take no notice except to inform their students when they are leaving about the difficulty they will face in getting a job on account of their chaddar. The duration of the bridge course is three years, at the end of which all the students have, till now, been taken on by local companies. The best among them bag the plum apprenticeships. Hermann Jung, Director of the Cologne Labour Office concludes that remedial classes do work and that everyone can be integrated into the labour market provided suitable openings are created. With the Brückkers, there has been a steady decline in the number of unemployed foreign youth. One thing all the instructors have to say is that those children who come straight from Turkey are better behaved, more eager to learn and more punctual than Turkish children from German schools. This paradox can be explained by anyone who knows anything about German public schools. Overcrowded classes and indifferent teachers leave no room for the special needs of immigrant children; as in France, mass education has only succeeded in marginalising them. So the factory proves to be a more effective integrator than the school. A lesson we would do well to bear in mind.

However the Cologne model does have its limitations. A pilot project, it requires the mobilisation of private companies that cannot expect much from the State, highly committed instructors and a fierce desire to move ahead on the part of the young foreigners. As well as a great deal of money. Brückkers are held for groups of six to eight students in training centres which normally have about eighty students on their rolls. Sometimes, individual German language classes are held for beginners. The Chambers of Commerce estimates that the cost for a single trainee is about twenty thousand Deutsche Marks per year; that is why this scheme is not feasible on a larger scale. The city can only provide training to three thousand students annually, a drop in the ocean considering twenty percent of its population is of foreign origin. Nonetheless, the Cologne experiment does tell us something about how to achieve economic integration. What is required is the will to do so and a relatively high investment. But can this be a profitable venture? In all probability the answer is yes, because companies will get qualified manpower and the threat of social tension will be minimised.

GERMANY, THE LAND OF IMMIGRANTS

Looking beyond Cologne, I think we can speak of a German integration model, based on economic rather than political citizenship. Even if they can't vote in Germany, the Turks are citizens in the companies they work in.

Can what holds good for the Turks in Germany be applied elsewhere? Perhaps, provided one is careful. The Turks did have some factors working in their favour to begin with. They come from a Muslim country no doubt, but one that has been greatly influenced by secularism, Turkey's national ideology for over seventy years. Besides, the Turks did not have any historical scores to settle with the Germans, unlike the Algerians in France. Independent Turkey was

Germany's ally , never its colony. These historical, cultural and religious circumstances made it easier for the Turks to integrate till such time as they came to Germany with the sole purpose of finding a job and the German economy was able to deliver the goods.

Furthermore, it would be wrong to think that Germany does not have a tradition of immigrants. Without going back as far as the Jewish settlements in the Middle Ages or the Huguenots in Prussia, Germany has, since the beginning of the nineteenth century, absorbed three major waves of immigration: first, the English workers who came to the Ruhr in the early nineteenth century, followed by the Poles and the Italians towards the beginning of this century. All of them eventually became naturalized German citizens, though the process of integration had been a slow one.

But are we speaking of the same Germany? Now that is not so certain. Till 1945, Germany was a remarkable mosaic of varied provinces and cul-tures; language, accents, customs, Catholicism, Protestantism divided the Germans as much as their citizenship bound them. After 1945 began what the writer Heinrich Boll called the 'great displacement'. Traditional barriers crumbled one after the other with East Germans bringing in their Protestant faith to the Catholic West and the Aussiedlers (ethnic Germans) bringing back oriental and Slavic customs from Romania, Poland and Russia. By the time the Turks arrived, history had already taken its toll of the German sense of identity. This made it somewhat easier for them to integrate.

And so the saga of Turkish immigrants to Germany is not as original as it seems. But then what are we to make of the increasing instances of racial violence since 1991? They are limited to the new arrivals,

Gypsies and Blacks in particular. The Turks, considered 'good immigrants', are hardly affected. In spite of living in Germany and being Muslim, it does seem that the Turks will eventually become full-fledged Germans without having a drop of German blood.

THE CITIZENSHIP TEST: BLOOD OR PLACE OF BIRTH

Ruddie Kemal lives and works in Berlin. He was born there. He speaks only German and cannot conceive of living in any other place but Germany. For him, Berlin is his 'Heimat'. Thirty-five years ago, Ruddie Kemal's father left Turkey to come to Germany. That makes Ruddie a Turk. He could apply for German nationality, which he may well get, but the complex paper work involved is forbidding. Ruddie will have to undergo a stiff test to prove that he is fully integrated. This is how citizenship by blood, *jus sanguis* works, in contrast to citizenship by place of birth, as is the case in France, Great Britain and the United States. So, despite having been born and brought up in Germany, Kemal is not German.

Ulrike Frockhof is not required to prove anything. She is an ethnic German even though she hasn't a clue about German culture. When she arrived in Berlin in 1991, she could not speak a word of German. She still can't and I could only communicate with her through a Russian interpreter. Ulrike Frockhof was born in Kirghiz. For fifty years, she raised geese near Frunze, some five thousand kilometers away. Her ancestors had left Germany in the middle of the eighteenth century in response to an appeal made by Empress Catherine of Russia, who granted them lands on the banks of the Volga. In 1941 Stalin, suspicious of these

Germans from the Volga, inspite of their impeccable Bolshevik credentials, had them deported to Kirghiz and Kazakistan. But by virtue of her ancestry, Ulrike Frockhof remained German. Under German law she can return to the land of her forefathers whenever she wants to. All she has to do is to invoke her *Deutschtum*. The proof of her *Deutschtum*: her Russian and Kirghiz neighbours believed Frau Frockhof was German and hated her for it!

Citizenship through ancestry and Germaness were all very well as long as it was only the Ubersiedler or East Germans who crossed over to the West. Neither was the principle questioned when Germans from the Valleys of the Danube, the Banat and Transylvania - who had been living for centuries in what is now Hungary and Romania - came back. For these communities, whose lives revolved around the parish, the bible, their schools and their pianos, have remained more German than the Germans. But the collapse of the Soviet Union complicated matters, as millions of ethnic Germans whose existence had been forgotten suddenly woke up to their ancestry.

How many Aussiedler are there in Germany? Going by the German authorities definition of Deutschtum, the figure varies from anything between two and twelve million, more likely twelve than two though, if the former Soviet economy continues to slide at the rate it is and anti-German xenophobia in Central Asia remains as virulent. The German Government hopes to keep some of them where they are by reestablishing the German Volga Republic as it existed between 1921 and 1941, though it seems rather unlikely that the tide can be stemmed midway between Frunze and Berlin. To check the influx, the German government requires applicants claiming

Deutshtum to go via Moscow, where they are made to fill a plethora of forms. Outside the embassy, German speaking Moscovites offer their services to Germans who only speak Russian. In exchange for a few roubles, they will fill up a fifty page long questionnaire intended to verify the genuineness of a claim. A sample of the questions asked: 'What was the typically German thing your grand-mother did on Christmas Eve?' I am not making it up, the question is very much there and I suppose the right answer must be 'decorating the Christmas tree'. The return of the natives has had mixed reactions in Germany. Peter Schneider calls it a case of 'Deutschmelei' or Germanomania. The Conservatives, on the other hand, are full of nostalgia for these lost tribes; their German may not be much to write home about but their religiosity is as strong as their hostility to Socialism. They are proof of the enduring character of the German race. That is all very well, but they are still immigrants. In the autumn of 1991, Springer, a conservative paper, ran the following title: 'Do we give German citizenship to every Aussielder whose grand-mother had a German shepherd?'

The left is in the same quandary. Daniel Cohn-Bendit, Deputy Mayor of Frankfurt in charge foreigners, says, 'I would much rather German nationality be given to a young Turk born and brought up in Germany than to some non German speaking descendant of a distant Saxon coloniser who went off to Russia in the eighteenth century.' Peter Schneider is of the same opinion. He is unhappy about the fact that citizenship based on ancestry confers German nationality to any exile who can prove that his father was an SS man, while denying it to a Polish child whose father fought against the Nazis. Cohn-Bendit says that anyone wanting to leave Poland to come to Germany can buy a German grand-mother for a thousand Deutsche Marks in Warsaw! In fact, this business of verifying the genuineness of Deutschtum claims has set the German authorities on an ancestry hunt, reviving memories of the obsession for racial purity in the Spain of the Inquisition and Nazi Germany.

Thus defining citizenship on the basis of ancestry which seems so appealing, especially to certain French right-wing circles, is not as uncomplicated as it looks. In fact, it is not much better than defining citizenship on the basis of place of birth, as is being done in France and Britain. If by any chance the kinship principle were applied in France, it would lead to an irretrievable situation. Would the pieds-noirs still remain French if their parents turned out to be Spanish? And the Québecois, what would become of them? In Germany, naturalization by kinship has resulted in an Aussiedler invasion while jeopardizing the integration of five million foreigners who, for the most part, have no intention of leaving the country. The German experience therefore illustrates that naturalization by birth does not curtail the number of immigrants be they Turkish or African. People come to Germany not to get German nationality, but to flee poverty and persecution. The kinship principle is not going to deter a single immigrant from entering Germany or for that matter France.

3

THE RUSH TO THE WEST

Between Germany and Poland flows the Neisse - the Neisse which, since the collapse of the Berlin Wall, separates East from West, Slav from Occidental. Is this then the new frontier between the civilised and the barbarian world? In the West, there is affluence, in the East, scarcity and fear. The Neisse, a border arbitrarily chosen by Churchill and Stalin, reminds one of another river, the Rio Grande which divides the Americas into the rich, white north and the poor coloured south just as arbitrarily. However, this is where the comparison ends. The Rio Grande is bristling with barbed wire. Every day and night, U.S. Border Patrol jeeps and helicopters push back thousands of illegal immigrants. A losing battle, though. For in terms of sheer staying power, the immigrant has an edge. In contrast, the Neisse peacefully meanders through open fields; what the Germans call the Green Border is hardly visible to the naked eye. Border checkpoints are miles apart, manned by nonchalant guards of the former Federal Republic who are waiting for the Russian influx. But the Russians don't come; the only ex-Soviet citizens who manage to find their way in are the 'Aussiedler'.

The threat of a massive Russian exodus towards Western Europe is being kept alive by the Russian leadership to extort financial help from the West, Germany in particular. 'If you don't help,' Gorbachev let it be known, 'I will let loose my migrant hordes on Western Europe.' A figure of twelve million was bandied about. Where could it have come from? The KGB, in all probability. Which didn't stop Boris Yeltsin from making political capital out of it.

Will they come at all? Perhaps, if the Republics went to war with Moscow or a famine broke out. For the moment the Russian exodus is proving to be more illusory than real and the only people who are pouring in are Gypsies from Romania. In 1991 alone, a hundred thousand of them crossed over. You don't have to be particularly resourceful to enter Germany without papers; all you need to do is get to the first checkpoint or policeman and utter the password 'asylant' or asylum-seeker. The Gypsies may not speak German, but this is a word they all know. Once they have crossed the border, they are taken to a reception centre at Eisenhüttenstadt. What used to be the steel capital of East Germany has been converted into a refugee processing centre. The Romanians will be packed in abandoned army barracks along with Vietnamese, Turkish and Yugoslav refugees. Sixty-four nationalities were present the day I went there.

In Germany, asylum seekers enjoy special status. They are not only protected by the Geneva Convention, but also by the 1949 German Constitution. The constitution, adopted at a time of denazification, by virtue of its Article 16 binds the Government to take in any asylum seeker, even criminals excluded under the terms of the Geneva Convention, regardless of whether their application has been turned down by any other country. Historical and legal circumstances can however only partially explain the warm welcome extended by the German Government to asylum seekers. There are, as we shall soon see, other reasons which determine the attitude of German officials looking after refugees.

At Eisenhüttenstadt, an immigration hearing can go on for several days. Asylum seekers are assisted by an interpreter, a lawyer if they ask for one, and a representative of a humanitarian organisation. The Gypsies, in order to gain sympathy, testify that they are being persecuted by the 'Securitate', this despite the fact that two years have passed since Ceausescu's fall. And then the charade begins: the official in charge pretends to believe the asylum seeker who pretends to be a political refugee. The lawyer pretends to believe that his client is being persecuted and the humanitarian organization's representative pretends that Germany is on the brink of fascism. In point of fact, the Gypsy has nothing to worry about. He will never be thrown out from Germany.

After the Romanian, a Zairian walks in. How he got there is any one's guess. He is accompanied by his wife and four children - all the makings of a family saga. He vaguely mumbles something about political persecution in Zaire, not sounding too convinced himself. That hardly matters, he is well received nonetheless. The Zairian can't believe his luck. He applauds the German officials, who beam back at him. 'I had thought of going to France, but we've been so well looked after in Germany that I think we'll stay here.' Not for a moment does he doubt the final outcome of his odyssey. His confidence is not misplaced.

Once the paperwork is through, the Romanians, Vietnamese and Zairians will be sent off to a refugee hostel of the kind that exists in every German district. There, the government will take care of them till their applications are processed. This can take upto two years and more. After which, applicants whose cases have been turned down can appeal in the courts. And so it goes on and on. While the authorities decide their cases, asylum seekers are the responsibility of the host Lander; they are provided with accommodation and an allowance equal to what Germans get by way of social security. These refugees have the right to work provided they get a special permit, which is always given. This marks the beginning of their integration into the German economy. When their applications for asylum are rejected - which is more often than not - the fake refugees are not deported. The Lander governments which in principle ought to go ahead with the deportation refuse to do so. How can you expect German soldiers to drive Gypsies back to the border in the full glare of world television cameras? Germany, with over a million applicants for permanent asylum in 1992, has thus become a prisoner of its own laws. Unless of course the government and the major companies have entered into a tacit agreement. Public opinion is hostile to immigrants whereas employers are looking for cheap labour; so fake refugees are the convenient way out. Anyone who has been refused asylum is given the status of a turned down refugee. This is enough for him to be able to work and thus become an economic refugee, which is in principle not possible as a political refugee cannot legally become an economic migrant.

The director of the Eisenhüttenstadt reception centre, Reinhardt Seel, is wise to all these games. He knows for a fact that ninety-two percent of the asylum applications will be dismissed in the last instance.

Then how does he accept or at least pretend to accept the stories the Asylanten make up for his benefit. Reinhardt Seel is not amused. Any asylum seeker, he explains, is presumed persecuted till proved otherwise. No German official would take the responsibility of verifying a claim on his own. That would be acting against the Constitution, the law and the Statute books. Would it also mean stirring German guilt? Evidently, officials more than make up for Germany's past with the attention they shower on their visitors.

Does not Reinhart Seel fear a deluge? What would he do if the expected Slavic influx were really to occur? Oh well, then the authorities would just have to increase the number of reception centres, interpreters, officials, lawyers, all those in fact who live off and for the refugees. The people working at the reception centre, far from being hostile to asylants, seem to like them. Because they are coloured, exotic or different? Because those working here are anti-racist activists? Because they want to make amends for Germany's historical blunders? Or is it simply because the continual influx of refugees gives their office stature and funds? What would become of Reinhardt Seel if the stream of refugees were to dry up?

He admits that before the reunification he was just another policeman at Eisenhüttenstadt; now he heads a huge department. In true bureaucratic tradition, the officials dealing with refugees have used Article 16 to feather their own nests. The greater the problem, the more they stand to gain.

But the mood is very different behind the line of bureaucracy.

RACIST GERMANS

When I met Irena Runge in February 1992 in Berlin,

she had just come back from a study trip of Hoyerswerda
schools in Lower Saxony in the former Federal Republic.
Irena Runge is a well known East German sociologist.
A survivor of the Nazi onslaught, she lived through
communism, holed up in her tiny, decrepit apartment
with her books, her postcards from all over the world
and her seven branch candelabra. Now that Germany
is reunified, she misses - though not overly - her
cocoon and the old regime: the GDR, the 'unGerman
perhaps even anti-German Germany'. Her life was
frugal but at least there was no racism, which is not
the case any longer. Irena Runge is still shaken by
what she saw at Hoyerswerda.

Hoyerswerda has become a symbol of sorts since
September 1991 when crowds cheered on as a group
of skinheads dressed up as Nazis set a Gypsy refugee
camp on fire. The police did not intervene. Whether
out of choice or because it was ill equipped to do so
is difficult to tell. For Irena Runge what is far more
worrying is what followed. Though the President of
the Republic, Richard Von Weiszacker, expressed his
solidarity with the refugees, he did so only in his
personal capacity. The Kohl Government did not
condemn the attack but blandly stated that the influx
of asylum seekers was a matter of serious concern. The
Government admitted it had a problem on its hands.
Were the skinheads seen as an answer? Moreover,
instead of sending in police reinforcements to
Hoyerswerda to protect the Gypsies, the Government
chose to evacuate them from the city and pack them
off to another refugee camp. The assailants felt they
had scored a clear victory, gleefully declaring their city
'Auslanderfrei', or cleansed, reminiscent of the 'Judenfrei'
call in the Nazi times. At Hoyerswerda, Irena Runge
asked children how they felt about foreigners. 'All

communists, Jews, foreigners and Blacks must be shot,'
they declared in unison. Irena Runge is Jewish; she
told the children so. They had never seen a Jew in
their lives and hadn't imagined them to be like her.
They had never even seen a Black either. And a
foreigner? There are hardly any in Lower Saxony.
Then why did these children say what they did? Irena
Runge explains that they have completely lost their
bearings. Previously the former communist regime
thought for them, now they have to think for themselves.
And as they don't think at all, nor for that matter do
their parents, the only thing they can do is to glorify
their identity. 'We are Germans,' they say. But saying
one is German is not saying very much. What do a
Jewish woman from Berlin, a Rhinelander and a Saxon
have in common? Very little, apart from the language.
Irena Runge emphasises that there is no such thing
as a German identity. That is why the Hoyerswerda
children can only define it in terms of hatred for the
other. Irena says the situation is just the opposite in
Berlin. At the University of Humboldt where she
teaches, students claim to belong to the liberal left;
they abhor all that is 'Deutschtum', swear by
multiculturalism and say they prefer Turks to Germans.
They also prefer Jews. Such excessive philosemitism
is most unnatural and equally worrying for Irena
Runge.

So this is the story of the erstwhile East Germans,
destabilised by reunification and torn between a lack
of identity and an overdose of nationalism. However
racist attacks are not confined to East Germany alone.
After Hoyerswerda, there have been numerous such
instances all over Germany including the former
Länders. Two hundred incidents were recorded in the
last six months, which makes Irena Runge think it is

a well organised operation. Whose is the hidden hand behind the plot to destabilise the country, the former East German secret police or ex communists? Irena Runge is convinced that though East Germans are being pushed forward, the conspiracy has been hatched in the West. A case perhaps of a leftist intellectual's nostalgia for the past, unable to shake off her distrust of capitalist Germany. West Germans are no less racist, she says, only they manage to hide it behind a bourgeois veneer.

Daniel Cohn-Bendit does not agree.

NON-RACIST GERMANS

Daniel Cohn-Bendit is twenty years younger than Irena Runge and does not share the concerns of the old lady. He refuses to accept that Germany is by definition eternally suspect. He reminds us that xenophobic parties in Germany have had less success than those in France, Austria, Flanders or Italy for that matter. Hoyerswerda was no conspiracy, says Cohn-Bendit; the skinheads acted under the influence of beer and gang emulation. They only went on the rampage when they realised there was no police around.

Cohn-Bendit asking for the police ? The man has turned into a full fledged politician. In Germany, Daniel Cohn-Bendit is not known as the May 68 agitator alone. He is quite a respectable figure who has won his spurs in politics. A councillor in Frankfurt's town hall, the Mayor has given him a difficult charge: the Office for Multicultural Affairs. An office that gives him considerable clout, given that one fourth of Frankfurt's population comprises of foreigners. Cohn-Bendit is of the view that xenophobia thrives in those regions where the Germans have had little or no contact with foreigners, as in the case of the new Eastern Länders. In West Germany which has had a long tradition of immigrants, coexistence is much easier. So it is not so much having foreigners as not having them which brings racism to the fore. The imaginary fear of immigrants is more likely to spark off violence than immigrants themselves. And as several million refugees — economic and political — as well as a couple of million ethnic Germans are going to settle down in Germany in the next few years, racist violence, paradoxically enough, ought to decline. Germans will then, according to Cohn-Bendit become 'normally xenophobic', neither more nor less than other Europeans. There still remains the task of organising the coexistence of Germans and foreigners on the same soil: that is what Cohn-Bendit is doing in Frankfurt.

'Cranky ecologists like us hadn't anything to do with the foreigners coming into Germany !' exclaims Cohn-Bendit. 'Immigration in Germany is the direct consequence of the market economy, a purely capitalist by-product.' Cohn-Bendit rightly points out that German employers had been the victims of Marxist ideology when they thought that the Gastarbeiter would be a pure factor of production, cheap labour and no more. But Marx was wrong, and so were the employers: foreign workers were human beings too, with feelings; they did not rest till they had brought across their wives and children. The Deputy-Mayor rejoices in this great melting pot of races, peoples and languages that Frankfurt has become. Having partaken in three cultures - French, German and Jewish - Cohn-Bendit is at a loss to understand how people are happy being just French or German. Nigerians, Turks and Sri Lankans add so much colour to Germany. In any case, the modern world is multicultural.'Why not just accept it,' suggests Cohn-Bendit. 'The Germans and the French who do not want to do so in the name of national identity refuse to acknowledge that they have lost their identity a long time ago, what with rock concerts, Italian restaurants, marijuana joints and vacations in Bangkok.' The multicultural revolution needs no stimulus, it just happens of its own accord. Only, the Germans have to be convinced that being modern is being multicultural. Now who can convince them better than Cohn-Bendit. He has launched a series of anti-racist campaigns in Frankfurt, using TV spots to drive home his message. For example, there is a globe with the slogan 'Every where else but in Germany, we too are foreigners', very similar to the May 68 'We are all German Jews' call. At the time the French Government had tried to deport the student leader to Germany. Another favourite slogan of Cohn-Bendit is 'Please don't leave us alone with the Germans', intended for foreigners in Germany.

But Cohn-Bendit does more than come up with catchy slogans; the Deputy Mayor of Frankfurt has the very laudable ambition of keeping his city free of violence. The coexistence of so many different communities in Frankfurt is difficult but manageable.

The proof is that Germany has never in the thirty years it played host to the Turks known ethnic clashes of the kind that broke out in the suburbs of Paris or London. For Cohn-Bendit, this is testimony of the fact that Germans are not more xenophobic than others; in fact they are given to greater introspection than even the French: their history compels them to do so. A multicultural society requires organisation; Cohn-Bendit has no single solution to offer - there is no one solution - but a combination of strategies to 'ease the tension', unlike other politicians who have nothing to offer.

THE COHN-BENDIT METHOD

Step One: Enlist foreigners in the democratic process.
Difficult, considering that most of them will not get
German citizenship. The Cohn-Bendit plan consisted
of setting up a foreigners' Parliament in Frankfurt. In
October 1991, the Office for Multicultural Affairs sent
a voters card to every foreigner whose papers were
in order and who had been living for at least three
months in Frankfurt, covering about a hundred and
fifty thousand people. Elections took place for the first
time on the 30th of November. There were fifty-six
lists contending for the fifty-one seats, the same
number as in the Municipal Council of Frankfurt. Each
one of these lists was headed by the leader of a foreign
community. Cohn-Bendit rued the fact that the lists
were all drawn up on ethnic or religious lines -
Croates, Greeks, Serbs, Muslims, etc. There was only
one exception, the Social Democrat Party, which got
the highest percentage of votes - 12%. Cohn-Bendit's
rivals chuckled over the low turn out with 80% of the
voters abstaining. Cohn-Bendit had an answer to that.
The first minority groups to settle in Germany came
out in fairly large numbers. 35% of the Turks voted
and this was quite good for a first time, especially as
they were electing a purely consultative body. Cohn-
Bendit emphasised the need to maintain democratic
norms while electing the Parliament so that it did not
suffer the same fate as other consultative bodies in
German and French cities; universal suffrage is what
makes the difference.

When the Parliament (Kommunalen Auslander
und Ausladerin Vertretung, or KAV) met for the first
time in February 1992 in the main hall of the Frankfurt
Council, it was clear that Cohn-Bendit's gamble had

paid off. While he came sporting his oldest green tee shirt and worn out jeans, the foreign councillors arrived formally dressed in coat and tie. Each tried to outdo the other in Germaness, each was more courteous than the other, using the German 'Lieber Kollegue' to address his colleagues. Even the long procedural wrangling was typically German. Cohn-Bendit was tickled pink. "Sie sind so Deutsch'! (How German can they get!), he kept exclaiming as he moved around the hall. At the same time, he felt a tinge of regret: these foreigners had already become far too German for his liking.

What was going to be the shape of an assembly which comprised of only ethnic parties? The right wing and the Frankfurt press predicted the emergence of an 'Islamic block', Cohn-Bendit having unwittingly provided it with a platform and legitimacy. They were proved wrong. The KAV split into two groups, the religious and the secular. The religious coalition brought together Albanian and Turkish Muslims, Orthodox Greeks and Roman Catholic Italians. The Chairman Grigorius Zarcadas, a Greek Social Democrat, beat his Kurdish Muslim rival who had the support of the Italian Roman Catholics, by a single vote. In the months to follow, the foreigners' Parliament of Frankfurt got bogged down in procedural matters relating to the appointment of committees and rapporteurs. However what counts, Cohn-Bendit hastens to add, is not so much what is happening in the Assembly, as the fact that it exists at all. The democratic process has been set in motion, and as an old hand at revolution, Cohn-Bendit can tell you that the parliamentary duties of the leaders of foreign communities will leave them no time for other forms of protest. Practicing democracy makes for integration.

Step Two of the Cohn-Bendit Method: Propagating Multiculturalism. All over Germany, Cohn-Bendit is mobilising multicultural teams - Greens or Social Democrats- to take control of the municipal corporations. We may see replicas of the Frankfurt Parliament mushrooming wherever there are a large number of foreigners and the left is in a strong position. While waiting for the nationality laws to be amended, Cohn-Bendit, a staunch advocate of multiculturalism, is not averse to multiple nationality. 'Why force such a difficult choice on young Turks. Let them have both Turkish and German nationalities; by being both Turkish and German they can have the best of both worlds.' This has been the Turkish experience - the law ultimately has to catch up with the times.

Last step : quotas. Cohn-Bendit says there is no point denying that Germany still attracts a large number of immigrants: in numerical terms, it is second only to the United States. Germans would do well to accept this fact rather than repeatedly denying it. Besides, Germany still has a lot of space, 'The boat is half empty, it needs people to fill it up.' The population is aging and Germans have stopped producing children. Some one has to perpetuate the species, so welcome to immigrants, refugees and the poor; Germany has been chosen to take them in. And if in the process Germany becomes less German, why worry. A little intermingling will do no harm; on the contrary it will probably reduce the chances of a return to Nazism. For this purpose Cohn-Bendit suggests American style quotas. The debate would thus shift away from immigration per se to the merits and demerits of the quota system. It would focus on concrete problems and lead to interesting realignments, 'Employers favouring immigration for economic reasons would join hands with the human rights groups and the Greens in asking for an increase in quotas.' He feels however that, due to public pressure, a dispassionate debate on quotas would not be possible in the Federal Parliament. So the issue should be referred to a council of wise men, a common practice in German and Swiss institutions. The council, after discussion, could fix the quotas. In Switzerland, parliamentary debates do not always end in a vote but are used to evolve a consensus. In 1991, the Bern parliament spent a long time discussing a government sponsored policy for taking in immigrants without putting it to vote. Were quotas to be fixed by a European council of wise men, it would go down much better according to Cohn-Bendit, as a national policy on immigration and asylum no longer has any meaning. A European solution would be more readily accepted in the member countries as each government would be able to hypocritically hide under Europe's petticoats. In the face of this well thought out offensive by the new German left, what does the right in power have to offer? Not much, by the looks of it.

THE CHANCELLOR'S PREDICAMENT

Chancellor Kohl was on time. I wasn't. Europe's forever crowded skies made me reach Bonn two hours late. Any other head of government would have cancelled the appointment: not the German Chancellor. Bonn has never stood on protocol, a far cry from the Elysée. Minus the usual army of ushers, the Chancellery looks more like the head office of a company. The Chancellor's office is a picture of discretion, very much in keeping with a bourgeois democracy. Helmut Kohl apologizes for the modest decor. He needn't have, long live the modest state! My being French gives the Chancellor a good reason to order a bottle of Moselle white wine. By three o'clock in the afternoon, he has polished off most of it.

The agenda for our meeting is immigration. 'Germany is not a country of immigrants,' says the Chancellor. Indeed. The same is said of France. But that does not alter the fact that Germany has five million foreigners on its soil. 'You are confusing the issue,' retorts the Chancellor, not in the least put out. He says a distinction has to be made between the 'good' immigrants and the rest. To begin with, Aussiedlers, or ethnic Germans, are not foreigners. They are part and parcel of Deutschtum. The government looks after them, provides them with accommodation and finds them a job; till date, their return has not led to any hostility. How many are likely to return? The Chancellor puts their number at somewhere between five and fifteen million. Then come the 'genuine' immigrants, treated by the government 'with affection'. The Chancellor is referring to the Gastarbeiter called in by companies between 1961 and 1973. They will stay on in Germany, they are almost German. The government wants their integration and naturalization. Nationality by ancestry has been made less exclusive since 1991 in order to facilitate the naturalization of young Turks. But the Turks do not seem overly enthusiastic; they would like to be both Turkish and German. They'll have to choose, says Kohl. For the moment, there seems to be a stalemate.

Kohl is quite clear though that there is no question of going back to economic immigration and the Gastarbeiter. It is wrong to say, as the left is doing,

that Germany will run short of manpower. The
population has stabilised and technical innovation will
make up for the shortfall, 'Germans don't want to be
prolific, they want to be happy.'

Listen carefully, for this is more than just a catch
phrase. For a long time, immigration found favour in
Western Europe because of conscription. The same is
no longer true. In the modern world numbers don't
count. Kohl is thus implicitly rejecting the idea of
'demographic necessity', often put forward by
statisticians. Today it is little more than an attachment
to the great countries of yore. Some people in Germany,
including the Christian Democrats, would like 'to
invite' a couple of million workers from the East,
Russia for example. Kohl doesn't agree. Germany has
already experimented with the Gastarbeiter. You think
you are calling in one worker and lo and behold three
years after his arrival, you have the whole family
coming in, demanding decent accommodation. If
Germany is truly short of manpower, the Chancellor
feels that free movement should make it possible for
others from the European Community to fill up the
vacant slots.

We get down to brass tacks: the asylum seekers.
Kohl says Germany will remain committed to the right
of asylum, as the Germans are strongly in favour of
taking in political refugees provided they are genuine.
But how do you decide who is genuine? The Chancellor
would like to amend the Constitution so that the
screening can be done at the border itself. But he is
not in a position to muster the two thirds majority
required for such an amendment. No political party
wants to appear hostile to human rights. One could
perhaps think in terms of drawing up a list of

countries whose citizens can under no circumstance seek political asylum in Germany. But then by imposing a blanket ban on all Romanians, isn't there the risk of turning back the one genuine refugee? Not necessarily. The Poles are no longer eligible for refugee status but can get short duration work permits. As a result, not a single Pole has asked for asylum and all of them have become legal immigrants, though Kohl admits it would be difficult to implement such a policy on a wide scale. Speeding up proceedings so that asylum cases are settled within six months is another option available to the Chancellor. However, this too does not seem very feasible. First, it means impinging on the freedom of the judges, for whom the government cannot stipulate any time frame. Second, the fact is that till date not a single refugee, legal or illegal, has been deported from Germany, a trend likely to persist. In any case, the Chancellor does not think that legislation, however good it may be, can stem the rising tide of immigration. Socio-economic factors are pushing foreigners towards Germany and Europe must act collectively to change conditions in the sender countries; they have to be made to control their population and adopt viable development strategies. These words ring hollow. In spite of all the European aid, not a single African country has developed to such an extent that Africans don't feel the need to immigrate any more.

What will happen at German borders were a civil war to break out in Russia? The Chancellor prefers finishing what is left of the white wine. I join him. I am not likely to get any new insights from him. The seat of power is never conducive to thinking, so let us to move on.

IMMIGRATION IS UNNECESSARY

'Europe's decision to take in immigrants was based on an economic miscalculation. Her industries could have run perfectly well without immigrants. In fact, not a single European country had any need for them.' This statement, designed to provoke, comes from Professor Klaus Werner Schatz. Schatz heads the Kiel Centre of World Economy, founded at the turn of the century by Emperor William II. Kiel, an isolated outpost of the Communist system during the cold war, now finds itself at the heart of our brave new world: William II chose well. This is one of the rare economic research centre's in Europe free from State control, a point worth noting. There are very few European institutions capable of stating things as they are and dealing with sensitive issues - immigration, social protection, education - without getting swayed by interest groups and public pressure. Had Klaus Werner Schatz said the same thing in France, he would have been immediately labelled suspect. But at Kiel his analysis is judged on its merits and not used to fuel partisan rivalries. Schatz says, 'The Gastarbeiter have certainly benefited from their migration; had they stayed on in Turkey, they would have remained poor. But what has Germany gained?'

If it hadn't been for the immigrants, how would companies have managed to compensate for the low German birth rate? Who would have done the menial jobs turned down by the Germans so cheaply? This is what most people think, replies Schatz . But this is not true. Let us just suppose that Germany had not imported labour, 'then the concerned companies would have had to invest in more efficient technology and capital would have replaced labour. Productivity would have gone up and menial jobs been done away with thanks to new technology.' One thing that emerges from Schatz's analysis is that immigrant workers cannot be accused of depriving Germans of jobs: they are doing work which 'would have disappeared' had immigration not existed. The experience of the Japanese automobile industry is a case in point. For want of immigrant labour in the sixties and seventies, the Japanese replaced unskilled workers with robots; Japan's technical superiority is perhaps a result of non‾ immigration. Schatz feels there is no task which cannot be performed more efficiently by better technology than cheap immigrant labour. Take garbage disposal for instance. Current methods of disposal could easily be replaced by robots. This kind of work will only continue as long as a cheap supply of immigrant labour is available. Schatz is in no way advocating an end to immigration; this is an issue for politicians to decide. All he is saying is that the economic justification for immigration has been and will remain untenable. The same holds true for the demographic rationale which postulates that the aging of the population must necessarily be compensated by immigration. Here again, technology can replace labour. In the ultimate analysis, the immigrant still remains the sole economic beneficiary of immigration; the host country gains nothing. Neither does the sender country, as it is deprived of its most motivated and qualified manpower. Driving home this economic truth in no way dilutes the case for a redistribution of wealth between the industrialised and the Third World countries. International trade can achieve this at a lower social cost than immigration. It would be better to export investment and import goods rather than the men who produce them. The only way to check immigration -

even though it is not the most liberal one - is to enter into an agreement with sender countries in the South as in the East within the framework of a global 'settlement'. All aid to the Third World would henceforth be subject to two conditions: governments of receiver countries would have to switch over to a market economy and would have to hold back their emigrants.. Another utopia? Not really. The attempt on the part of the German and Russian governments to re-establish a Volga Republic in 1992 is a step in this direction; a few million ethnic Germans who would have otherwise emigrated will be settled here in exchange for investment. Similarly, the Americans have set up 'Maquiladoras' (companies) in Mexico to keep the population from crossing over; in this way goods and not men are imported. The Schatz's model is the blue print for a new North-South, East-West relationship. We shall discuss it later when we come to the chapter on France.

4

THE LAST ENGLISHMAN

In the tranquility of his Kensington house, an elegant old parliamentarian of eighty has become the symbol of all that is detestable for the British left: Enoch Powell is his name. For his Conservative colleagues, on the other hand, he has belatedly acquired the stature of a statesman denied to him when he was in Parliament. Twenty-five years ago, Powell was slated to become Prime Minister. However, a single speech of his scotched his chances, and it was with this same speech that his name went down in history. The year, 1968. The representative from Wolverhampton, regarded as a somewhat eccentric staunch Tory, had warned a party congress against the perils of immigration. His speech was the first anti-immigration policy declaration ever to have been made in contemporary Europe. Since then, any organisation using 'national identity' as its main plank has acknowledged Powell as a pioneer. His only mistake was to have spoken too soon; to top it all, he addressed his colleagues in Latin. 'I see,' he declared, 'immigrant communities organising and consolidating themselves, using our laws to serve their own interests and dominate us.' He carried on with a quotation which was to ruin his career: Like the Roman, 'I foresee that the Tiber will be transformed into a river of blood.' Both Parliament and press did not realise he was quoting Virgil. Powell was accused of inciting his fellow citizens to murder, an accusation that is still leveled against him by all anti-racist movements.

Powell does not appreciate being called a Conservative. 'I am,' he tells me, 'a Tory and belong to a tradition much older and much more British than Conservatism,' which he finds somewhat 'continental.' 'A real Englishman does not innovate,' explains Enoch Powell. 'An Englishman never acts, he reacts. Tradition, in our country, is the real fount of authority; it is enough to say that it has always been so to legitimise our actions.' Powell is anti-liberal. 'Liberalism is a continental tradition which places the individual above and beyond society.' For Powell, society comes before the individual and man can only be the product of the place he was born and brought up in. Is it not possible for man to change? No, people change little or not at all. Culture and traditions are immutable except at the surface. 'When the English change, they only seem to change; and thus feign to be Europeans, which they will never become.' Enoch Powell justifies himself by saying that in 1968 Great Britain had no laws on nationality: all subjects born under the Crown in any part of the Empire could freely settle in Great Britain. The Empire had ceased to exist but Parliament did not take this to its logical conclusion. It did not close British borders to the citizens of its former colonies. At that time, Powell had warned that Britain would have four million immigrants. Today, twenty years later, his predictions have come true. The concept of integration, he adds, is an imposture. 'One is born

British, one does not become British.' Once again, twenty years later, the fact that immigrants in Great Britain have fallen back on their own communities seems to prove him right.

Will the English remain forever English? Enoch Powell has his doubts. He feels that immigration will get the better of them. How? By virtue of their geographical concentration and the rate of growth of their population, 'these communities will take over our institutions - beginning with the local bodies - and subjugate them to their own specific ends.' And so the very nature of English democracy which is based not on written law but tradition will be distorted and crumble. Without a common tradition, democracy will vanish. What does Enoch Powell suggest? Nothing, obviously. Tories are by nature pessimists. It is too late to act or even react. The harm has been done. All is lost, except perhaps the traditional evening tea. We move to the library. Mrs Powell dips two tea bags into a silver teapot. 'Teabags', I exclaim! 'My parents' admits Enoch Powell, 'would have been horrified.' In front of his South Eaton Place house, two policemen stand guard - 'They are there to protect me against leftist threats' - or perhaps they are curators, protecting the last representative of a fast disappearing England. 'The English have never known defeat at the hands of outsiders,' observes Enoch Powell. 'Neither Hitler, nor Philip II of Spain could defeat us. But this time we will be beaten: from within.'

THE MUSLIM PARLIAMENT

Allah ho Akbar! On the second of January, 1992 at Kensington, Enoch Powell's prophecy seems to be coming true. A mullah in a white and golden turban crosses the hall with painful slowness and places the Koran in front of the Speaker. Then without a word, he goes back. The first session of the Muslim Parliament of Great Britain may begin its proceedings. Is it a genuine Parliament? That is what the two hundred odd delegates gathered together in a West London Kensington town hall room call it. They have got their mandate not through universal suffrage, but through a system of cooptation from amongst the Muslim community in Great Britain, 'a council of wise men', according to Kalim Siddiqui, the man behind the Parliament. Or, if one were to listen to his rivals, a fundamentalist conspiracy whose sole purpose is to impose Muslim law and customs on Great Britain. Kalim Siddiqui is also the man behind the Salman Rushdie affair. He had ordered the auto da fé against the Satanic Verses. Ayatollah Khomeini's fatwah against the author only came later. This very same Kalim Siddiqui, a Muslim fundamentalist, has very British habits, as the Kensington Parliament will show us. Except for men in turbans and women in veils, the Muslim Parliament adopts all the rites and rituals of Westminster. Kalim Siddiqui goes as far as not addressing his colleagues; he directs all his comments to the Chairman of the Session, prefacing them with 'Mister Speaker'. The proceedings are conducted in English, the only language Commonwealth Muslims have in common. The Muslim parliament is very much in keeping with British community organisations and their way of functioning. 'It would be abnormal if two million British Muslims went unrepresented.' The purpose of this gathering is to preserve the cultural and religious identity of the Muslim community and to resist any attempt to try and integrate it. It was for this reason, explains Siddiqui, that Salman Rushdie was denounced. 'Muslims have shown the way to the Christians'. After the Rushdie affair, the BBC refrained from screening 'The Last Temptation of Jesus Christ' by Martin Scorcese so as not to offend the sensibilities of the faithful. Siddiqui insists that British institutions are in no way being harmed. In point of fact the Muslim community is helping in keeping them alive by reminding them that a civilisation is threatened when it abandons its moral and religious roots. For Siddiqui though, the West is fighting a rearguard battle as from now onwards Islam has become the sole custodian of morality in a decadent West. 'The proof being that only Islam is fighting against homosexuality and liberal deviance.' The West is the sick man of the modern world, 'it will,like Marxism, be consigned to the dust bins of history.' In fact Kalim Siddiqui's dialectics are very similar to Marxist dialectics after the collapse of the USSR. 'Islam is perfect', he explains, 'even though there is no historical proof. It is not Islam which is at fault, but those who are practicing it. All you have to do is to restart the experiment.'

The Muslim parliament intends to take under its wing the entire British Muslim population in order to prove the superiority of Islam. 'We will build,' announced Siddiqui, 'the best schools, the best universities, the best social institutions and the best factories.' Where will the money come from? The zaquat, that is 2.5% of the annual income of each Muslim, shall be given to the parliament. Siddiqui however foresees neither secession nor an Islamic revolution. 'The Muslim community is British and we have no intention of leaving Great Britain.' Muslim piety and the community's intellectual and economic success - 'We need million-aires,' the speaker proclaims - will perhaps save Great Britain from herself and her liberal gravediggers. In

Siddiqui's lexicon, liberals are those who defend free speech, the separation of religion and the State, and democracy. What is being suggested in place of democracy? Communities governed by their own laws coexisting on British soil, like the Western concessions in China or the Christian capitulations in the Middle East. This time, however, it will be the other way around, because henceforth it is the West which shall be occupied by a 'superior' society.

THE ANTI RACIST-BUSINESS

Let us continue our journey in British Islam. At Bradford, the old textile capital of Yorkshire, the signboards are in Urdu and the grocers are called Qureishi, Kakar or Mahmoud; you hardly come across a Smith or a Brown. It is like being in Karachi. It was here in 1987 that the 'Satanic Verses' were burnt. Anglican churches have been converted into mosques, and schoolgirls wear the Islamic headcloth. In former Victorian residences abandoned by British industrialists, live scores of families of Pakistani and Bangladeshi origin. All the symptoms that ravage 'invaded' European cities are present here: unemployment, violence, degradation of the town centre and the collapse of public education. Who is to blame? The Blacks, say the Whites. The Whites, because they are racist, reply the Blacks, who don't seem very black to me.

'We call ourselves Black,' explains Mohammed Naem, 'because we are non-white.' And to express solidarity with other ethnic minorities. 'Black is a political colour.' Naem himself was born in Pakistan. Covered with rings, necklaces and bracelets, he seems more gold than anything else. He heads the Council for Racial Equality at Bradford. The Council is funded partly by the State and partly by local bodies. There are about two hundred such councils in Britain, spread over all her cities. The Council is a large undertaking. Its offices, though not luxurious, are overstaffed and all the employees are of Indian origin. Naem likes to play the heavy boss. He deals in anti-racism. The Council he heads is responsible for implementing the 1976 racial equality law; this charter for ethnic minorities in Great Britain has no equivalent elsewhere in Europe. It is based on the recognition of racial differences and the resultant inequalities. The British model stands in sharp contrast to the French tradition of non discrimination or rather non differentiation.

Even though I can see Mohammed Naem's skin is the colour of coffee, being a Frenchman it means nothing to me. My colour-blindness, explains Mohammed Naem, is pure hypocrisy, typical of the French, who pretend not to notice race and who are as a result more racist than the most confirmed racist. Being colour-blind is the worst form of discrimination because it denies the obvious. In Great Britain, each one is recognised according to his or her race, white or non-white. If you are not white, you are black, or at the most defined as an 'ethnic minority', the term used for the Turks and the Poles. The minorities are further classified according to their degree of visibility: as a Pole, you belong to a 'non-visible ethnic minority'; as a Turk, you are 'a visible ethnic minority'; as a Pakistani, you become black. Another distinctive feature of the British model is that the State deals with communities and not individuals. It is up to the community to organise itself and appoint its 'leaders' with whom the authorities can negotiate. Integration policies, especially those pursued by municipal bodies, are community based. This is in contrast to the French model which assumes the spontaneous integration of individuals of indeterminate race.

There is another major difference between France and Great Britain. Communities, be they black or ethnic minorities, are almost all of British nationality, subjects of the Crown who legally entered the country in the fifties and the sixties on a Commonwealth passport; today their children are British citizens. And so now the Empire has 'colonised' the motherland. Great Britain's main concern is not immigration - stopped about twenty years ago - nor naturalization but the integration of coloured nationals, which is proving to be a difficult task indeed. The communities suffer from educational backwardness, police violence, bad housing, poverty and unemployment. At Bradford, a Black with the same qualifications as a White is four times more likely to be unemployed; a quarter of British prisoners are black, whereas they only represent five per cent of the total population. For Mohammed Naem and his ilk in Bradford and elsewhere, all these evils can be attributed to a single cause: racial discrimination.'White racism is the sole reason for all black problems.' Mohammed Naem firmly believes in what he says. Though he doesn't seem to bear any of the scars and makes his pronouncement with all the arrogance that my French skepticism warrants. This bothers Naem. He points out that the British are the only people in Europe to deal squarely with the question of racism. Like all professionals in the human rights business in Great Britain, he is afraid of what he calls 'Euroracism'. The British anti-racist left-wing is worried about the effects of the European Union on race relations. What the British persist in calling the 'Continent' is perceived from London and Bradford as an open field for the National Front to indulge in its fascist antics and the neo Nazis to go on a Gypsy hunt. These British leftwingers are extremely wary of the 'continental' left. For the latter, observes Naem, anti-racism is merely a talking point. No comprehensive legislation has been drawn up, nor is there any special department to fight against discrimination. What the European left has failed to realise is that as long as racial discrimination is not clearly defined as in Great Britain and Europe does not adopt a common strategy to deal with it, all anti-racist discourse will be counterproductive. In Great Britain, the whole interventionist rationale is based on the acceptance of discrimination as being the main reason for black backwardness. The Commissions for racial equality are waging a legal, political and media war against bad landlords, bad employers, xenophobic teachers and racist policemen. At Bradford, there is no shortage of clients. The ethnic communities in Britain are far more militant than their Dutch counterparts; perhaps because of their British nationality they have no fear of retaliation. But black activists are not content with militant anti-racist rhetoric alone. Through 'positive action', they want to corner as many jobs as possible.

THE LEEDS MODEL

Leeds, like its neighbour Bradford, used to depend on textiles for its livelihood. So too did the Pakistani immigrants. And then the factories closed down. Industry gave way to the service sector which required more qualified manpower. In the seventies, the Anglo-Pakistanis lost their jobs. Their children, born in Great Britain, are also jobless. Some of these Bradford teenagers are half-heartedly looking around for a job. Only the girls manage to pull through, doing secretarial work.

And so begins the long tale of woes: unemployment, dependency, poverty, violence, drugs, religious fundamentalism, cultural conflicts in Muslim families - a scenario all too familiar in the West.

Jobs, it does seem, are the only way out. This is where 'positive action' has a role to play. British racial equality laws call upon employers to make a special effort to engage minorities, but these are not binding. Furthermore, the law prohibits any form of discrimination, even positive discrimination, likely to favour a particular race or sex. So there can be no question of preferential recruitment, special favour or quotas. This narrows down the scope for positive action, limiting it to the pre-recruitment stage; for example, getting applications from people who would not have thought of applying on their own. This is what the Leeds local council - the biggest employer in the city - is doing. It handles all public services and employs thirty-seven thousand people out of a population of two hundred thousand. Ten percent of the Leeds population is black. So since 1990, the local council has set itself a target of 10% black recruitment; initially, only 5% of its staff was black.

Phase I: Inviting applications. The local council advertises vacant posts in the ethnic press and puts up notices in community centres. All over Great Britain, minority presses are thriving on these classified ads. Phase II: keeping qualifications down to what is strictly necessary for the job. For instance, a bus driver does not need to know English to drive. Very often, I am told at the Leeds personnel office, the minimum qualifications stipulated at the time of recruitment are implicitly discriminatory; this is true too for the private sector. Phase III: once the candidate - preferably black or at least a woman or a disabled person - has crossed all the initial hurdles, it is generally found that his or her qualifications are not up to the mark. He or she will then be taken care of and 'nursed' as a trainee for two years. In most cases, after such extensive nursing, the Black will get a job, not through any preferential treatment which is legally prohibited, but because of the constant care given. In this way, about two hundred people are covered every year. Once recruited, Blacks continue to receive the same attention to ensure that they are not discouraged or harassed by their white colleagues and guaranteed the same promotion avenues as their white counterparts - this without being shown any undue favour. Fifty civil servants are needed to carry out the whole exercise. They work at the Leeds Town Hall in the Equal Opportunities Department headed by Lyn Alderton, an anti-racist activist with a vaguely Trotskyist background, a species that always manages to thrive in Labour Britain.

A Black walks in with sandwiches and tea with milk for us. It must be four o'clock. 'Even though it's been three years since she's gone, we are still besieged by Thatcherism,' declares Lyn Alderton. 'In the name of a balanced budget, the Conservatives are dismantling all our social institutions.' But with its fifty civil servants, isn't the Leeds Equal Opportunities Department a wee bit overstaffed? Lyn Alderton concedes that the fight against discrimination is an expensive business. Apart from the Department, there are also the numerous voluntary advisory committees with a permanent secretariat managed by the Mayor's Office. All this to recruit two hundred Blacks a year! 'Well, you have to look for them,' admits Lyn Alderton. The press and the Conservative opposition members on the local council never fail to denounce such wastage. Lyn

Alderton like a true anti-racist, agitprop activist has found an unassailable argument: the Equal Opportunities Department not only defends the cause of the Blacks but also that of women and the disabled. Now who would dare begrudge women and the disabled?

Even with the limited financial and legal means available, Lyn Alderton feels that positive action can succeed. It is a question of political will. To prove her point, Lyn Alderton tells me about the work she was doing previously in the coloured municipality of Haringey in North London. Haringey was the first municipality to adopt in 1982 the principle of ethnic accountancy and commit itself to an active policy of racial equality. This decision was taken at the initiative of an extreme left local committee. At Haringey, Blacks constitute 40% of the population. 'How many black municipal employees do you think there are after ten years of positive action?' she asks me. 40%, I reply. I guessed right.

Lyn Alderton had planned to help gays and lesbians by the same means but she left Haringey too soon. Will she succeed at Leeds? Probably not, for she admits that times have changed. The fight against discrimination is no longer the great political cause it used to be in the early eighties: today, it's more a question of management than revolution.

THE SIKHS VS ALL

Positive action as a means for integration does sound convincing. As discrimination is believed to be the main cause for unemployment, a vigorous policy of training, recruiting and promoting the minorities looks like the right way to integrate the Blacks. What I had actually seen and the impassioned arguments put forth had more or less won me over to positive action. That is till I met Montek Bhasin.

He has a pompous sounding title: President of the Gurdwara. What exactly is a gurdwara? The address seemed distinguished enough: Barry House, Sussex Place, Kensington, a good locality in London. Having reached the appointed place, for a moment I thought I had come to the wrong address. Barry House is a small hotel of the bed and breakfast kind that proliferate all over London. But Montek Bhasin was very much there at the doorstep, wearing a black turban. This was his hotel and the gurdwara, a Sikh religious congregation, was seated in the basement dining room. While Mrs Bhasin was plying us with French toasts, so very British, President Bhasin was instructing me in the three basic tenets of his faith: always remember God, work hard and help the poor.

'We are,' he added, 'the Jews of the Indian world: our community is well knit, we believe in education and carry our faith with us wherever we go. And we hope to succeed as well as the Jews.'

There are about a hundred thousand Sikhs in Great Britain. For many years, their fortunes depended on the British whom in India they used to serve as chauffeurs and soldiers. What makes them stand out is that not a single Sikh is unemployed in Great Britain. Bhasin explains that a Sikh would rather do any job than be idle. He will never accept dole or live on public money. At the very worst, he will seek help from the charitable institutions of his own community. The members present nod their heads in agreement. Mrs Bhasin serves a second round of French toasts, even more oily than the first lot.

Unlike other minorities, are the Sikhs immune to discrimination? On the contrary, their beard and turban single them out, exposing them to ridicule right from the time they go to school. Because of their visibility, they have to bear the brunt of the contempt in which the British seem to hold Indians in general. The average Britisher, for whom all Asians are alike, calls them Pakis, the diminutive for Pakistanis, even though they are not so. Montek Bhasin explains that as the Sikhs are so easily identifiable they have to behave in an exemplary manner, unless of course the reputation of the community is at stake. Bhasin is certainly embroidering facts. However, it is quite true that very few Sikhs have been found committing offenses in Great Britain. Their beards and turbans making it difficult for them to get jobs, they have been forced to turn to businesses: the head of every second family is either a trader or an entrepreneur and employs other Sikhs. As they have difficulties in being accepted as tenants, they have had to buy their own houses.

But are these economically well adjusted Sikhs (better off than most Blacks) British? Apart from their passports, there is hardly anything British about them. At the Barry House Gurdwara where Sikhs continued to stream in as our interview progressed, conversation did not take long in turning to a question of real interest to the community: the political situation in India and other Sikh diasporas in Canada and Australia, even more prosperous than those in Great Britain. Today in London, the Gurdwara could well shift to Toronto, Sydney or even New Delhi, should it be prompted by economic considerations. What lessons does this unusual community, comparable in certain respects to the overseas Chinese, hold out for us? In the first place, by overemphasising white racism we tend to forget that to a certain degree the Blacks are responsible for their own fate. Secondly, the culture of a minority plays as much of a role in shaping its destiny as the conditions obtaining in the host country. The Sikh example brings out clearly the limitations of viewing discrimination as the sole cause of social marginalisation; that does not mean however that we give up the fight against discrimination. As all Blacks are not Sikhs, it is to no earthly purpose to regret the fact that they do not share the same work ethic. Positive action in favour of non Sikhs may not yield great results, but that does not mean it is not worth a try. In any case no one in Great Britain plans giving up positive action; today, the debate centres more around whether it should be extended to the private sector. The left is for it and is asking companies to maintain ethnic accounts and recruit their staff on racial lines; somewhat like in Ulster where companies have to show a religious balance sheet in order to prove that they are not discriminating between Catholics and Protestants. Positive action is likely to make more demands on companies, considering the number of Blacks in Great Britain is hardly likely to stop growing.

ENGLAND, INSULAR NO MORE

England's former colonies have always flocked to her shores. But now, people are pouring in from all sides; the South and the East, the Balkans and French speaking Africa, communities that have no historic or linguistic ties with the Commonwealth. Britain is having to bear the brunt of tighter immigration policies on the Continent. Even in the heart of Africa, asylum seekers know all about immigration procedures in Europe and go from one country to the next, depending on how they are going to be received. The immigrants have understood the nature of European space before the Europeans themselves. British authorities have the reputation of being more vigilant and less corrupt than those on the Continent. Their borders, easier to guard, are better protected. But immigration, forbidden in principle, continues unchecked through the usual channels: family reunions, tourism and asylum applications.

First, let us look at family reunions, supposedly subject to many restrictions in Great Britain. On paper, there is a primary purpose clause which allows the authorities to refuse entry to a husband or wife if the primary purpose of the marriage is to facilitate immigration. No doubt arbitrary, this clause has had human rights associations, the Asian community and the Labour Party up in arms. Which makes it virtually inapplicable, affecting not more than two thousand people a year.

What about refugees? Towards the end of the eighties, there were about four thousand a year. In the nineties, the figure shot up to fifty thousand. Of these, eighty per cent will be refused political refugee status, but only after a long process, one that could go on for four to five years. All refugees are looked after by the municipalities. They are provided accommodation, schooling, health care, and the State gives them 90% of the minimum welfare allowance. Humanitarian organisations, extremely powerful in Great Britain, are always on the watch. After six months of their arrival, asylum seekers are authorised to work; after four years, they can bring in their families. And hardly any one is likely to be deported even after being denied the status of political refugee.

Finally, illegal immigration is so much easier in Great Britain as identity cards do not exist and there is no way of bringing employers to book if they employ illegal immigrants.

In 1991, the Conservative government had decided to speed up procedures for deciding asylum cases and to take the finger prints of asylum seekers to avoid welfare frauds. Even this innocuous step raised a storm of protest from the anti-racist movements, the churches and the Labour Party. Needless to say, it had to be abandoned. In Great Britain, the fear of immigration does not make political capital. Anti-racism does. Immigration will therefore continue till as long as the South remains poor and war ravaged, British companies recruit cheap labour and public authorities bear the expenses of refugees. What else can be done? No one in Great Britain has any radical solution to offer. The main thing, explains an Immigration Director at the Home Ministry, is to stay calm, be relaxed and ensure that the tea break carries on. It's more important for the English, he concludes, to safeguard their civil liberties - no identity card, no finger prints, no unwarranted police checks - than to check immigration.

WHAT IS A NATION?

Can the British model be applied to the rest of Europe as anti-racist activists claim? Or is it historically specific and non transferable? There is something to be said for both. Community based organisation is rooted in imperial culture, a product of English history and colonisation. The British subject traditionally belonged to a religious or ethnic community. Unlike in France where nationhood is based on the idea of individuals entering into a social contract, in England the nation is the aggregate of communities which organically participate in its life. A British subject

quite willingly identifies himself first as a Welsh
Catholic or a Scottish Presbyterian, then as a British
citizen. Nationality is a fairly new idea, a non essential
one at that. The same principle is at work in the case
of immigrants who are asked to incorporate themselves
into their own communities and stay put. This
community structure which, with immigration, has led
to racial conditioning, has shades of apartheid. This
is all the more true because race often determines
where one lives. Even on the Continent, immigrants
from the same community tend to group together in
the same locality. Still, they find it easier to escape
from their milieu than in Great Britain. London's
community neighbourhood makes it difficult for an
individual to move out and integrate into the white
mainstream. A Jamaican is tied down to Brixton very
much like a South African Black who cannot leave
Soweto. Identifying individuals with their community
can lead to strange paradoxes, especially as people
from the former colonies come from very diverse
backgrounds. At the time of a census, an Indian from
Jamaica could be listed as an Asian, even though his
roots lie in America; a Hong Kong Chinese may find
himself in the same category as a Guyana born
Pakistani and a West Indian Black could be clubbed
together with a Nigerian. But aren't those at the
forefront of the fight against discrimination using the
community structure to consolidate their own power
base? The meticulous classification of society into
communities, tribes and ethnic groups on the part of
the Whites is an obvious reminder of the former
colonial practice of divide and rule. How the English
were able to rule over millions of Indians for more
than a hundred and fifty years with only a few
thousand civil servants is well known. Today, the

Indians have come to the Metropolis and become British citizens; but they are still being governed in the same way. With the State financing the fight against discrimination, haven't the leaders of dispersed communities been bought off with positions in the innumerable official organisations? For many black leaders, racial equality has become a thriving business, entirely dependent on the bounty of the State. These leaders have just about as much freedom as the Maharajas of yore vis-à-vis the Vice-Roy of India. Who else has gained anything from the public campaign against discrimination, launched fifteen years ago? Black unemployment and imprisonment have not fallen; the jobs generated by positive action have only benefited the black nomenklatura, which has wangled posts for itself in municipal departments and anti-racist committees.

Only a handful of intellectuals, often of West Indian origin - Harry Golbourne is one of them - have attempted a critique of positive action and the community structure. They are arguing in favour of French style individual integration. But the white and non-white establishment - right and left alike- is quick to put them down. For curiously enough, all political forces are clamouring for strengthening the community structure, though motivated by different reasons. The left-wing Labour Party, because it supports multiculturalism and protects the identity of minority communities. The Conservatives, because they are convinced of the impossibility of black integration. From their point of view, 'East is East and West is West and the twain shall never meet'. This rationale implies that Blacks can never really become British. Or perhaps one should think in terms of a situation in which the Whites will be considered just another ethnic community. In both cases, Goulbourne wonders what will become of the nation. If the Whites are its sole custodians, then nationhood can no longer be defined in terms of citizenship. On the other hand, if the nation belongs equally to all communities, it will loose its identity, reduced as it will be to a mere piece of land on which different cultures coexist. Is the British model, so far removed from French practice, another one of those quaint English traditions like boiled lamb and double decker buses? Is it a Conservative strategy used by the Whites to maintain their privileges while paying lip service to minority equality? Or could it be the shape of things to come, where the nation will be nothing more than a territory on which various communities and tribes happen to coexist; where each group will pursue its own aims, respecting some form of collective ownership so as not to be perenially at war with its neighbours? The prophets of doom are likely to invoke the spectre of balkanisation. Others will see this as the dying away of the nation-state, a nineteenth century invention, and the beginning of a post-modern, individualistic and diversified society.

5

THE AMERICAN TRIBES

Stephen Carter will never know whether he got into Yale because he was good or because he was black. He went on to teach there and recounts how he got admitted in his book, 'Affirmative Action Baby', published in 1991. This hard hitting account of his experience evoked a mixed response in the U.S.

In the early eighties, after graduating from Stanford, Stephen Carter applied to the Law Schools of Yale and Harvard. Yale accepted him immediately on the basis of his past record. Harvard turned him down. Stephen Carter was mortified. A couple of days later, he got another letter from the Dean of admissions at Harvard. 'Sorry, we didn't know you were black. We would be happy to have you.' Since then, Stephen Carter has come a long way with many degrees and legal research papers to his credit. Yet in spite of all his achievements, his peers still believe Stephen Carter got his law degree from Yale because he was black. Carter can't help but wondering: did he get his job at Yale on merit or because the Whites wanted to make up for all those years of black slavery? Fellow Blacks find him equally suspect. They feel he betrayed their cause by playing the game according to white rules instead of trying to change the game itself.

Stephen Carter's personal odyssey sums up all the dilemmas of affirmative action, the American way of integrating minorities into colleges, universities, the administration and private companies with government dealings.

Defining affirmative action is by no means easy. The way it works depends not only on the law, but also on how judges interpret it. Over the last thirty years, the 'rule of judges' as established by the Supreme Court of the United States has drastically changed the definition of racial equality. To avoid being accused of racism or sexism, it is not enough for a company or institution to demonstrate its willingness to take on minorities; it has to show tangible results. Now racial equality can no longer be equated with traditional notions of equal opportunity and equality before the law: only results count, intentions are of no consequence.

For equality to be achieved in terms of results, the law and the courts do not in principle allow reverse discrimination; this means that quotas for a given minority or recruitment policies biased in favour of a minority are not legally acceptable. So courts condemn positive discrimination, in other words voluntary or implicit racism; they also come down on negative discrimination or favoritism, though not as heavily. A narrow, torturous path indeed!

Who stands to gain from affirmative action? It is supposed to guarantee equal opportunity to the 'protected minorities': Blacks, Hispanics, Asians and American Indians. And women, of course. Amazingly, the law offers the same protection to new immigrants such as the 'Chicanos' - second generation Mexicans

- as to the Blacks who came to the continent three hundred years ago. This is because discrimination and not immigration is the criterion for protection. Blacks are regarded as 'domestic' immigrants, just recently 'arrived' in American society. From the thirties to the fifties, several million Blacks left the agricultural belt in the South and moved to the industrialised North East, very much like the current influx of Mexican immigrants. In some ways Blacks living in cities are like second generation immigrants. The same can be said for the American Indians who gave up their reserves to join mainstream America. Women, also victims of discrimination especially in the workplace, have stood to gain in the bargain, getting the same concessions as the minorities.

All in all, affirmative action is not a theory but something which is actually being practiced. The ultimate purpose is to make objective conditions comparable for all races. There is no single method. Each institution - be it a company, university or town hall - has evolved its own system; there are considerable variations depending on the region and the power structure. For a Frenchman, trained as he is to think logically and used to administrative uniformity, it seems like a morass of regulations and communities. America is somewhat puzzling, to say the least.

A MULTICULTURAL UNIVERSITY

'Stephen Carter's book,' protests Sharon Parker, 'is part of a reactionary, racist plot hatched by George Bush and conservative intellectuals like Irving Kristol and Allen Bloom. Their sole aim is to restore white privileges.' Stephen Carter's criticism of affirmative action is not valid, it is an individualistic point of view and shows Carter's lack of solidarity with his own people. The Blacks have the right to be compensated for the years of slavery and discrimination they have had to endure. On the affirmative action issue positions immediately harden, each side accusing the other of an anti-white or anti-black conspiracy. Sharon Parker is neither black nor white. Born of black and Indian parentage, she is married to an Indian. She couldn't have done better. In the sixties, she was an Indian rights activist - sorry in PC that should read native American rights activist - and since 1990 she has been in charge of the Multicultural Office at Stanford in California. This is a key post of symbolic value in the American controversy over affirmative action, as for the last fifteen years Stanford has been at the forefront of the crusade challenging white supremacy. One of the most radical, left-wing universities in the U.S., Stanford also happens to be among the most expensive. When it comes to worthy causes, the students and teachers of Stanford have left no stone unturned. Be it the whales, the ozone layer, boycotting South Africa, unilateral U.S. disarmament, the campaign against Eurocentricism in history and literature courses, saving the spotted owl from Oregon woodcutters - they have fought for them all.

Stanford has come to represent an America which is no longer fully white. Thanks to one of the most vigorous affirmative action programmes, forty-five percent of the students enrolled here belong to the 'minorities'. Sharon Parker informs me that this is in keeping with the state's demographic composition. But Conservative Whites see in this coloured outbreak a plot in which affirmative action has become a tool in the hands of activists like Sharon Parker. 'It's no plot,' she retorts, 'only demography.' She does however concede that a little prodding is required to get the right demographic mix. You have to scout out Blacks, Hispanics, Chicanos and Indians, as they hesitate to apply on their own to a university as elitist as Stanford. The University sends coloured recruiting agents to high schools in California to look for potential students from their own community and offer them scholarships. But what guarantee is there that these coloured applicants will clear the entrance exam? It seems as if quotas have been fixed implicitly. 'Quotas, how dreadful!' exclaims Sharon Parker. The word is taboo and such practices illegal. Perhaps, she concedes, some small universities hard pressed to get good students do have some kind of black quota; a pity, but that is not the case at Stanford.

Which brings us back to square one. How does one guarantee that non white students, often from underprivileged backgrounds and poor schools, get into Stanford? What you need is a 'diversified' admission policy, says Sharon Parker. When scrutinising applications, the committee does not only consider scholastic achievement but looks at the overall personality of the applicant. One's qualities as a human being, sportsmanship, artistic ability and capacity to contribute to the cultural life of the university all matter. The aim of this exercise is to ensure that Stanford's student population be as interesting as possible. The admission form contains questions like: 'Describe an old family custom', or 'What kind of relationship do you think you will have with your room-mates?' Were scholastic achievement the only yardstick, Sharon Parker explains, it would be tantamount to discrimination in favour of the Whites, 'as exams are based on a specifically white world view'. As a matter of fact, 'the Whites who criticize affirmative action for the minorities do not

realise that the entire American society is geared
towards Whites: what comes naturally to the Whites,
what they consider normal is actually a permanent
form of discrimination in their favour.' Affirmative
action for coloured people is only a very modest way
of compensating for the immense institutional preference
given to Whites; the day these preferences go, there
will be no need for affirmative action.

Once enrolled at Stanford, it is important that
coloured people and minorities feel good. This is also
part of Sharon Parker's job. Her Department for
Multiculturalism finances black, Mexican American
and Indian clubs and shows. The Association of Gays,
Lesbians and Bi-sexuals felt that it was being
discriminated against because it had no premises. That
was no problem, Sharon Parker simply converted a
closed down fire station into a club room for them.
The Whites can claim no special rights; it is time the
superior race learnt humility. The old fraternities have
been banned as they have been rightly suspected of
perpetrating racist traditions.

And then you have the Asians, who've proved to
be most embarrassing. Chinese, Japanese and Vietnamese
students apply en masse at Stanford, pass all the
exams, snap up all the prizes and tread on the
preserves of other coloured people. Should there be
a *numeres clausus* in order to check the flow? Such was
the case in the seventies, when big universities limited
the number of Jews they took in. Sharon Parker
wonders whether the admission criteria are somehow
biased in favour of the Asians. Oh well, they will just
have to be diversified!

There is however one small hitch on the road to
minority success and that is getting the degree. 45%
of the new admissions are minority students, but only

20% of them leave the university with a degree in hand. That is because the exams are the same for everyone, at least till now. Should the criteria be diversified at this level too? Some second ranking universities do so if only to attract minorities. Stanford hasn't followed suit as yet.

THE WHITE WOMAN'S LAMENT

'We are guilty, we must make amends,' proclaims Maureen O'Connor, the Mayor of San Diego, one of California's most prosperous cities. An ultra-conservative Republican, Ms. O'Connor feels that there is nothing leftist about affirmative action. 'I want my government to be clean, a model for our society and a mirror of the people who elected me. 20% of my voters are Hispanic, so my office employs 20% Hispanics, and women hold 46% of all jobs.' Maureen O'Connor has opened a municipal school for women who want to work in the fire brigade. Why the fire brigade? Because in all the cities which follow a policy of affirmative action, the fire brigade and the police force happen to be high on the list of minority preferences. Both are high visibility jobs, traditionally occupied by Whites, and both wield considerable political clout. Firemen's unions are the main electoral agents in American town life. Every three months, Ms O'Connor asks all her departmental heads to give her a progress report on minority integration for the ten thousand employees taken on by the city. Their promotion depends on how far they succeed with affirmative action, not only in quantitative but also in qualitative terms. Recruiting at the bottom of the ladder is not enough; Ms O'Connor aims to achieve 'vertical parity', as management is still a white male prerogative. I notice that the Mayor doesn't say white but 'non minority'. Nowadays, this is the politically correct term in California.

San Diego also has a politically correct motto: *Diversity brings us together.* Certainly 'diversity' sounds much better than 'quotas reserved for ethnic minorities'. Then how does one 'manage diversity'? This is phase 2 of affirmative action. How do you teach a male white foreman not to look a Mexican worker straight in the eye as this goes against his culture. How can you make a Laotian firewoman work with a Filipino, a Mexican and an Irish captain when they don't share a common language? There are no ready made solutions. You just have to play it by ear. 'We are very attentive to what the minorities have to teach us. Believe me, it's fascinating.' I ask her whether departmental efficiency ever suffers on account of too much 'diversity'. 'Of course,' admits Maureen O'Connor, 'but then there are things more important than efficiency. The minorities and the non minorities have to work together.'

A SWARTHY SHERIFF

On the 2nd of January, 1992 Julia Cordero was appointed Deputy Sheriff at Santa Anna in California. I was there that day. Her colleagues, white males, were not overly enthusiastic about her promotion. For the first time in the history of Santa Anna, a woman, a Mexican at that, had become deputy sheriff. 'If only she had been taller,' the men told me. Julia Cordero was barely 5'3"; so for her to get the job, the minimum height required had to be changed. Cordero, countering the criticism of her sexist and racist colleagues, retorted, 'I am as American as you, and that too for much longer!' The other policemen were not just complaining about Cordero's sex and height. They were questioning her ability, hinting that she got her promotion only because she was a woman and coloured. They accused the County Sheriff of reverse discrimination against white males and were threatening to go to court. But did Jim Roache, the county sheriff, have any choice in the matter? He is due for reelection soon and his electorate comprises 35% Mexican-Americans who are closely watching his minority record to see if he deserves a second term.

Moreover, since 1975 the county has been placed under the supervision of the court. At the time, *Raza Unida*, a Hispanic anti-racist group had filed a case against the county, accusing it of racial discrimination: all the sheriffs were white and male and so were all the firemen. The suit resulted in the Court giving a consent decree by which the county undertook to respect the equality of race and sex in matters relating to recruitment and promotion. The judge fixed quantitative goals for each profession and department so they reflected the race and sex composition of the county. As a result, 21% of the deputy sheriffs had to be Hispanics because they represented 21% of Santa Anna's population and 46% had to be women. The same was the case for the fire brigade. Though the judge did not set any time limit, he constantly reviews the situation to see whether the authorities are moving in the right direction.

Achieving these targets is a difficult proposition, as women of Hispanic origin are not exactly falling over to apply for such jobs. So, explains sheriff Roache, you have to work on these communities. Julia Cordero will serve as a model and be called upon to make speeches to young Hispanic high school girls. Now supposing some girls do apply, will they be able to

clear the same exams and aptitude tests as their white
male competitors? Californian law - though this is not
true everywhere- does not allow different criteria for
different categories of applicants nor does it allow
quotas for minorities. Sheriff Roache hit upon a novel
solution: he simply did away with all the tests which
put women at a disadvantage, particularly those
relating to minimum height and physical fitness,
qualities not strictly necessary for becoming a sheriff.

And if, in spite of all this, not enough Blacks,
Hispanics or women get the minimum score required
to be eligible for recruitment or promotion, what then?
After a protracted legal battle started by some black
or Hispanic civil rights group, the exam will probably
be declared discriminatory, the results proving it to
be biased against the minorities. In such cases, the
judge, in order to meet the quantitative goals, will
simply 'broaden' the result and let through a certain
number of protected minorities candidates who failed
to clear the test. This is how Julia Cordero's name
appeared on the deputy sheriff's aptitude list and the
sheriff was able to appoint her. He was under no
compulsion to do so. In fact, admits Roache, there
were other more qualified candidates. But affirmative
action brought in a new distinction: the choice between
more qualified and better qualified. Julia Cordero was
not more qualified but better qualified to the extent
that she had what the department was lacking,
'diversity'. Finally, even though the sheriff was in
principle free to choose anyone, had he not taken on
Julia Cordero, the only Hispanic candidate on the
aptitude list, he would have had to justify the 'reasons
for her non selection' in writing. If someone from a
'protected minority' fails to get selected in spite of
having the minimum qualifications, a written explanation

which is 'rational, in good faith and specifically related to the job in question' is called for. This rule does not apply to the Whites.

Yet Sheriff Cordero feels this is not enough to compensate for the hundred and fifty six years of discrimination suffered by Mexican Americans. A hundred and fifty six years? I ask. In 1836, Davy Crockett died defending Fort Alamo and a defeated Mexico surrendered her north western territories to the United States. In this way Julia Cordero became a minority and acquired the right to compensation!

ONE OUT OF EVERY TWO POLICEMEN IN BOSTON

Affirmative action is not always as subtle in achieving results. Wherever political equations allow, the term quota is used without any reservation; this is the case in Boston.

For over two hundred years, discrimination was as brutal in Boston as it was in the South. However twenty years ago, the Blacks, on account of their numerical strength, came to play a decisive role in politics. Expectedly, the 'communities' went to court to settle their scores. A simple rule was adopted: ever since 1978, one out of every two posts in the police force, the fire brigade, the bus services and the city's teaching staff has been reserved for a Black or a Hispanic. All those who apply for the same job have to take the same test. But there are two aptitude lists: one for Whites, another for the rest. The Mayor, the police and fire brigade chiefs are obliged to recruit an equal number from each list. Vietnam and Gulf war veterans are the sole exceptions, as they have top priority. Once the veterans and the minorities have been taken in, there are not too many posts left for the Whites. As a result, white Unions in Boston are now complaining about reverse discrimination.

Boston's Mayor Ray Flynn, of Irish origin, justifies the quotas: 'We had to catch up on the accumulated backlog.' Blacks now constitute 23% of the police force as against 1% fifteen years ago. But the city has a new headache: the Asians! Their numbers are on the increase, they have colonised some Boston quarters and seldom speak English. It wouldn't be a bad idea to recruit Asian policemen but neither the Whites nor the Blacks nor the Hispanics are willing to give up even a single job from their quotas and the Asian community is still too fragile to wield any electoral clout.

Isn't it possible to put an end to quotas, as discrimination is on its way to becoming extinct? Out of the question, declare the leaders of the Black community. Ray Flynn agrees with them, not just because of electoral considerations. The level of education of the Blacks and Hispanics when they leave public schools is so low that if quotas were scrapped, they would never be able to clear the same exams as the Whites. Affirmative action in the civil services is just a way of catching up on the disastrous education that the minorities have been given.

Since the last fifteen years, Boston is the one American city where affirmative action has been practiced systematically; it is also the city where criticism against quotas is at its most virulent. According to the Conservatives, quotas only serve to further the political aspirations of minority leaders and appease the white sense of guilt. Quite true, but what would have become of Boston without affirmative action? Who can tell. Perhaps racial integration would have come about of its own accord, as the Conservatives claim. Perhaps not. In the sixties, like many other large American cities, Boston had witnessed violent clashes between young Blacks and white policemen. Since affirmative action, such incidents have not recurred. The Black and Hispanic riots that broke out in Los Angeles and Atlanta in May 1992 did not reach Boston. The cause and effect relationship between the calm and quiet in Boston and the police recruitment policy cannot be proved but nor can it be discounted. Perhaps affirmative action is the price, however high, that has to be paid to maintain urban peace.

A HARD WORLD

The Mexicans have recaptured Dallas! Domingo Garcia, one of the city's municipal councillors informs me that till 1988, the Mayor's Office - an unwieldy bureaucratic apparatus with a staff of seventeen thousand of which eight thousand belong to the police force - was in the hands of the Anglos. Anglos? In Texas, this is the term used to describe all Whites. Garcia himself is a 'Mexican American'. Though they constituted only 50% of the population, by joining forces, the Anglos always managed to keep out Mexican Americans and Blacks from the municipal council and the local administration. Discrimination! shouted minority leaders. Domingo Garcia, one of them, was a lawyer. The matter was taken to court and in 1991, a federal judge divided the city into fourteen ethnically homogeneous districts so that each community could appoint its own representatives. The ploy worked: Domingo Garcia was elected by fellow Mexican Americans and the town council came under the control of a coalition of elected Blacks, Mexican Americans, feminists and progressive Anglos. Since then the administration did a turnaround in favour of the discriminated minorities. Domingo Garcia calls it reverse discrimination which will ultimately 'put an end to all discrimination'.

But affirmative action is not merely limited to municipal jobs. Companies dealing with the Mayor's Office are also expected to apply it: we are talking about a sixty-three million dollar gold mine every year. The municipal council has set a target (not a 'quota') of reserving 35% of the city's contracts for the disadvantaged business enterprises or the DBE. What is a DBE? Any company run by a member of a protected minority - Mexican American, Black, Red Indian - or a woman. Though not a legally protected minority, Asians in Dallas are treated as an 'informal minority'. A municipal department decides whether a firm is a DBE or not. Its job is to ensure that the firm is genuine and not a front. Can an Anglo entrepreneur run a DBE? Yes, if the entrepreneur happens to be a woman or disabled. The 35% of contracts kept aside for the DBE's should not however violate the law stipulating that every contract must go to the best bidder. To keep Anglos at bay, Domingo Garcia and his black colleagues declare them ineligible on the pretext that they do not fulfill all the tender requirements. In case no certified DBE is capable of satisfying the technical specifications of the contract, the Anglo entrepreneur is asked to subcontract whatever possible to DBE's...

What can one say about this odd mix of political patronage and capitalism which passes off as a minorities integration policy? On the debit side, there is widespread corruption; the DBE certifying authorities, the elected representatives who award contracts and the Anglo companies which operate behind ethnic fronts all want their share of the cake. Domingo Garcia concedes that maybe the city is paying its suppliers a little more than it would have had to without quotas, but this is the price to be paid for the fight against discrimination. On the credit side, we have seen the emergence of a new social group, as a number of small companies have been set up by minority entrepreneurs. They recruit their staff from among the coloured people most hit by unemployment. And then there is that sweet taste of revenge Domingo Garcia so savors, 'For more than a hundred and fifty years, the Americans have been lying about Alamo. Davy Crockett's men were not Americans but Mexicans, fighting against General Santa Anna's dictatorship. Davy Crockett did not die a hero in the ruins of the fort, he was shot down on his knees, begging for mercy from the Mexicans!' In the hard world of Dallas, whom do you believe?

MULTICULTURAL CAPITALISM

It is time to move to the next airport in this tribal America where dreary urban suburbia and fast food chains are consuming the vast, open spaces. As you enter Detroit, a gigantic illuminated board flashes every minute the total number of cars produced since the beginning of the year. On the 7th of January 1992, the number of cars manufactured rose to 37,869. Detroit still is the car capital of the world, Japanese or no Japanese. Or perhaps because of them, for it was the Japanese who shook the three American giants out of their slumber.

At the Ford head office that morning, Louis Camardo was meeting with the members of two civil rights groups, the Push Movement founded by the Reverend Jesse Jackson and the Hispanic Association for Company

Supervision. During the meeting - an annual feature at Ford - Camardo discussed the company's performance. The report he presented was neither commercial nor financial; instead he gave an 'ethnic balance-sheet', highlighting the steps taken by the company to ensure black and Hispanic participation in Ford's development. Camardo stated that in 1991 the company had exceeded its target by recruiting 18% of its skilled workers from among the Blacks in an area with a 14% black population. Yes, but the same cannot be said for the management, was the Push repre-sentative's polite rejoinder. Camardo agreed and said he was sorry but neither the public schools in Detroit nor the engineering schools in the U.S. trained enough Blacks qualified for the automobile industry. Ford, Camardo added, was not satisfied with just recruiting Blacks and Hispanics. When selecting suppliers, subcontractors, agents, adver-tising agencies, banks, insurance agents and lawyers, the company saw to it that the minorities were equitably represented. In all Ford literature, advertisements in particular, the minorities have been given their rightful place.

Will the company reserve quotas for Blacks, Hispanics and women? 'Out of the question,' says Camardo. 'Let's say that targets have to be met.' Because Michigan has a 14% Black population, it stands to reason that Ford has 14% Blacks on its payrolls. If this doesn't happen, it means there is discrimination somewhere which has to be corrected through affirmative action. Camardo is quite clear this will not result in Ford hiring Black workers less qualified than their white counterparts: affirmative action does not mean reverse discrimination and different standards for Blacks and Whites. On the other hand, there is nothing wrong in sending out recruiters to schools to look for minority employees, if they do not apply themselves. Ford is also working towards reducing discrimination at the upper levels through scholarships and training programmes for the minorities - mainly Asians and women - traditionally under-represented in the automobile industry. Thus affirmative action is very much a part of company strategy; it needs an entire department, currently headed by Camardo, the equal opportunity planning manager.

Why try so hard ? The answers vary, depending on whom you ask. The Push Movement representatives will tell you that as Ford had been indicted in the early seventies by the American law ministry for racial discrimination, it is now compelled to support affirmative action. Not true ! retorts Louis Camardo. The company has been taking on Blacks since the thirties. Recognising that his workers were also his clients, Henry Ford wanted his staff to be a faithful picture of the nation (even though he himself was a wee bit racist). In any case, these are non issues for Camardo. 'In a market economy, morality and business are not contradictory, capitalism reconciles both.' Ford takes on minorities because the company's managers have a sense of social responsibility. This is not merely an act of altruism but one of enlightened self interest: minorities represent the bulk of the available labour force and will continue to do so. Besides, the minorities are also potential clients. Alienating them - some American companies did this - is an expensive proposition in terms of clients lost, what with boycott campaigns. The minorities certainly know how to organise themselves. No wonder companies are so whole-heartedly taking to affirmative action.

In Detroit, the meeting between the Ford managers and the ethnic associations ended in mutual backslapping. Each side felt it had got a good deal. That morning, capitalism did seem to have effectively reconciled social harmony with trade and morality with business. However, let us not make generalisations: an affirmative action as subtle as the Ford kind is more the exception than the rule in the private sector. Among the five hundred top American firms, only Chrysler and Rank Xerox have made a comparable effort. And among these five hundred, not a single one has a black president.

At Ford, every one seemed happy. At the Boston Mayor's office and Stanford, it looked as if the disadvantages outweighed the advantages. How does affirmative action work so well in a private company when it only gives rise to controversy in universities and excesses in administration? In the private sector, economic considerations govern affirmative action. Had Ford or any other employer gone too far in lowering recruitment standards, the company would not have been able to survive in the long run; the market succeeds in rationalising affirmative action. When all is said and done, a preferential policy in favour of minorities reconciles justice and utility as long as it takes into account the economic interests of all parties concerned. Conversely, if market forces do not regulate these preferential policies, then they are governed by the might is right principle.

BLACK VS BLACK

'In the name of which principle and for how many generations must today's Whites continue to pay today's Blacks for the misdeeds of their grandfathers?'

asks Glenn Loury. Affirmative action is the only issue
which divides America down the line, though much
of the criticism against it, especially white criticism,
is hackneyed and entirely predictable. I shall limit
myself to the most original points of view. It so
happens they have been expressed by black intellectuals;
they have no reason for self-recrimination. We shall
be meeting the economist Glenn Loury, the sociologist
William Julius Wilson and the philosopher Thomas
Sowell.

Glenn Loury began resisting affirmative action on
moral grounds: he has had enough of race! 'Race has
become the working capital of black intellectuals and
politicians.' On the Boston university campus where
Loury teaches economics, his stand has not exactly
made him popular. 'Behaving like a victim,' he says,
'is both comforting and reassuring. While waiting for
reparation, every Black is absolved of personal
responsibility.' For the black elite, nothing could be
more handy than self-victimisation; this way, they can
get the Whites to give them jobs, emoluments and
political representation. On the other hand, Loury
claims that Blacks who makes good on their own
merit are immediately suspected of betraying their
race, as refusing to play the victim is denying one's
race. The affirmative action rationale is this: a real
Black is one who remains poor and resembles the
archetypal victim. So, explains Loury, the social success
of some Blacks, instead of serving as a model for the
rest of the community, becomes a source of opprobrium.
If you have made it in white society, say professional
anti-racists, it is because you have sided with racism,
you have abandoned your brothers, you have become
an Uncle Tom. The only individual success accepted

by black revolutionaries as being politically correct is paradoxically the racist stereotype success story: sports persons, musicians and entertainers. Glenn Loury finds this attitude difficult to understand. 'Unlike other minorities, our leaders are asking us to look down rather than up, to identify with the poor Black rather than the Black who succeeds.' The role model of the victim appeases poor Blacks, as then racial identity compensates for lack of social status, even though it keeps them poor. On the other hand, successful Blacks are made to feel insecure till they begin to doubt their own ability. They never speak of their achievements, preferring to keep them hidden. Black children who do well at school are teased by their black schoolmates. They call them 'brainiacs' and force them to choose between their community and good grades, good grades being part of the white value system. According to Glenn Loury, self-victimisation is the root cause for the socio-economic backwardness of the Blacks. All affirmative action does is to legitimise the belief that black is synonymous with victim.

'A generation after the civil rights struggle and thirty years of affirmative action, the African-American has become a proletarian, violent, welfare dependent, drug taking inhabitant of the ghetto.' More than half of all black American children are not recognised by their father. Teenage African-Americans are twice as likely to find themselves in prison while in college. In the big cities like Chicago or Atlanta, 80% of American prisoners are black. Half the African-American population lives off state subsidies; welfare dependency - a new social ailment - is a term often heard when referring to them. These are not the findings of a white racist but an eminent black sociologist from the University of Chicago, William Julius Wilson. He was the first to have identified what he called a black 'underclass'. It has two distinctive features: economic degradation and geographical concentration. In Chicago, both these features are very clearly in evidence.

Has affirmative action been a failure? Should the U.S. give it up and should it be rejected elsewhere as well?

Wilson's answers are more subtle than my questions. Affirmative action has one major achievement to its credit: within the space of just twenty years it has given rise to a black elite and middle class, especially as far as the administration and the teaching profession is concerned. This would otherwise have been painfully slow or even impossible. However, creaming off the elite has not benefited the black community as a whole. Worse still, those who gain from affirmative action move out of the ghetto at the first opportunity, leaving the underclass without leaders or easily identifiable role models. The other drawback is that Whites start feeling they are the targets of reverse discrimination. Their passive resistance acts as a break on Black integration. All in all, Wilson is just as opposed to doing away with affirmative action as to extending its scope. Extending it would mean making quotas compulsory everywhere, which is what the black leaders are asking for. According to Wilson, such quotas would further widen the gap between the black elite and the black people as well as between all Blacks and all Whites. Can affirmative action be given up? This would be vindicating the racist reaction of the Whites. What is required is a different kind of preferential policy.

William Wilson thinks to get a policy of active racial integration accepted in a democracy, it has to be called by another name. He advocates a policy of full employment; in principle this would be applicable to all, but really it is the weakest sections - namely the Blacks - who would stand to gain the most. Experience tells us the Blacks are the first to be fired and the last to be hired by companies. There are several reasons for this: black and white racism, lack of work ethic and inadequate training. If the total number of jobs were to go up, the Blacks would benefit as they are more vulnerable to unemployment. A full employment policy not intended for Blacks alone but for all the underprivileged would go down better with the Whites and as a result be better for the Blacks. This is a lesson we would do well to remember when we discuss the Beurs in France.

Wilson's strategy is pragmatic but it is interventionist and community oriented. That is why Thomas Sowell is vehemently opposed to it. Sowell is an unusual intellectual; a misanthropist, he doesn't give interviews easily and never answers letters or the telephone. At Stanford's Hoover Institute- a high spot in ultraliberal research and ideology, where Milton Friedman had also worked - Sowell, to avoid meeting his colleagues, comes in only at night. Perhaps his aloofness is what makes his analysis so intransigent. Sowell starts with the assumption - this is what he has gleaned from the history of the United States and other mixed populations - that racism is not an obstacle to economic integration. In the course of American history, the Jews, the Irish and the Italians have all suffered persecution but it did not stop them from integrating. In other words, for Sowell, there is no better integration mechanism than the market economy. On the other hand, State interventionism, even in the name of anti-racism, always has the opposite effect. Black Americans have become an underclass not because they are black, not because the Whites are racist - the Whites are racist but that is inconsequential - not because they had been enslaved, not because African-American culture represents an obstacle to their integration, but because the State wanted to help them! It is this do gooding demon that is at the root of the Blacks' misfortune, for it has set them apart as a community.

Let us explain this Sowellian paradox. A white employer is not a priori enthusiastic about engaging a Black. More often than not, Blacks are underqualified and their reputation as workers is not the best. Still a White will take on a Black if the money he is paid is low enough to compensate for his lack of skills. So in the nineteen fifties, when there was no such thing as a minimum wage or affirmative action in the U.S., there were proportionately more Blacks on the labour force than Whites of the same age. Once they joined the labour force, these Blacks made economic progress like the other minorities before them. Unfortunately, according to Thomas Sowell, since 1963, at the behest of the American left and Presidents Kennedy and Johnson, the legal minimum wage and affirmative action were introduced with a view to protecting black employment. What happened in fact was that Blacks were taken off the labour market. For the white employer, the economic cost of employing a Black became too high. For a young, unskilled Black, affirmative action seemed to confer privileges : right to compensation, right to a high salary, right to job reservations. Between white refusal and new black demands, the natural adjustments of the market place have been replaced by conflict, growing racism and violence. Instead of affirmative action based on state intervention and community belonging, Thomas Sowell is suggesting a return to the market and individualism. Each one for himself and the liberal economy for all would be far more beneficial for the Blacks than the illusory protection of preferential policies.

Is Sowell's analysis accurate? Any answer can only be hypothetical, as society never repeats itself. What would have happened in the U.S. without affirmative action? Who knows. There might have been full black employment. Or perhaps the black elite might have brought about the social revolution that affirmative action stalled.

The misfortunes of another community, the Puerto Ricans, seem to confirm the harm done by welfare aid that Sowell has decried. As American citizens, the three million Puerto Ricans residing in the U.S. are entitled to all welfare benefits; and yet they are the poorest community in the U.S., worse off than even the Blacks. Is discrimination the reason? The Puerto Ricans are more white than black and they have never been slaves. Is their culture to blame? It is no different from the culture of other Latin Americans in the United States. But other Latin immigrants do not get citizenship. So they do not enjoy the same kind of welfare benefits and have no choice but to work. On an average, a Latin American who has stayed in the U.S. - legally or illegally - for ten years is twice as prosperous as a Puerto Rican who has been there for thirty years. Q.E.D.? Or then... It so happened that during the sixties, most Puerto Ricans worked in the New York garment industry; once this fell apart, they became the victims not of their Hispanic culture nor of social welfare but of an economic accident.

The problem with the Sowellian analysis is that it tends to give too much weight to a single factor in explaining the complex phenomenon of the marginalisation of a tribe be it Black, Hispanic or other. Even if we were to assume that Sowell is right, can his theory be put into practice? Which democratic government in the world is capable of taking such a radically liberal stand and allow itself to be ruled so completely by the laws of the labour market? Now even in the United States a 'welfare garb' seems mandatory. Finally, one does not know if all minorities, all forms of racism and all historical experience have enough in common for us to conclude that the market can always be assimilated in the same way, everywhere, by everyone. Will what was true for the Jews and the Irish also be true for the Blacks, or for that matter, the Beurs in France? Thomas Sowell, who has written about preferential policies in Israel, India and Kazakhistan, has yet to write and think about European immigrants: we just happen to be too far away from California!

MODEL OR ANTIMODEL?

Can affirmative action serve as a model for Europe? We have seen it become a reference point for Holland and Great Britain. On the face of it, affirmative action is based on universal principles: the quest for equality and social justice. The political and psychological motives are just as universal: a social tool for some, moral guilt for others. On the other hand, its dynamics are not so easily transferable as they are closely related to the specific nature of American democracy, a

democracy based on the interplay of various lobbies.
Political clout in the United States is a tool in the
hands of communities and pressure groups. What has
become of the general good? In the words of one of
the founding fathers of the Constitution, James Madison,
it flows from the sum total of individual interests.
There is nothing shocking nor undemocratic about
organised groups taking over a town hall office or a
state in order to serve their own interests. Another
unique feature of American democracy is the active
role played by the judges. Federal courts impose
affirmative action and follow up its implementation
to such an extent that in some cities, Boston for
instance, there has been a real transfer of power from
the mayor's office to the judges. This in turn presses
into service thousands of lawyers and leads to innumerable law suits. So with affirmative action we shall
discover a new face of America unknown to Europe.
This socio-democratic America is profoundly
bureaucratic; it is enmeshed in rules and regulations,
legal pettifoggery, and is waging a constant war with
the other face of America, that of savage capitalism
and the conservative revolution.

Just as American democracy differs from ours, so
too does their idea of integration. In France, the
individual is called upon to integrate into a national
culture; integration and assimilation tend to overlap.
In the United States, integration takes place at the level
of both the community and the nation. One never
ceases to be a member of one's community, bound as
one is by common customs, culture, religion and a
certain attachment to the native land. The American
melting pot is more an ethnic alloy than a fusion of
individuals. Obviously, some ethnic groups feel more
American than others; each one stakes its claim; some

talk of precedence, others of their contribution. Whatever be the case, till now the supermarket civilization has assimilated all immigrant communities within the space of a single generation. Except for the Blacks! Social issues in the United States - poverty, homelessness, drug addiction, urban violence, gangs, ghettos, unemployed youth, school violence and racism - are in fact and for the most part a Black problem; affirmative action covers all 'protected minorities' but without the intractable black problem, affirmative action would never have been. And as this policy has not been an unqualified success, black leaders and their white allies are now tempted to experiment with another model: the Black Revolution.

6

THE BLACK REVOLUTION

'The Black Revolution needs more leaders like Malcolm X,' says Ali Mazrui, all affability. Mazrui, an easygoing, greying intellectual, was born in Kenya sixty years ago. Currently he is the Director of the Department of Black Studies at the State University of New York in Binghamton. All major American universities have a Department of Black Studies where black teachers are being recruited to teach black history and black literature to black students to restore them their respectability. 'Afrocentrism' has become a lucrative academic business. Black intellectuals with the right qualifications are a rare species indeed; universities are doing their best to grab them and are willing to pay them the earth. When the press got the story of how the Governor of New York enticed Ali Mazrui away from the University of Michigan at a fantastic price, it created quite a stir. But what could they say against a professor so politically correct. 'My being paid more than my white colleagues is part of the compensation Whites owe African-Americans,' Mazrui tells me.

Ali Mazrui is a Muslim. A look at his office leaves you in no doubt about his religion: Koranic verses decorate the walls; the calligraphy on the table, the carpet and the coffee cups is all in Arabic. A return to Islam, explains Mazrui, is necessary for the reafricanisation of black Americans. Malcolm X was the first to have understood this. 'Martin Luther King with his Christianity, non violence and championing of individual effort was on the side of the Whites. Our real hero is Malcolm X.' A reprobate, a guerrilla who embraced Islam and was slain by an assassin, 'he had understood that for the Blacks to be free, white society had to be destroyed.' Luther King thought white; Malcolm X thought black.

THINKING BLACK

What does it mean to 'think black'? For Mazrui, thinking black is taking an Afrocentric view of history. So far, the history of America has only been written by white masters; to be Afrocentric is to reread American history, this time from the point of view of the slave. Elsewhere too, Afrocentrism is reversing roles and looking at history from an African perspective: France did not give Algeria its independence, the Algerian uprising revolutionised French political institutions. Fascism was overthrown in Portugal by Mozambique and Angola. In such a scheme, Africa becomes the force that propels the Western world. Similarly, it was African slaves who built America just as Egyptian slaves before them built the pyramids. Thomas Jefferson or the pharaohs being at the same place and the same time as these slave-protagonists of history was nothing more than a coincidence. What is true for history can also be applied to literature.

Afrocentrism is studying literature with African sensibilities and looking for new texts of African origin. Mazrui is not quite so categoric when it comes to science; he feels the history of science ought to be taught from an African perspective, not science itself. Other African-American academics, less cautious than Mazrui, hold the view that there is such a thing as African mathematics.

At Binghamton, there are not too many takers for Ali Mazrui's course. This black Muslim professor happens to teach in predominantly Jewish university where Afro-American history programmes are certainly not a big draw. When the university reopened in 1991, Mazrui decided to teach the history of Black Africa in order to woo students, but the benches remain as empty as ever. Is this the reason for his anti-Semitism? Like many other African-American leaders, Mazrui can't stop writing about the Jews. 'I find it hard to accept this Jewish monopoly over the concepts of diaspora and holocaust. The mass deportation of Blacks to America and their enslavement were no less of a holocaust. There are Africans on every continent, how is it that no one speaks of an African diaspora?' It seems strange, this rivalry between Blacks and Jews for the role of history's victim. Jewish merchants actively participated in the slave trade, continues Mazrui, whereas white history only speaks of Muslim traders. Is that Mazrui the anti-semitist speaking? 'No I am just anti-Zionist and pro-Palestinian. The Jews can't stand the fact that African-Americans have their own point of view on every subject including the Middle East. They'd like to see the Blacks confined to their ghettoes.' Hatred, fanaticism, perhaps, but also grudging admiration. ' We Blacks should learn a lesson or two from the Jews and use their tactics of conquering America by taking over finance, academics, the media and cinema.' Interestingly enough, the 'Jewish question', whenever and wherever it is raised, reveals the desire to return to ethnicity and the cult of the origins. But before conquering America, the Black Revolution is for the time being training itself on conquering the minds of the very young.

INFUSION AT SCHOOL

Emily is barely seven years old but already she knows her hieroglyphics. 'Who wants to come to the board and write the figure 2427 the way our ancestors did in Africa?'asks the teacher Etolie Williams. Emily raises her hand. She takes a piece of chalk and draws two lotus flowers, four coils of rope, two yokes and seven sticks. Etolie Williams compliments her pupil. When Emily grows a little older, she will learn to count in Swahili and Roman numbers; only then will she be taught the decimal system. This is not happening in some remote corner of Africa but at the Cleveland Avenue primary school in Atlanta. All the children and teachers of this school are African Americans.

Atlanta, like Chicago, Detroit and Portland, is a black city. Thirty years ago, it was here that Martin Luther King began his struggle for black civil rights and desegregation in schools. It was here that he made his famous 'I have a dream' speech; the dream of an America in which white and black children would have equal rights and equal opportunity. In the seventies, it had looked as if his dream was going to come true. Children of all races were systematically 'mixed' in public schools in the hope of achieving a homogeneous society. The school bus had become an instrument of social change as well as a symbol of racial mixing. Black children were bused to white schools and white children to black ones. Unfortunately busing made white families flee from the city centres; and African-American children were left to themselves in schools abandoned by the Whites. Forced integration in schools was a failure. The new generation of African-American political leaders and intellectuals felt no regret; instead they chose to glorify their difference. Reverse racism became the politically correct credo of this community. Black leaders, fully armed with statistics to back their claims, point out that black children in fully black schools are doing much better than those in mixed schools. The reason: there is no conflict with white classmates to throw them off balance. Black parents associations support this new form of racial conformity; black schools in the United States refuse to admit Whites. Integration is dated, as African-Americans now worship at the altar of their origins. This cultural reconversion began in Atlanta; the Cleveland Avenue school serves as a model for black America.

In Etolie William's class, African mathematics is not just another fad, it is part of a general effort to africanise school curricula in Georgia. The minute I uttered the word 'Afrocentric', a term which is not politically correct, my slip drew from Etolie Williams a condescending smile of the kind she reserves for the non-initiated. The new teaching methods, she explains, are not Afrocentric. The right term is 'infusion of African culture'. In principle, the curricula for black public schools are drawn up at the national level but they are 'infused' locally. The extent to which African culture is infused has become the criterion for judging merit and determining promotion of teachers and pupils alike. Etolie Williams teaches hieroglyphics, wearing an African boubou; she is thought to be the most 'infused' teacher at the Cleveland Avenue school and has been declared 'the teacher of the year' by her colleagues. This is for Afrocentrism what the Oscar is for films.

The fundamental difference between 'infusion' and Afrocentrism, explains Eunice Robinson, Director of Atlanta's school district, is that 'infusion' does not exclude but includes the other; the idea is not to create a new form of segregation but to move from 'white curricula' to a more 'global teaching'. Infusion of this kind is particularly important when teaching the history of the United States. In traditional textbooks, African-Americans only appear after they had been enslaved. 'We did exist before that,' protests Eunice Robinson. She is right. So on Cleveland Avenue, classes from kindergarten to the sixth grade are 'infused'.

Maps of Africa hang on the walls. There are posters of all the great African-American heroes who helped make the history of the United States. Some are well known figures even amongst the Whites like Frederick Douglas, the abolitionist, and James Baldwin, the writer. But who is Benjamin Banneker? The children know and enthusiastically explain to me that this brilliant black mechanic was the man who built the first ever fully American clock around 1780. And Garrett Morgan? 'He invented traffic lights in Cleveland a hundred years ago. The gas mask too!' The children are proud of their new found science.

A look at the new curricula, completely revised for Atlanta schools by a group of black professors under the black psychologist Asa Hilliard, reveals a certain number of syllogisms: Africa is the cradle of mankind; civilization was born in Egypt; as Egypt is in Africa, Africa is the cradle of European civilization. Then there are statements of the kind: Africa is deeply united in spite of superficial differences; Africa has always been besieged or colonised but the Africans have always resisted in spite of a history of martyrdom; the Africans have never ceased to contribute significantly to culture, science and art. By reappropriating history in this way, the Blacks have come up with an ideology as farcical as the Eurocentrism they claim to oppose. Eunice Robinson agrees. But she tells me it is more important for the children to feel good! When little Emily drew hieroglyphics, her teacher was all praise so that the child felt good. Is school just therapy to feel good?

Well at least these children will have known a few moments of pride and happiness, feels Eunice Robinson. For most of them, school will only lead to a dead end. Hardly anyone will go to college. Most of the young ones will have problems finding a job, starting a family and escaping urban violence: in Atlanta one out of every four black teenagers goes to prison. The purpose of Afrocentric teaching however is not to integrate African-Americans into white America but to change America itself. A cause, we shall discover, even white intellectuals are helping.

CLEOPATRA'S SKIN

We knew that if Cleopatra's nose had been longer, the face of the world would have changed; what we did not think was that Cleopatra was black, because we knew she was Greek. Martin Bernal asserts however she was black or almost black. Bernal himself is white and of English origin, something that goes down very well in American universities. He teaches political science in the heart of the State of New York at Cornell. He is the Guru of Afrocentrism and his book, *Black Athena,* a radical revision of the origins of Western civilization, has become the cornerstone of new black education. *Black Athena,* the monumental research of one man, runs into several volumes and a few thousand pages. It has become the standard reference so long awaited by the black community in the United States. In his book, Bernal 'proves' that Greek civilization is Egyptian in origin. Bow down, all ye Whites to your ancestors! Bernal vouches for the rigour of his work; however, he is much less emphatic about the title of his book. He had originally suggested 'African Athena' but his publisher felt 'Black Athena' had more punch. His publisher's argument was unassailable: women don't sell, Blacks don't sell but a black woman does. The African-American organisations jumped at the title and made it their banner for obvious reasons. Prior to Bernal, Afrocentric historiography was based on the research of an erudite Senegalese scholar, Cheikh Anta Diop. Diop was the first person to assert, in the nineteen fifties, the Africaness of Egypt and, on the basis of some linguistic traces, show that Egypt owed much to Black Africa, a debt Egypt passed on to Greece. Not many historiographers outside Africa took his work seriously. Another scholar Van Sertina, an African-American, was similarly dismissed. He had claimed that West Africans were navigators and had discovered America a hundred years before Christopher Columbus. Bernal is more rigorous and he is white, which makes his arguments all the more irrefutable. In his conclusion, Bernal had written that the purpose of the book was to 'lessen European cultural arrogance'.

What does Bernal have to say? The Greeks, he tells me, willingly acknowledged their debt to Egypt. Several historians of antiquity, notably Herodotus and Strabo, made a mention of it. This is also borne out by archeology and linguistics. Bernal himself relies heavily on linguistics to prove his point. If he is to be believed, the names of practically all Greek cities and gods are Egyptian in origin. Two thousand years before Christ, the Cretans and Phoenicians had carried Egypt's cultural heritage across to Greece. At the time, Egyptian priests had already spoken of the soul as being distinct from the body and life after death, ideas later taken up by the Phoenicians, the Hebrews and finally the Greeks. Plato himself was supposed to have been educated in Egypt; there are six ancient texts testifying to this. For Greeks desirous of studying philosophy, mathematics and astronomy, a journey to Egypt was a must. Till the nineteenth century, this was commonly accepted by European historians. Bernal calls it the 'ancient model'. He explains. Towards the middle of the nineteenth century, this model was deliberately occulted and replaced by the 'Aryan model', a German and Anglo Saxon invention. Racism, the dominant ideology of Northern Europe, was directly responsible for it. Historians, carried away by the times, did their best to prove that all civilisations came from the North and could only be white. The contributions of the African, Egyptian, Phoenician and Semitic civilisations were systematically suppressed and any text seeming to belittle the Aryan model was deemed a legend or a myth. Some historians like

Victor Bérard resisted and held on to the ancient model, acknowledging the Semitic contribution. However, by and large teaching in Western schools and universities came under the sway of the Aryan model. What is Bernal trying to prove? That no historian can be free of ideological bias . What does he offer? A 'revised ancient model' based on recent linguistic research which sets out to reestablish the relationship between the Egyptian-African civilisation and our Greek one.

Let us suppose, as Bernal does, that Plato was educated in Egypt. That metaphysics is Egyptian in origin. That Egyptian had been the language of the clergy in ancient Greece. Did that make Egypt African and the Pharaohs black? Most certainly, declared Cheikh Anta Diop. The frescoes and tombs in Egypt bear witness to this fact. Bernal is more guarded: the Egyptian language was an African one but race was not a discriminatory factor in Ancient Egypt. In all likelihood, the Egyptians were of mixed blood. An idea abhorrent to the Aryan school, which was striving to prove that racial purity was the precondition for the creative genius of the Greeks. It was the Aryan school's bad luck that the Greeks were mixed both genetically and culturally. The Greeks made no bones about it; in fact they boasted that they combined the warrior like qualities of the North Europeans with the intelligence of the Egyptians. It so happens, adds Bernal, that even African-Americans are genetically and culturally mixed, just like the Egyptians and Greeks. A fortunate coincidence indeed!

Bernal's *Black Athena* raised a storm both in academic circles and the American press. It figured on the October 91 *Newsweek* cover and took up several pages of the *New York Times*. Why argue so fiercely about something that happened four thousand years ago? Because Bernal is providing scientific legitimacy to the desire to return to the basics, the quest for roots, the worship of origins and the exaltation of relativism. Biologists and paleontologists have told us the homo sapiens first appeared in Africa; now Bernal is proving that culture began there too. If what he says is true, then the West owes not only its genetic heritage but also its philosophical and cultural heritage to the Blacks. If you think like Bernal, then you are genuinely multicultural and 'politically correct'!

THE PC IDEOLOGY

'Are all cultures equal?' 'Should black or Asian students be forced to study Western history and culture?'

These are some of the questions put to students at the admission test to the Duke University in North Carolina, one of the most selective universities in the United States. At Duke, tuition fees and other expenses run upto twenty thousand dollars a year. The purpose of the admission test is to check whether candidates abide by the University's new motto: 'multiculturalism.' Being multicultural is saying all cultures are equal - especially white and ethnic minority cultures - and that there should be no hierarchy among them. All cultural attitudes, no matter which civilisation they belong to, are equally respectable.

If you haven't understood multiculturalism, it means you're 'unicultural', a blasphemy on the Duke campus. A unicultural is treated as a mentally retarded person, someone who must have voted for Ronald Reagan or George Bush; a unicultural still thinks white civilisation is superior to Swahili civilisation or the civilisation of the Amazonian Bororos. Such a person believes that literary and artistic works are the creation of individuals. Whereas for a multicultural, the creator is only the voice of a given social or cultural group. A creative work is simply a manifestation of the desire of one group to dominate over another. The unicultural fails to understand that what goes by the name of white culture is in truth nothing more than a form of white male oppression of non-Whites and women. Uniculturals are automatically branded racist, sexist and homophobic by their classmates and teachers. On the other hand, those who embrace multiculturalism and give the right answers are considered PC or politically correct.

On many American campuses PC has become the law. Being PC is joining hands with feminists, pacifists, ethnic minorities and all 'victims' of male imperialism and white chauvinism. Conservative professors and students are on the defensive. If they so much as mention Plato or Shakespeare, the PC immediately hoots them down: you can hardly call Plato and Shakespeare universal, they were nothing more than dead white European males. If you are not PC, friends and colleagues give you a hard time at Duke. The University president set up a 'committee for the fight against discrimination', a moral watchdog which has taken it upon itself to root out even the slightest trace of racism among the professors. When it can't find any case of blatant racism, it directs its ire against those whose facial expressions or body movements could be construed as being disrespectful to black students.

James Barber, an eminent political scientist at Duke, has joined the PC Resistance. He gives us a few examples of 'crimes', as defined in the code of good conduct that some universities have drawn up. The following are reprehensible : 'ageism' - oppression of the young and old by young adults and the middle-aged; heterosexism - attitude critical of sexual orientations other than heterosexual and not acknowledging the right to be different (Smith College's code is particularly harsh; those feigning ignorance about the existence of gays, lesbians and bisexuals are also deemed guilty of heterosexism). Lookism is another serious offense whereby some people are considered better looking than others (in some places the code urges students to not only stop differentiating between the good looking and the ugly but to suppress altogether the temptation to do so). Then there is ableism - students must understand there are no disabled people, only the differently abled with qualities just as commendable.

'Finding the right politically correct word,' says Barber, 'has become an intense intellectual activity in the big American universities.' Never ever use the word 'black'. The PC term is African-American. Never call a thirty year old student old. 'Non traditional age' is the right PC term. Feminists are particularly vigilant over pronoun usage. It is strongly advisable to use 'she' as frequently as 'he'. For instance, when you refer to God use 'she'. On the Duke campus as elsewhere, the issue of how to address women is a hotly debated one. The word 'woman' contains 'man' so the recommended PC spelling is 'womyn'. James Barber, the Chairman of the Political Science Department, had to change his designation: from chairman he became chairperson (just 'chair' is better still). Even so, a student pasted on his office door an invitation to a Gay and Lesbian awareness evening to rid all those who considered themselves normal of such ideas. In his buttonhole, Barber wears a badge of the American flag.

'It may not be politically correct,' says Barber,'but it is "patriotically correct.", Barber's anti-PC PC is provocative. On the other hand, a peace badge is politically correct. Being anti-American is PC; being patriotic is not. The PC code also prevails at the time of selecting teachers. In November 1991, the University of California put out the following advertisement for a history teacher : 'Preference will be given to coloured persons, members of a cultural minority, women or the disabled.' The educational qualifications required for the post were not mentioned.

PC may not be as strong in other universities as it is in Duke. But no university has remained untouched by such activism. 'You have to be careful when they tell you PC was thought up by the Conservatives', says Dinesh D'Souza, a sociologist of Indian origin and the author of the well acclaimed book 'Illiberal Education.' 'If you want to really be PC, you have to say PC does not exist.' It is true that all the PC professors I met in the United States denied the existence of the movement; all of them said they were the victims of a white, anti-minority, racist, anti-feminist conspiracy, hatched by powerful conservative foundations. The success of D'Souza's book is proof enough of the anti-PC conspiracy.

According to D'Souza, the intellectual climate currently prevailing on American universities is reminiscent of the fifties when the Communist witch hunt was at its peak. Now it is the Conservatives, the victims of black fundamentalism, who are being hounded out. At Harvard, Stephen Thernstrom, who has been teaching the history of American settlements for the last twenty five years, had to abandon his course in the face of continual harassment from anti-establishment students, black for the most part. They resented Thernstrom's use of the term 'Indian' instead of 'native American'. Thernstrom tried hard to explain to his black censors that even the Indians call themselves Indians, but to little avail. 'This is just like the Ku Klux Klan the other way round!' exclaims Thernstrom. While on the subject of Harvard, Derek Bell, a black professor of law there, has stopped taking classes for several years, as a mark of protest against the absence of any 'black female' law professor; this, he says, is discrimination. The Harvard president has been desperately looking around for a suitable female candidate; to date he has not managed to find one with the requisite qualifications. The students, at least those who show up, support Derek Bell.

DECONSTRUCTING WHITE CULTURE

Henry Louis, better known as 'Skip' Gates, is the intellectual leader of the politically correct movement. He too teaches at Harvard where he heads the Department of Literature. An African-American, Gates' rise in the academic world has been meteoric as university after university has lured him away with mindboggling salaries. One would have expected either an economist or a political scientist to head the PC movement. Instead you have Gates explaining that literary criticism is at the heart of the controversy concerning white culture. Traditionally, all literature students in the U.S. were expected to read the Classics which included Shakespeare, Plato and the Bible. These were considered the canon of university teaching. Under fire from the oppressed minorities, the 'canon', according to Gates, is exploding. Women, who account for more than half of all literature students, were no longer willing to go on accepting a 'canon' that did not include female writers. The Blacks too began to realise that not a single text from Africa or for that matter the Third World had been prescribed. 'It's high time Third World feminist literature was incorporated into the curricula', says Gates. It does exist, the only problem is finding the right texts. For Gates, there is no disputing the fact that classical culture as we know it is based on a social falsehood; it merely reflects the preferences of a privileged minority at a given point in time. One culture claiming precedence over all others and asserting that it is 'the' American culture is ignoring women and the oppressed and denying them the right to make their voice heard. One of Gates' favorite ploys while teaching - this has made him extremely popular with the students - is bringing out implicit racism and sexism in the Classics. 'You cannot deny,' adds Gates, 'that the most interesting teachers are on the side of multiculturalism. The Conservatives are bores.' What he says is not untrue.

In this endeavour to demolish classical culture, French intellectuals have often played - though sometimes inadvertently - a decisive role. From Claude Levi Strauss, quoted every now and then, the American PC movement has taken the idea that there is no intercultural hierarchy. No people are more civilised or more savage than the other. There are just different civilisations, all equally respectable. This has led the PC movement to the conclusion that cultural relativism can be applied to everything. Jacques Derrida, deeply involved in the movement, is the real PC guru. It has become virtually impossible to teach literature in the

United States without referring to Derrida. Known only to a small elite in France, this French philosopher rules supreme over the best American universities. His method, known as the deconstruction of the text, brings out the radical instability of meaning and favours the reader over the author. Derrida's epigoni have reduced deconstructionism to trivia, making it seem like an appeal for unrestrained narcissism: what the student thinks of the author becomes more important than what the author has written. So Shakespeare is read not so much to understand Shakespeare as to understand the self and heighten one's self-awareness instead of increasing one's knowledge. Rejecting learning has become a legitimate form of defense against the 'oppressiveness' of truth and rationality. Truth, according to the deconstructionist theory, is not the truth. It is merely hierarchic discourse, logocentrism, or better still, phallogocentrism of 'old dead white males'. Thinking PC and swearing by Derrida is tantamount to denying that the Good, the Beautiful, the True and the Just exist as absolute categories; all of them become relative values; what was said to be the truth is nothing but a form of oppression. Clearly, the self becomes the sole object of study.

What is left of classical culture once it has been put through the mill of deconstructionism and relativism ? Nothing, Gates admits, but it doesn't matter. What we called culture, values, morality were nothing more than the imposed ideology of yesterday's masters on the oppressed minorities. Now, it is the turn of the minorities to have their say. It is true they are polemical and aggressive, but isn't that normal in a revolutionary period. 'A look at the history of mankind shows that dispossessed elites have always talked about dying values. Just go through the Ecclesiastes and Juvenal once again.' For Gates, culture does not die, it changes. 'We have stopped reading some books because we'll be reading other books. We are not witnessing the death of a culture but its reconfiguration along new lines.' For over a hundred years, he explains, the United States has lived with the myth of the melting pot. Today this myth has outlived its utility - at least in the minds of the PC academic elite - and has been replaced by a hymn in praise of difference. Concludes Gates, 'My students are all looking for some kind of minority ancestry; if they find even a drop of Indian blood, they go mad with joy and change their names! They are no longer just American but multicultural.'

Why this wave of PC and why now? Being PC is being fashionable, a convenient fashion, both radical and conformist at the same time. Besides PC methods do not tax the intellect. You don't have to strain yourself studying to be PC. It is enough to be a Black, Asian, pacifist, feminist or, if nothing else, an ecologist and oppose all forms of elitism. The cult of the self and one's origins has replaced exams as a yardstick for success. PC appeals to coloured people and Whites with a guilty conscience alike, in other words to the majority.

An interesting sidelight: today's professors were yesterday's rebels, the 'enfants terribles' of May '68. They were the ones to have set ablaze Berkeley and Stanford. These greying enemies of imperialism and capitalism - called the Mister Sixties - are carrying on the revolution exactly where they left it twenty five years ago.

FROM CLASS TO RACE

Revolutions are not always born in the smoke filled inner rooms of Zurich cafes. Nor are they always a blood, sweat and tears affair. The idyllic surroundings of Berkeley could do just as well. It was here, under blue skies, at the foot of the California Hills facing the San Francisco Bay, that one of the most authentic revolutions of our times began. In 1967-68, a heady cocktail of affluent students, leftist professors imported from Europe (Herbert Marcuse for instance), psychoanalysis, sexual freedom, mystic music, psychedelic drugs and Marxist vulgate was to hit Berkeley first before spreading to the rest of America, Japan and Europe. As this was not a strictly political revolution but a moral (or immoral?) revolution, its long term effects are still to be fully measured. '68' nonetheless did radically transform the industrial society, undermining traditional values such as the family, accepted codes of sexual behaviour, child-parent and man-woman relationships, as well altering the relationship of those in authority, whether at the work place, the university or the church, and those under them.

At Berkeley the transformation is very visible. They say things are back to normal on the campus. What has happened in reality is that the revolution has got institutionalised. Almost all the community activities financed by the University are in the hands of Blacks, Chicanos and native Americans, or then gays, lesbians and bisexuals. White males still put up token resistance but their supremacy seems doomed. 'Demography has sealed the fate of the white man,' feels Troy Duster. Demography has become history's new goddess.

Troy Duster, a black sociologist, does not throw bombs nor is he an aging hippy of the kind you still find hanging about the campus: he is just taking stock of the situation as it is. In 1969 when he was appointed to teach at Berkeley after having studied there, there were only five Blacks among the thousand six hundred and fifty odd professors on the teaching staff. At the time, less than 3% of the students were black and 1% of Latin American or Mexican origin. The wave of Asian immigration had not yet begun in California. Now twenty-five years later, one third of the student population is of Asian origin, one fourth is black and the Whites are in a minority. Troy Duster observes, 'The Whites are sandwiched between the Asians who achieve better scores at the admission test and the Blacks and Latinos who benefit from affirmative action. White students, who for the most part come from white schools, are for the first time in their lives confronted with the fact of being a minority and of being white. Never before in the history of America or Western Europe have Whites had to ask themselves what it meant to be white; it was up to the others to define themselves in relation to the Whites, not the other way around.'

Troy Duster feels the adjustment was all the more painful as being white was not enough to find one's bearings. Blacks are black not only because of the colour of their skin but because they share the same cultural outlook and generally come from an underprivileged social class. They have common ethnic, cultural and social reference points. They are not 'lost' at Berkeley, where they naturally gravitate towards their own community. The same is true of the Chicanos, the Chinese and the Indians. But a white student has to come to terms with being white alone.

How are the Whites adjusting to this new environment? They are finding it difficult and often seek refuge in alcohol. Some of them naively try to make friends with coloured students. They are being naive because however well meaning they may be, Whites fail to realise that they still represent a system condemned by history; they are not befriending a coloured individual but the member of a revolutionary class.

The PC discourse sounds very much like traditional Marxism. In Troy Duster's scheme of things, history moves in given direction as is the case of Marxism. In the multicultural vulgate as in the Marxist one, the individual cannot escape his or her condition; one who tries to do so is either naive or a traitor. But necessity is no longer defined in terms of economics, it has become cultural or demographic. The class struggle has given way to a race struggle which is just as inevitable. The proletariat has been replaced by the coloured people; they constitute the new exploited class which will in time become dominant.

It is unlikely that the new PC ideology and the black revolution will remain confined to the United States. America has been in the past and still is the laboratory of all social experiments. There is nothing to stop a French Bernal from appearing on the scene and reminding us of our debt to Islam. Today the 'Blacks' of West Europe are increasingly identifying themselves with American Blacks. Be it London, Amsterdam or Paris, they have taken on all their symbols: baseball cap worn backwards, unlaced sneakers, tags, hiphop, rap and Zulu bands. From their French suburbs the Beurs look to Bronx. The writing is on the wall: if we do not act now, we will be in for the same kind of violence. In New York, students have to go through a metal detector before they can enter class to make sure they are not carrying arms. Will Sartrouville and Argenteuil go the same way? If things continue as they are - the failure of integration, unemployment, welfare dependency and drugs - we can expect the same fate in France: our cities will be colonised by a new tribal culture.

7

RECONQUERING
AMERICA

His brown Stetson pulled low down, over dark Rayban glasses, his military shirt well cut and well pressed, William Doelittle, a lieutenant in the U.S. Border Patrol, stands guard at the Mexican border. In front of him, the brightly coloured pink and purple shacks of Tijuana mark the boundary between the two Americas. To the north, lies the prosperity of the Anglo world; to the south, the poverty of Latin America. Nowhere else does such an arbitrary frontier- three thousand kilometers defined by the fortunes of war and the vicissitudes of history - separate the wealthy from the Third World in such stark contrast.

Twenty years ago, Doelittle was fighting in Vietnam. Today, the Colt pistol on his belt is just a deterrent, but he has the same missionary zeal: he has to protect the free world, white civilization, material prosperity against ... what exactly?

On the Mexican side, I can see hundreds of men wandering on the narrow strip of land that separates the edge of Tijuana from U.S. territory. They huddle together in small groups, scrutinising the horizon as if something extraordinary was going to happen. In fact, they are only waiting for the U.S. lieutenant to get back in his car and check on some other illegal border crossing. Doelittle is familiar with the tactic; he calls for backup and, with four vehicles and six men, forms a thin line. The two groups observe each other: one thousand to six. Overseeing the operation, a noisy border patrol helicopter flies back and forth along the line, goes up to the Pacific coast and comes back again in what seems a pointless manoeuvre. The game carries on until dark when it comes to an abrupt halt, for night falls suddenly in these parts. But the darkness actually helps the border police to better observe what is happening on the other side, as it is equipped with infrared binoculars. The Mexicans don't know this. They start running straight toward the United States, thinking they are under cover of night. Doelittle and his men shout at the invaders to stop. Curiously they all stop, as if obeying some unwritten rule of the game; or perhaps they simply panic, a reflex action of Mexican peasants when confronted by 'officiales'.

That night, fifteen hundred illegal immigrants must have failed in their attempt to cross over; they must have been taken back to the border patrol station at Chula Vista, but twice or thrice that number must have suceeded, swelling the human sea that rises and flows over the border between Tijuana and the Rio Grande. This invasion, not of an enemy, but of poverty, of hunger, of the determination to break through obsesses and frightens the North Americans. According to various estimates, between two and four million Mexicans live illegally in the United States. In addition, a million seasonal migrants come for six months, return to their homes, and come again the following year.

Doelittle says he no longer recognises his white America: everything in Southern California - the architecture, the faces, the colours, the sounds - seems Latin American. Nevertheless, the lieutenant is not thinking of quitting the border patrol. For twenty thousand dollars a year, he will go on waging this absurd guerrilla war, a war that will do nothing to stem the tide of northward migration. For, along with poverty, the men and women of south are also rejecting brutish police forces, despots and omnipotent bureaucracies. They come to the North not just because it is richer, but because it is freer, more respectful of human dignity.

RETURN TO TIJUANA

This is an account of events that took place in 1986, events I have already recorded in my book, 'The New Wealth of Nations'. Six years later, I went back to Tijuana. Lieutenant William Doelittle has retired. His place has been taken by Clark Messer. Messer did not fight the Vietnam War; for him, patrolling the border is just another job.

All roads still lead to Tijuana. Since that night in 1986, some five million Mexicans and a million Latin Americans from other countries have illegally entered the United States. Most of them have settled there for good, some legally (thanks to an amnesty law), others not. I had returned to Tijuana to see how the Border Patrol was faring and whether it had really managed to stem the tide of illegal immigrants. I was curious for several reasons : in 1986, Washington had declared that it would seal the border with a hightech barrier and Congress had passed a law making recruitment of illegal immigrants a punishable offense for employers. Another new development was that illegal immigration had become a national issue ever since Patrick Buchanan joined the race for the White House and made it one of the planks of his campaign. Was America too succumbing to xenophobia and the fear of the new barbarians?

Sergeant Clark Messer takes me with him on his inspection round in Doelittle's battered but sturdy 4 x 4. We drive down the dusty track along the border. The car is not quite the same though: the rear has been turned into a Black Maria to pick up 'customers'. There is however no pursuit; it is more a question of not crushing the illegal immigrants, as young and old alike spring up from all sides. When they see our patrol car, they come up to greet the 'official' from the United States and then get into the back. I ask a Mexican why they are so 'passive'. He answers, 'No son dociles, son nobles.' Clark Messer deposits his group at the central border station. There the American police force, much the wiser since 1986, makes no attempt at checking identities which are fake in any case. The only question asked of the illegal immigrants is whether they will return willingly to the other side. The answer, a unanimous yes, makes it possible to dispense with all legal procedures. The bus simply takes everyone back to Tijuana, only to start all over again a few hours later. 'We arrest,' Clark Messer tells me, ' six hundred thousand people a year, around two thousand a day and we reckon that around thrice that number successfully cross the border.' What about the famous wall that was to have been built along the border, the wall the left-wing press in America had

derisively called the 'new Berlin Wall'? 'Come and
have a look,' suggests Sergeant Messer.

I find it hard to believe my eyes. In 1986, an old
wire fencing ran across the dunes, cut at some places
by illegal immigrants. Now the fence has disappeared
altogether, replaced by a stockade hardly two metres
high, made of scrap material, clumsily held together
with rusty, badly welded stakes. Well, admits Clark
Messer sheepishly, the border patrol had to do a
makeshift job at the weekends with whatever was
available. 'You know these Washington politicians talk
a lot about protecting the border, but when it comes
to giving the money they refuse to cough up.' Messer
adds that though the fifteen kilometer long stockade
may not deter anyone from crossing over, once spotted,
it's impossible for any one to get back. And then a
minor high tech addition has been made. Sensors have
been planted on the no man's land between the
stockade and the first houses in San Ysidro on the U.S.
side. These sensors can detect any border movement
and send back signals to the central computer located
at the patrol headquarters. So the border patrol gets
to know at once when a large group is crossing over
and can immediately send out cars or even helicopters.
Time is of essence, especially as there has been a cut
in the number of vehicles. Often while a patrol party
is intercepting one batch of immigrants, a second batch
has the time to cross over and reach San Ysidro. The
local population, also of Mexican origin, is in connivance
with the illegal entrants, which does nothing to help
the 'officiales'. Nonetheless, the wall did manage to
curb somewhat the number of illegal entrants. Not to
be outdone, the Mexicans came up with a simple
alternative: they enter through the city's gate. On

highway no.5 which leads to San Diego, a sign board asks motorists to slow down for pedestrians. The new Mexican strategy is to cross over to this highway which runs parallel to the border and then walk against the traffic. Patrol cars are forced to abandon their chase for fear of causing an accident. All along the twenty kilometer stretch to San Diego, hundreds of ragged, empty handed Mexicans - women, children, old and young - can be seen marching determinedly towards the city. Each one of them has somewhere to go: a hurriedly scribbled address of a remote cousin, a farm somewhere in California or a laundry firm in Los Angeles. Most of these immigrants belong to village clans with a long tradition - sometimes spanning several generations - of emigrating to California. Even those who come on their own - mostly from the towns - don't have to wait long before meeting an employer in the street markets of Los Angeles or San Diego. It is not welfare that brings these people here but the fierce desire to escape poverty.

THE OTHER SIDE OF THE WALL

Walls are always an invitation to trespass: what does the Mexican side of the 'wall' look like? Well crossing over to Mexico is certainly much easier than coming in to the United States. As you move southwards, there are no checks, the Americans ask no questions and the sentry box on the Mexican side is empty. Suddenly you are in the Third World. Only a minute ago, everything was clean and well ordered. As soon as you cross over, you are confronted with chaos, mess, hustle and bustle, noise, smell, pink facades, dazzling costumes and bazaars laden with shoddy goods. At the chemists, wonder drugs to cure AIDS

as well as all medicines for which a prescription would
be necessary in the U.S are sold freely. The office of
the Party of Institutionalised Revolution which has
been ruling Mexico for the last sixty years stands in
the heart of the town. It is not just poverty that the
immigrants flee; it is this despotism too. On the
American side, the stockade is just a sheet of rusty
metal; the Mexican side, covered with traditional
frescoes and graffiti, is much prettier. One of the
graffiti reads: 'American taxpayers, see how your
money is being used'. It's not very convincing though
as little money has been spent; in fact most American
tax payers would be willing to pay much more for
an impenetrable barrier. Another interesting slogan:
'We are not criminals, we are not illegal immigrants,
we are international workers.' This is how the clandestine
migrants see themselves.

The Mexican sociologist Jorge Bustamante explains,
'The United States government is being perfectly
hypocritical when it says Mexican emigrants are
offenders. They are the very international workers the
American employers are asking for.' Bustamante is in
charge of a specialised research centre on migrations,
'El Colegio de la Frontera Norte', situated in Tijuana.
If we were to follow Bustamante's analysis, then
hypocritical is putting it mildly; the term to use is
schizophrenic. 'The border patrol,' he says, 'is like an
actor playing two roles in two different plays, each
intended for a different public.' The first is being
enacted for the benefit of American public opinion,
traditionally xenophobic and hostile to immigration.
Playing at cops and robbers, rounding up people and
hurling impressive statistics are all part of this charade.
In any case, the figures are inflated. The two million

arrests reported annually include people arrested several times, very often on a single day. Each year, eight hundred thousand Mexicans enter the United States illegally whereas the quota for Mexico is only thirty thousand visas a year.

How is it that the border patrol can arrest only such a small fraction of those crossing over? Because they can't do any better? Because the government does not provide them with the means to do so? The truth, according to Bustamante, is that the border patrol switches roles, playing this time to a different audience: Californian employers who cannot do without Mexicans. If it weren't for the Mexicans, who would pick the fruit and vegetables, who would do the cleaning, the gardening, the repair work, who would toil in factories with little or no mechanization? That is the real reason why the border patrol allows so many Mexicans to infiltrate. Besides, whenever the federal government clamps down on immigrants to pander to public opinion, the employers lobby immediately raises a howl of protest against the closing of the border and speaks of the negative impact it will have on the local economy. As Governor of California, Ronald Reagan had supported immigration, something he continued to do even when he was in the White House. A fact oft forgotten by Reagan's French admirers! For Bustamante then, the real task of the border patrol is to keep the border both open and closed. It does not guard the border, it regulates the flow of migrants on the international labour market, very much like traffic policemen. Bustamante says, 'American employers have come up with the ideal worker: a Mexican without papers entitled to neither legal nor welfare protection.' For a pittance, the Mexican docilely accepts to do whatever work is offered, work that a White would turn down and no employer would offer a Black, even if the Black were willing to do it. The United States is the net gainer as it is Mexico which has to bear the cost - however modest - of educating the labour force. Furthermore, Mexico looses its most enterprising workers, as only they cross over to the North.

Is there any alternative to this 'invasion', slave market and mockery of the liberal economy?

In 1986, the United States government thought it would be able to put an end to illegal immigration by curbing demand. The Rodino law, named after the legislator who introduced the bill, made it illegal for American employers to engage immigrants without papers. At the same time, amnesty was granted to around two million illegal entrants who had been living in the country for at least five years. The outcome was entirely predictable: the amnesty caused an unprecedented rise in the number of immigrants, all under the illusion that they would benefit by it. And those granted amnesty called their families over, thus making permanent settlers of temporary migrants. As for the clause relating to employers, it deterred neither employers nor immigrants. Instead it gave rise to a thriving counterfeit business. A permit that used to cost four hundred dollars can now be had for just twenty dollars. The law does not stipulate that the employer verify the authenticity of the documents presented - this is simply not possible. And if employers do discover that their employees have false papers, it only strengthens their hold on the employees. In this struggle between the law and the market, it is the market that has won the day.

THE BORDER MUST EITHER BE OPEN OR CLOSED

Bustamante says, 'There is only one way to close the Mexican border: a two thousand kilometer long Berlin type wall, protected by a glacis and guarded by soldiers with orders to shoot at sight.' Is he being ironical? Not quite; there are some groups in the U.S. which favour 'protecting the American identity' through the militarization of the border (the most notable being the Californian association FAIR or Federation for immigration reform). Patrick Buchanan, who ran for the Republican presidential ticket, was to declare in March 1992 that the construction of such a wall would be less costly than the Gulf War and certainly more useful. But then wouldn't the Mexicans, like the Cubans and Haitians, find their way directly to Los Angeles and San Diego by sea. The very thought is enough to justify the present system. Another way out is to find genuine alternatives. One could be to open the border completely. A second possibility is to bring about the economic integration of Mexico and the United States.

Let us consider the first option. An American sociologist from the University of San Diego, Wayne Cornelius, has made certain projections: should border controls be removed, the scenario is not likely to differ very much from the current situation. Initially, the wave of immigration could rise, only to subside to previous levels after a few months. The demand on the labour market and not the border determines the inflow of immigrants. Only those Mexicans who can find a job will cross over; they are part of an immigrant's network or have some members of their family already settled in the States. This is a common feature of economic immigration the world over. So it hardly matters whether a border is open or closed.

The second option is to keep the Mexicans in Mexico. For this, North American companies would have to generate employment in the South. The experiment was tried out twenty years ago; it remains in an embryonic stage. 'Maquiladoras' or sub-contracting firms were set up in the free zones along the border. They work for American, Japanese and European principals. In this way, the industries of the North take advantage of the low wages and the skills of Mexican labour in Mexico itself. Both sides view this arrangement in a positive light; but has it managed to stop the exodus? Mexican employees use the skills they acquire in the 'maquiladoras' to cross over to the States and earn more money.

A more ambitious plan is the North American Free Trade Agreement. The three partner countries, Canada, the United States and Mexico hope to create the world's largest common market by mid 1993. A 'maquiladora', this time to cover the whole of Mexico! In principle, the free movement of goods- not of men, their movement has been excluded from the purview of the treaty - should encourage investors to set up factories in Mexico as long as wages for equal levels of productivity remain lower than in the United States. Currently, the difference is 1 to 10. Another advantage of relocating to the South would be escaping stringent U.S. pollution laws. But is employment generation in the South going to be enough to stem the tide of immigration? Jorge Bustamante calculates that five years after the NAFTA comes into effect, its impact will begin to be felt. The migratory flows will be down by 10%. They could come down by as much as 50% after ten years. In the best of cases, even if the South were to develop, the North would still require labour especially in the unskilled sector dominated by the Mexicans.

Would U.S. employers continue to call in Mexican workers if there was a recession in the United States? They probably would. In times of sustained economic activity, the demand for Mexican labour goes up in California; but demand goes up even further in a downswing phase as employers replace unskilled white and black workers by Mexicans who are cheaper still. Whether the border is open or closed, whether there is growth or recession is irrelevant. Migration will continue for as long as economic imbalances persist. So it seems that the common market does offer a long term solution even though its effect will be slow and uncertain. Unless... Gary Becker has another idea.

AN ULTRA RATIONAL SOLUTION

Gary Becker, a former student of the liberal economist Friedrich Von Hayek, has followed in the footsteps of his master and gone on to teach at the University of Chicago. In the seventies, he revolutionised economics and sociology with a new theory, the RAT or Rational Action Theory.

The Rational Action Theory holds that all individuals are rational, irrespective of where they come from. According to Becker this means that individual decisions are governed by cost benefit considerations: individuals act or behave as if they were calculating the future benefits likely to accrue from their present behaviour. To be rational is to try and maximise these advantages in relation to one's culture. Becker has thus 'proved' that decisions such as marriage, number of children, etc. are governed by economic factors. To give a few simple examples: when the cost of education goes up, the number of children goes down; when the price of a drug decreases, its consumption increases; with the death penalty, the number of crimes in the U.S. falls... These findings are the result of a massive statistical study undertaken by Becker and reflect neither his personal preferences nor his own thinking.

In what way is RAT relevant to immigration? For Becker, the immigrant is a rational being; so for that matter is the host society. If there was no welfare to distort the direct relationship between individual effort and reward, the laws of the market would regulate in a perfect manner the free movement of men from one country to another, just as free prices adjust the supply and demand of goods. The men and women who settled in the United States did so only after deciding that in spite of the risks, it was a worthwhile investment. In the nineteenth century, it was common for immigrants to borrow to finance their journey; they repaid their debt with their earnings of their first few years. The saga of immigration was a 'rational saga', both for the migrant and the host country. This equilibrium has been disturbed. Today, from the immigrant's point of view it is rational to go the United States or Europe which offer free social protection. However it is not so rational for the host country to accept them. Theoretically, there are two logical solutions which could help in restoring the balance. Either the host country lowers welfare assistance or makes it discriminatory by reserving it only for the nationals of that country. In practice however, neither of these options are feasible.

Becker has a third solution. The immigrant should be made to pay an entrance fee to take care of the initial expenses incurred by the host country. Doing so will disarm the opposition to immigration, as the immigrant will have to pay to join the labour market and use public services and amenities.

The idea is not as absurd as it seems. A rational immigrant is fully capable of calculating whether the investment is worthwhile or not. In the Becker system, each State could fix its own entrance fee and the immigrant could choose accordingly. For instance, entrance to the United States would be very expensive, but the immigrant could hope for a high rate of return. The same would be true for Japan and Switzerland. Canada and Argentina would be less expensive and so on and so forth. Wouldn't that be pro-rich? 'So what! Their investment would be beneficial to the host country.' What about the talented, deserving poor? 'The host country could apply differential rates, taking into account the immigrant's qualifications, give loans on easy terms or for certain categories waive the entrance fee altogether.' Not everyone who enters through Becker's system of rationing will be entitled to citizenship. This not out of cultural or ethnic considerations - the votaries of RAT are not xenophobic - but to remain consistent to RAT logic. As citizenship entitles one to public services and welfare assistance, it has a quantifiable economic value. It stands to reason that the immigrant work for several years before being able to enjoy the common heritage built collectively by the citizens of a particular country.

Would this not be immoral? No, says Becker, for he believes that morality and rationality are not contradictory. Somewhat fantastic? When the governments of Canada or the United States keep aside a quota of resident permits for certain investors (in the United States you have to bring at least one million dollars to qualify for such a permit), or when the French government charges the Algerians an exorbitant amount for an entry visa, they are tacitly part of the Becker system; but they refuse to see this and only apply it in part. Does anybody have anything better to suggest, given that the idea of putting a complete ban on immigration is neither desirable nor tenable. By taking the economic argument to its logical end, the votaries of RAT are widening the scope of the debate and suggesting new tools to overcome the open or closed border dilemma.

The late Friedrich Von Hayek was fond of saying, 'It is the duty of liberal intellectuals to prepare alternative utopias for the time when policies go bankrupt. The utopias of today are the realities of tomorrow.'

8

THE YELLOW PERIL

To each their Blacks! The yellow peril, which for a long time had haunted the Europeans, is now beginning to obsess the Japanese. One will always be a Black or a Yellow for someone else. In the eyes of the Japanese, the Chinese, the Vietnamese, the Filipinos and the Koreans are all 'yellow'. Try and see it the Japanese way: they have a billion odd Chinese at their doorstep and their own numbers are dwindling. Ever since they became affluent, they have stopped producing children. Work too has ceased to interest them. Contrary to their much vaunted reputation as the proverbial ants, any holiday - traditional or not - is excuse enough to take a long weekend, go golfing or seek the pleasures of night-life. The young prolong their studies to put off as far as possible the nine to five routine. Besides, there is no question of a Japanese taking a three K job. The three K's stand for Kitsui, Kitanai, Kiken - dirty, tiring and dangerous. Three K is only fit for immigrants.

Immigration is not completely new to Japan. In the twenties, the military government forcibly brought in two million Koreans, Taiwanese and Chinese workers

to the replace the soldiers who had gone to war. After
the defeat of 1945, only the Koreans stayed on. In spite
of moving up socially, the community has yet to
acquire Japanese nationality. But the Koreans are no
ordinary immigrants. 'Who colonised whom,' they
ask. Where did the Japanese get their customs, art and
Buddhism, if not from the Koreans. The relationship
has become all the more complex with Korean industries
competing with their Japanese counterparts. The one
million odd Koreans in Japan are more a nation within
a nation, even if the Japanese do despise them. The
Japanese attitude towards the Koreans reminds one of
the white American attitude towards the Blacks and
the French attitude towards the North Africans; the
Japanese are only willing to accept Korean success in
sports and music, fields in which talent is more natural
than acquired. The real immigrants in Japan then come
from the Third World countries of Asia: Thailand,
China, the Philippines, Iran and Pakistan. They enter
the country on tourist or student visas, huddle together
in their own community neighbourhoods and form
their own cultural associations. They are confined to
menial work - labourers in small companies, construction
workers, waitresses and barmen. All illegal immigrants
have to work for a living; there is no welfare assistance
in Japan. But how do you tell the difference between
a Japanese and a Chinese?

MAKING A FINE ART OF DIFFERENTIATION

The Japanese can never go wrong. For centuries they
have been practicing the fine art of differentiation.
Before the immigrants, three million Burakumin - low
caste ethnic Japanese - were marginalised and treated
as untouchables. Was it because Japanese society was

fed up of its own homogeneity that it decided to designate a caste of pariahs from within? Pariahs who outwardly looked the same. The Burakumin were allowed to perform only the most degrading tasks - animal slaughter, removal of corpses and garbage collection. Though they were emancipated a hundred years ago, the Burakumin have not moved out of their localities; their children are still made to feel outcasts at school, they find it hard to get jobs in companies and rarely marry out of community. Very often, families and employers engage specialised detectives to check out the antecedents of candidates suspected of being Burakumin in disguise. Why did the Japanese choose other Japanese as their barbarians? Racism is never more virulent than when the difference is almost imperceptible.

Even though the Burakumin are a typically Japanese phenomenon, the political response to it is fairly universal. For the last forty years, the Japanese right-wing has being saying, 'The Burakumin are different because of their culture. Time alone will narrow the gap. Meanwhile the government is doing all it can to integrate them: the Burakumin are living in subsidised accommodation, their children are getting scholarships.' The Japanese left is quick to counter, 'Those in power - be it the Emperor in ancient Japan or the capitalist backed government of today - have always wanted to discriminate against the Burakumin.' The Socialist deputy, Tatsukumi Komori adds, 'The Burakumin are not a legacy of Japanese culture, they're a proletariat who are being deliberately exploited to keep wages low.' Komori's conclusion: capitalist employers can now apply to the immigrant population the methods they have tried out on the Burakumin. Japanese company bosses claim that immigration is necessary

as Japan's economy is short of manpower. But is not
the need for immigration more psychological than
economic? Does not every nation need its pariahs to
perform the three K jobs, a caste to be looked down
upon?

THE INVISIBLE WORKERS

'Immigrants? What immigrants? How can Nissan employ
immigrants when the law in Japan forbids immigration.'
Takashi Ishihara is furious. My questions do not
amuse him. This industrial baron is used to fawning
admirers, not impudent foreigners. I go on regardless,
though it is perfectly obvious that Ishihara wants to
change the topic and speak about European
protectionism, for instance. The three secretaries, his
principal private secretary, his press secretary and the
inevitable note taker, all look aghast. Have I forgotten
that I am talking to the Napoleon of the automobile
industry? I continue undeterred as I know for a fact
that Nissan does employ foreign workers. By then
Ishihara has recovered. He admits, 'You're quite right,
Nissan did employ fourteen foreigners last year. They
were not immigrants, they were trainees. In any case,
they have all gone back to their own countries.' That
is the end of our interview. I am served a final cup
of green tea and bowed my way out to the lift. I leave
none the wiser, though one thing is becoming clear
to me: when in Japan, do not ask any questions about
the Emperor's intelligence, the Burakumin and
immigration.

A little later, Hisashi Osawa, the official looking
after foreigners at the Japanese Ministry of Justice
explains, 'Japanese firms cannot hire immigrant workers
as we have no law which allows immigration.' After

much pressing, he finally concedes that since 1991, there exists a law regulating entry to and exit from Japan. This is what I must have meant when I wrongly used the term 'immigration.' I let him score this point on terminology before shooting the next question. 'Won't foreigners take advantage of this law to come and work in Japan?' Osawa's normally impassive face brightens, 'Oh, you are talking about trainees. It is true that the entry-exit law allows foreigners to come in as company trainees.' Osawa takes it upon himself to arrange a visit for me to three of these companies so I can see for myself that trainees are not immigrant workers.

I cannot decline such a courteous invitation. As a result, I am forced to spend the next three days commuting in Tokyo's suburban trains, my hosts having taken great pains to see that the companies I have to visit are furthest away from the city centre. Courtesy the Ministry, I have the pleasure of meeting two Chinese dressmakers in a garment factory in North Tokyo, an Indonesian in a engineering workshop in Yokohama, and two dozen Thais at the electronics giant NEC. Hardly enough foreigners to warrant the fear of an invasion in Japan.

But, as is often the case in the course of an enquiry, the Chairman of NEC quite inadvertently let the cat out of the bag when he told me, 'Our trainees are real trainees.' What does that mean, I asked Hiroshi Shigehara. The trainees spend a few weeks at the company's training centre before returning home. When they go back home, some of them will be using the NEC computer or telephone equipment that the company sells in their countries. Some have come as part of a technology transfer programme; this is Japan's way of furthering third world development and ... its own markets. This mixture of marketing and philanthropy does honour to NEC, but why is Mr Shigehara so keen to clarify that his trainees are 'real'? If his trainees are real, then who are the fake trainees? The Chairman had heard somewhere that some Japanese companies used the term 'trainee' for people who are in fact immigrant workers. At last, we are getting to the truth, even though it has been a long wait. That is Japan for you. Nothing is ever said, everything is hinted at: a fascinating game provided one has the time and the patience for it. We have just been told that there are no migrant workers in Japan. So how many 'trainees' who are not quite trainees are there?

When I put this question to Hisashi Osawa at the Ministry of Justice in a subsequent meeting, pat came the answer of this seasoned bureaucrat, 'A hundred thousand'. As for political refugees, according to the last count in October 91, there were a 147. Obviously, the official statistics have to be taken with more than a pinch of salt.

Kazuaki Tezuka, a professor at the University of Chiba and one of the few economists to take an interest in the new sociology of migration, estimates the number of immigrant workers in Japan at around six hundred thousand; two hundred thousand Chinese, two hundred thousand South-East Asians and Filipinos and two hundred thousand Nissei or Brazilians of Japanese origin whose forefathers had emigrated at the turn of the century and who are now trying to come back. In spite of their fully Japanese appearance, they only speak Portuguese and are viewed as foreigners. Then there are six hundred thousand Koreans and six hundred thousand clandestine workers. Not that many in relation to the total population. But all the large cities, particularly Tokyo and Osaka, have their immigrant neighbourhoods; with the coming of Pakistanis and Iranians, immigrants have become all the more visible. So the figures are not quite as negligible as one would think, given the closed, 'tribal' character of Japanese society.

IN PRAISE OF ALL THAT IS NEBULOUS

What is the policy of the Japanese government towards immigration? A typically Western question to which a clear cut answer is unthinkable in Japan. A policy assumes that there is choice, something alien to Japanese culture. The ruling classes prefer the nebulous, which Western observers sometimes refer to as consensus. But I think nebulous is a better term. The Government turns a blind eye to immigration because immigrants keep employers happy and they are the ones who finance the Liberal Democratic Party (LDP) that has been in power for the last forty years. Shizuka Kamei, the LDP's man in charge of immigration, says the government is being flexible in enforcing the law.

Shizuka Kamei is very much the stuff legislators and ministers are made of: years of uninterrupted rule have allowed the LDP to function virtually as a single party, churning out bureaucrats and demagogues who all look and sound alike. 'The law,' explains Kamei, 'prohibits immigration; public opinion is hostile to immigrants but the employers want them. At each and every election meeting, I have had to face groups of small employers demanding foreign manpower.' As for the large companies, they need immigrants to do the menial work, keep wages low and impart flexibility to an otherwise rigid system, given the 'employment for life' staff policy of companies. So how does Japanese society reconcile company recruitment with

the law? First, the police never inspects work premises.
Second, for as long as the company has a clean record,
no checks are possible. Kamei adds ,'Foreigners are
always welcome in Japan, provided they work and
leave the country after a couple of years. But we don't
like foreigners who settle down for good.' By that he
means the Koreans. 'We do not want to create a
subclass of immigrants, confined to the three K's and
ghettos of the kind you see mushrooming in the
United States and Europe.' Now don't leap to
conclusions, the Japanese are not racist. Kamei is at
pains to emphasize the long Japanese tradition of
cultural and religious assimilation. 'We are a mixture
of all the cultures and civilisations of Asia: Mongoloid,
Chinese, Korean and Buddhist.'

I remark that this was the case till the sixteenth
century, after which the Japanese have been
systematically victimising the Koreans and Chinese.

Kamei's rejoinder, 'That was the war. War is a
confrontation between states, not between races or
nations. In wartime, the enemy is faceless.'

- The brutality with which you colonised Korea
does not augur very well for your future relationship
with immigrants.

Kamei is not a man to get flustered easily.

- Colonisation and imperialism are purely European
constructs. Unfortunately, we were influenced by them,
and subsequently made a mess. Now Japan is rejecting
these Western ideas and trying to renew her tradition
of assimilating what comes from outside.

THE MITI ANSWER

Public opinion is hostile to immigration; employers
need immigrant labour; is there any way to reconcile

the two? Shoichi Ikuta says he has the answer. Which is just as it should be, considering he is a bureaucrat with the Ministry of International Trade and Industry. MITI is supposed to be the real brain of the Japanese administration, the author of Japan's forty year economic success story. It had foreseen and planned for every eventuality. Unfortunately for MITI, not all the Japanese - least of all employers bodies - share this perception of the economic miracle, though MITI is quite popular in U.S. and West European social democratic circles which favour planning. As always, there is something to be said for both sides.

The Japanese tax payer can certainly not accuse MITI of wasting public funds on luxurious offices: in Japan, civil servants work in the sublime obscurity of Dantean cells, unlike the palatial offices back home. To reach the corner where Ikuta sits with a dozen other colleagues, I have to make my way carefully through files and jump across cartons of documents. All Japanese offices are alike, as cramped and uncomfortable as the houses they live in. But like a true MITI bureaucrat, Ikuta makes up in arrogance what he lacks in material comfort. I had to wait several weeks before he condescended to meet me. Prior to the appointment, I had been asked to submit a detailed biodata testifying to my qualities and educational qualifications. Without a degree you just cannot meet a bureaucrat in Japan. The way they rate your degree is going to determine how you will be received: as an equal or as an inferior. As the Ecole nationale d'administration is considered at par with the University of Tokyo, from where all MITI bureaucrats are recruited, the possibility of a meeting could be entertained. But this is only the beginning. You also need to have the right contacts who will forward your name to the bureaucratic overlord you want to meet. Even then, the ordeal is by no means over. To sit through the meeting you need monumental patience. Questions, particularly direct questions, are never heard. Besides, asking a straight question shows lack of breeding. Prevarication and cliches are all you can expect in response. If need be, the bureaucrat will not hesitate to tell outright lies with a perfectly straight face. Should Westerners believe all they are told? It is up to them to draw their own conclusions after much questioning, cross-checking and comparing information gleaned from various sources.

I have no doubt been very harsh on Ikuta. But then even I needed a scapegoat on whom to take out my frustration and pin my fantasies. My outburst should therefore not be allowed to detract from the intrinsic merit of Ikuta's project.

'At the international level, migration has always had a negative impact: immigration has more disadvantages than advantages both for the sender and host countries,' asserts Ikuta. In Japan, immigrant labour will only delay modernisation: it would be much more profitable to invest in technical upgradation and put an end to the three K's rather than bring in the Koreans or the Chinese. Emigration also acts as a deterrent to growth in the labour exporting countries, as they are deprived of their most productive workers. Shoichi Ikuta's analysis has much in common with that of the German economist Klaus Werner Schatz. However, it assumes that workers would be as productive had they stayed in their own countries as they are in the countries to which they migrate. Now this is rarely the case. Even then Ikuta does deserve a hearing for he has definite plan to suggest.

In order to resolve the various contradictions, the plan provides for taking in a hundred thousand 'trainees' every year in Japan. This in fact has begun on an experimental basis since 1992. Large automobile, machine tool and consumer durable companies have been allowed to recruit trainees from South East Asia; they will be given a three year visa. During the three years of their stay, they will be under company contract. For the first year, the company will give in house training; for the next two years, the trainees will be put to work in the company. The company provides them with accommodation and pays them an 'allowance', not a wage. In this manner, employers pay less than the minimum wage, which is fixed in consultation with the trade unions. At the end of the three years, the trainees are legally bound to return to their own countries but they will have had the time to master the organisational and technical skills that Ikuta chooses to call Japanese 'work software.' Thus employers will be able to overcome the shortage of local manpower and create at the same time a potential reservoir of skilled labour in South East Asia. If the Japanese company eventually decides to relocate its plants in a third country, it can tap on this reserve and recreate the same conditions of efficiency as in Japan. In principle, every one stands to gain: the Third World benefits from Japanese investment and will be in a better position to reexport its goods as a result of this trained manpower; the immigrant workers will return to their country with a profession and, very often, a job contract in hand. The Japanese companies will manufacture for export the same products as they would have in Japan but at a much lower cost. 'Isn't it more rational,' asks Ikuta, 'to manufacture cars in a place where there is underemployment than in Japan where there is a shortage of manpower? Isn't it better to export factories than to import immigrants? Isn't it preferable to spare Japan social and cultural upheaval as well as the enormous cost of settling immigrant communities?'

Ikuta's formula is valid for multinational companies, but what does he have to suggest for the smaller firms which are heavily dependent on illegal immigrants. MITI has thought of a way out for them with the JITCO, the Japan International Cooperation Organisation. The JITCO is supposed to estimate the labour needs of small companies through the intermediary of their Chambers of Commerce, after which it matches demand with supply. This way the State will regain control over the foreign illegal employment market and companies and immigrants will get a chance to regularise their situation. All trainees who come through JITCO will be guaranteed training for one third of their stay and work for the remaining two-thirds. The one year contract will be renewable provided the trainee has behaved properly. What will they earn? They will be given a training allowance which naturally will be lower than the minimum wage paid to the Japanese. Is this not tantamount to legalising the exploitation of immigrant workers by small and medium industry? Yes, but it also means the immigrants will be integrated into the official labour market and will be protected against slave drivers. When all is said and done, the MITI and JITCO solutions, however imperfect, are still a practical attempt to reconcile hostility to immigration - forbidden in principle - with the integration of trainees through legally recognised work and the companies' demand for cheap labour. The Ikuta plan is at the same time a blueprint for a new kind of contract between the industrial North and the underdeveloped South.

Does MITI still have the power to impose its writ? It was all very well twenty years ago, but today Japanese society has become far too complex to be controlled by planners alone. Even if MITI succeeds in transforming illegal immigrants into legal trainees, does it have the wherewithal to regulate the inflow of migrants and stop politicians from whipping up public hysteria? For today immigration is being perceived as a threat to national identity and is one of the reasons for xenophobia. If the Japanese press is to be believed, Japan has even managed to throw up its own version of Le Pen: a certain Nishio Kanji. Only this Le Pen is supposed to have read Hegel!

IS THE JAPANESE IDENTITY IN JEOPARDY?

Nishio Kanji is a professor of German philosophy at the University of Tokyo. He is being compared with Le Pen because of his pointedly anti-immigration public stance. Now it is rare for someone to speak out in Japan; people may be hostile to immigration but they will never openly say so. Japan is not a country for intellectuals, even less so for committed intellectuals. The only forum they have to express themselves are specialised reviews; these are circulated confidentially and their political influence is negligible. The only reason why Nishio Kanji got such widespread media coverage is because he dared to say what many Japanese felt but never expressed.

Says Nishio Kanji, 'The Japanese race is a homogeneous race. Mixed blood is almost unknown. In the seventeenth century, the Japanese archipelago did take in a few thousand Chinese and Koreans, as they brought with them techniques which were superior to the Japanese ones. At the time, because they were so few in numbers, it was a case of cultural not racial intermingling.' On the other hand, continues Kanji, the current lot of Koreans are descendants of forced labourers who have nothing to contribute save Pachinko (a game) and crime. Furthermore, they refuse to assimilate, continue to stick to their community and remain loyal to their country of origin. Unfortunately, they have set a bad precedent, one that should make the Japanese tread cautiously.

Nishio Kanji denies being racist; all he is doing is trying to protect a culture which till now has been homogeneous. 'Non verbal communication and a common history,' he explains, 'have so far allowed Japanese society to function smoothly.' In all rela- tionships - husband wife, family, friends, companies, Parliament - what is left unsaid, hinted at or implied make for the consensus so typically Japanese. 'My country,' he adds, 'is the only non conflictive democracy in the world. By destroying homogeneity, immigration will lead to the break down of this communication network and common history; Japan will be compelled to function along Western confrontationist lines.' And isn't throwing Japanese society into disarray just what the Westerners want? asks Nishio Kanji. In any case, the Western experience of immigration should be enough to dissuade the Japanese from accepting immi- grants. Immigrants only spell ghettos, drugs, urban unrest, a proletarian sub-caste, evils Japanese society had so far managed to avoid. Last but not least, the Japanese are 'ill-equipped' to take in foreigners, as they have no experience of it. What is the point of forcing them to do something they can't.

All this is very well, but immigrants continue to pour into Japan. 'This is the doing of 'liberal employers' taken in by Western ideas of competition. Give these liberals an inch, and they will take a mile; soon you will have them importing rice into Japan even if it means ruining the peasantry, the true custodian of our civilisation.' expostulates Nishio Kanji. Rice is a big issue for Japanese nationalists. Though locally produced rice is ten times more expensive than imported rice, listening to Kanji fulminate, it is hard to decide which is worse, foreign rice or Korean immigrants. A typical xenophobic attitude you may well say, except that in Japan intellectuals do not usually express themselves in such a forthright manner. But then Nishio Kanji has studied in Germany, is particularly well versed in German philosophy and leaps to the defense of national identity, a concept, ironically, he has borrowed from Europe. His methods can hardly be called Japanese. Perhaps this is because he is from Tokyo, a city whose inhabitants have assimilated Western ways more than they realise. For their reaction against immigration is no different from that of an American or a European. It is different however when the scene shifts from Tokyo, the new capital, to Kyoto, the old capital.

ABSORBING IMMIGRATION

Kyoto is ancient, but only up to a point. The city's wooden temples and palaces have been buried below a hotchpotch of modern architecture. In Japan, customs not monuments, keep the past alive. Kyoto's intelligentsia - notably the Centre for the study of Japanese history - has taken up the task of defining and defending Japan's national identity. Founded in 1987 by Prime Minister Nakasone, the Centre is being generously financed by employers bodies and has become the Mecca of 'identity' thinking. Some of the best scholars in the country have gathered here to lead what has come to be known as the new Kyoto school. This brings back memories of a similar movement in the thirties which attempted to align the eternal Japan with modernisation. Hayao Kawai is undoubtedly the Centre's most original thinker. Kawai is a psychoanalyst by training, a rarity in Japan. Having studied in Switzerland under Karl Jung, Kawai shares his mentor's point of view: each culture is a relatively immutable structure, made up of intangible archetypes. These archetypes define the entire network of relationships with the other and explain the attitude towards immigrants.

For Kawai, Western culture is a paternal culture; mythology, religion, politics and family are all dominated by the father image. The father - Zeus, God, the boss, the chief, the President - is the fount of authority. In such a culture, conflicts with the outsider are inevitable. Eventually, there will be no immigrants, as they will have either been excluded or assimilated. In a paternalistic Western society, there can be no via media. By its very nature, Western society is ill-suited to cultural coexistence, which it perceives as a challenge to its authority.

Hayao Kawai explains that these traits do not exist in Japan, which is a maternal society. The mother is the central figure of Japanese mythology. According to medieval tradition, the mother is the guardian of all religious places and shrines; even today, she remains the head of the family and it is to her that the earning members of the family hand over their earnings. In Japan, the woman is first and foremost the 'mother' of her children and her husband and the Japanese do not feel the slightest need to tear themselves away from the maternal bosom when they enter adulthood. On the contrary, the key to the behaviour of a Japanese adult is this constant dependence on the mother or on surrogate mothers such as the clan and the company. In exchange for voluntary submission, the Japanese male is shown indulgence at all times by the mother- be it his wife, the company, the school or the State. The Japanese word for this is 'amae', a term crucial to the understanding of national identity.

In such a sheltered society, one that has known neither discontinuity nor charisma, there is no place for individualism. In no Japanese fairy tale will you find a handsome knight leaving his family to marry a princess. Such an archetype simply does not exist in the Japanese subconscious. On the other hand, in this society which rejects individualism, the individual is not punished. School children never fail as this will separate them from their group; judges do not sentence the guilty, they take them to task so that they may repent; and employers never dismiss their employees. Then from where is power derived in a maternal society? Power only exists in a hollow : 'the centre is a void.' In mythology, the incarnation of power is a woman, the Moon god. The Moon god does not do anything, that is her function. Her sceptre is a mirror which reflects the world. Power in Japan means conciliation, not decision making. It is symbolic that the Imperial Park, a vast open space, lies in the heart of Tokyo. The Emperor does not rule, the prime minister takes no decisions and employers have no charisma. Then who does decide? A futile question, as decisions are not taken, they just evolve out of a natural harmony.

What does all this have to do with immigration? Until you grasp the concept of Japan's identity, you can't understand Japan's relationship with foreigners, explains Hayao Kawai. The 'hollow centre'or 'maternal society' sucks in and absorbs all that can be assimilated. In this way, Buddhism was imported from Korea, rice cultivation from China and modern technology from the West. The Japanese gift for imitation which the West makes so much fun of is in point of fact absorption by the mother; according to Kawai this is much better than confrontation with the father. This archetype characterises the Japanese model of immigration - first sifting and then assimilating contributions from the outside world, provided they are considered useful for the nation as a whole. Fascinated by this model, Claude Levi Strauss had written, 'Only Japan has found the right balance between what to absorb and what to reject, between how much to let in and how much to shut out.' As a result, the terms used in the West to define the relationship between immigrants and the host country - multiculturalism, xenophobia, racism and integration - would be meaningless in Japan. You have to reason differently, with new concepts. 'Immigration will never be a threat to the Japanese identity as it is eternal and never comes into conflict with the outside,' says Kawai.

If Hayao Kawai's reasoning and conclusions seem irksome and lacking in conviction, then Kawai will have proved his point: the Japanese are different. At least this is what some Japanese believe and would have others believe. For not all Japanese subscribe to this ideal of a culture so perfectly impervious to time and outside influence.

JAPAN'S POST MODERNISM

Both Nishio Kanji and Hayao Kawai conform to the
image foreigners have of Japan, an image Japanese
leaders want to project of their country. Both represent
and support the imperial system, favour a hierarchical
society and modernisation by the state. For these 'old'
intellectuals, state and nation are one, and Japan can
only have a single culture which is at once modern
and rooted in an immutable tradition. But this is only
one face of the real Japan, for another Japan was born
after the war. Akira Asada is the spokesman of this
new Japan, one that belongs to the generation that has
just turned forty.

'What is all this nonsense about maternal societies,
the new Kyoto school!' exclaims Akira Asada. How
does one describe the protean Asada? Young philosopher
of the new generation, teenage intellectual idol, herald
of consumerism and hedonism or the darling of the
media? By the looks of it, his only concern is to be
seen at all the fashionable Tokyo cafes and to make
sure his Cashmere sweaters match with the colour of
his scarves and spectacle frames. He thinks it is stupid
to spend eighty hours a week working in a company
that is run like a barrack. Asada says Hayao Kawai
has been paid by Japanese employers to sell the idea
of pseudo-harmony between man and nature in a
supposedly eternal Japan. What we are witnessing, he
explains, is a rebirth of ideas fashionable in the
thirties, which the military dictatorship too used. All
discourse about Japanese distinctiveness, the once
Eastern always Eastern theme, the mother symbolism,
the critique of Western materialism, the mystification
of the past and indigenous philosophy, is music to the
ears of large employers. For it is with this ideology

that they counter the rise of individualism amongst
the youth.

- But Akira, I thought the tea ceremony has once
again caught the fancy of the young girls.

- The young are only interested in sex and cars.
The older generation pretends to worry about the
threat of immigration because this pretense lets them
keep alive the illusion that such a thing as Japanese
culture still exists.

'In truth the Japanese no longer know how to
identify themselves. The way they live and what they
buy have been completely westernised.' Classical culture
has not been taught since 1945 and history has come
to a standstill, religion is being practiced in name only
and tradition has been reduced to a farce. By the year
2000, the Japanese will have become rootless nomads
living in a maze of electronic goods, stuffed with a
surfeit of travel, and nothing in their heads. A couple
of million immigrants here or there will not make any
difference. The Japanese will have truly entered post
modernism and in the process shed their national
culture.

9

RACE AND CULTURE

The time has come for us to stop a while to define in as concise a manner as possible the basic terms that recur in the universal debate on immigration. Is it their race or their culture that makes immigrants different? For most people, the distinction between race and culture is very blurred. Nowadays, no one refers to race in public, even though people still have racism on their minds. What do the modernists who have substituted racial differentiation by cultural differentiation understand by assimilation? Is the 'Other', now different on account of culture not race, biologically capable of integrating into the culture of adoption? The latter, usually perceived as being superior, is obviously our culture! And how can we be absolutely sure that the Other will not transmit his culture to his descendants through some genetic determinism? To whom does one put these questions and should one expect a clear answer?

Strangely enough, very few scholars in the world have devoted much time to the distinction between race and culture, and cultural transmission. Both these subjects seem to have fallen between two scientific stools. Biologists, carrying on the work started by Darwin and Mendel, study the evolution of our genetic heritage; culture is not their field. Anthropologists, on the other hand, have little or nothing to do with evolution, as by inclination, they prefer recording 'cold' civilisations which have little or no history. Somewhere in the middle, a few socio-biologists, prompted by Konrad Lorentz and Edward Wilson, have tried to make the link between biology and culture, but so far their efforts have met with little success. Wilson himself has given up trying to show the relationship between genetic characteristics and cultural predisposition. Claude Levi-Strauss told me the person to meet was Cavalli-Sforza.

RACE IS INVISIBLE

Luca Cavalli-Sforza tells me, 'The "homosapien" is by nature a migrant and a half-caste. This is the only living species which has not stopped mixing since it originated, nor for that matter has it stopped moving.'

We are at Stanford where Cavalli-Sforza works and teaches. All new ideas find their way to Stanford which is the modern day version of Cluny; only the scholarly monks of today wear shorts and move about on bicycles under clear, blue skies. For Cavalli-Sforza, classification on the basis of race is not possible as there are thousand of races and no one knows where one race ends and the next begins. Some kind of natural demarcation among groups is possible but morphology is not the best criterion to go by. External traits are deceptive and reveal little about the homogeneity or heterogeneity of human groupings. Genic frequency or the frequency of certain genic types (blood groups, Rhesus, DNA nucleotide sequences) is the only scientifically acceptable method for grouping and cross-checking. What emerges from this is that there is no clear cut line of demarcation between two groups. Instead the transition from one race to another appears to be extremely blurred. The most common way of classifying people into races is by looking at external traits, but very often groupings on the basis of genic frequency tell a different story altogether. For instance, the distinction between Blacks and Whites is only skin deep. A study of genic maps has revealed that the American Blacks have more genes in common with the Whites than they do say with yellow Asians. Australian aborigines are closer to Asians than to African Blacks whom they resemble. Visible physical traits which shape popular perception of race are the most superficial features of a human group; they only reveal physiological adaptation to climate. This is how, through a process of natural selection, the colour of our skin changed gradually from black to white, for a white skin absorbs more ultraviolet rays than a black one, a natural advantage in temperate climates. Similarly the shape of the nose - broad and flat in tropical countries and fine in cold countries - was determined through natural selection to make air filtering easier. Physical appearance, which we set so much store by and which fires our imagination, is only on the surface. Physical traits tell us next to nothing about racial differences. When viewed on the human time-scale, physical changes are relatively recent. Ten to twenty millennia are enough to bring about a change in the colour of one's skin; it was only ten thousand years ago that the Europeans got their white skins.

HOW CULTURE IS TRANSMITTED

Genic maps are far more informative than visually

apparent racial characteristics. To those who know how to read them, they tell the entire history of mankind and human migration. The method used for making and reading genic maps is fairly simple to describe. Blood samples taken from various sections of the population are used to draw up planetary charts indicating the frequency of certain kinds of genes. The more frequently a genic type occurs, the closer it is to the geographical point of its origin. The rarer it becomes, the farther the human group has travelled and distanced itself from its source. The homosapiens, whose descendants we all are, seem to originate from a single place: East Africa. From here modern man moved out in all directions to colonise the entire planet in a hundred thousand years. Archeological findings in Tanzania bear out the genic analysis. The single and relatively recent origin of man explains the deep homogeneity of mankind. There are slight variations here and there, for instance, adaptation to climate and some illnesses like malaria. But it is these slight variations which tell us our history just as genic maps tell us of large migratory movements.

The great contribution of Cavalli-Sforza is to have matched the genic maps of several hundred peoples with their linguistic maps in an effort to see whether cultural history corroborates biological history. For instance, Cavalli-Sforza's maps show that the men who colonised Western Europe ten thousand years ago came from the Middle East. Genic frequencies of Middle Eastern villages spread all over Europe at the same time as their agricultural techniques. The migratory flow from Turkey to England and Sweden as revealed in genic maps lasted some four thousand years, at the end of which the whole of Europe was conquered and the population became a thoroughly mixed one. By this method, it is now possible to verify the Greek colonisation of Southern Italy twenty-five centuries after the event: genic frequencies correspond with toponymy. Genic frequencies were used to reconstitute the Magyar invasion of Hungary and to discover that the Magyars came from the Urals. A comparison of the genic and linguistic maps shows that though the Magyars were a minority, they were a conquering army, as the area of their linguistic influence is much larger than that of their cultural heritage. The opposite is true for the Basques whose genic frequency is much more spread out than their linguistic area. This means that the Basques, who occupied all of South-West France and Northern Spain, survived by partially giving up their language under the influence of a new set of colonisers.

What about Jewish culture, are the Jews a race or is it more a case of common genic frequencies? Most Jews - the Ashkenazim from Central Europe and the Sephardim of Mediterranean descent - have some common Middle Eastern genic frequencies and some genic frequencies of the countries in which they settled. In this manner, a Polish Jew has fifty per cent Jewish genic frequencies and fifty per cent Polish genic frequencies. Obviously these are group averages and the figures will vary from individual to individual. On the other hand, Ethiopian or Yemeni Jews do not share the same genic frequencies as other Jews; they are late converts.

We move on to the subject of black Americans. Luca Cavalli-Sforza is a living encyclopedia. 'A black American is on an average thirty per cent Caucasian, in other words white.' This genic evolution is the result of three hundred years of intermingling. If the trend persists, in another thousand years black Americans will be left with only fifteen per cent of their African genes. In another two thousand years, it will be hard to differentiate them from the rest of the American population.

Luca Cavalli-Sforza's maps have invalidated many generally accepted ideas about Europe. Genic boundaries have very little in common with cultural, linguistic or political boundaries. The only people in Europe with singular genic frequencies are the Lapps, the Basques and of course the Sardinians. Now we have just seen that the Basque 'race' no longer coincides with its culture. Similarly those who are Lapps 'by race' are scattered all over Europe and do not speak the same language. On the other hand, for Sardinians, 'race', culture and language remain closely linked. In the case of the French and the Germans, their genic homogeneity is almost complete; both these nations belong to the same race, their differences are only cultural. One of history's ironies is that the Rhine has never been a border but a fertile ground for intermingling. The language and culture of France or Germany are clearly a product of their respective histories; they are a political not a biological imposition.

Scientific findings and popular perception about race do not seem to tally. When we say so and so has typically German looks, we are actually confusing the natural with the cultural. We automatically equate attitudes that are really cultural in nature with physical traits, facial expressions being a good example of this. We tend to interpret in terms of race what is in fact determined by the cultural and natural environment.

What are we to conclude from all the examples Cavalli-Sforza has given us? Race and culture may or may not coincide. Each follows its own path and is governed by its own laws. Sometimes their paths meet, sometimes they don't. Only political history can decide.

THE IMPREGNATION THEORY

If culture is not transmitted genetically, then how is it transmitted? In truth, we can only guess. Cavalli-Sforza is of the view that very little theoretical research and only two empirical studies have been done on the subject. The first study deals with Pygmies and the second, students at Stanford. The Pygmies observed by Cavalli-Sforza offer anthropologists the advantage of living in isolated groups. When questioned about their cultural habits, Pygmies can tell you exactly when and how a cultural trait was passed on to them. Ninety per cent of their cultural traits came to them from their parents and ten per cent from other Pygmies. From the study carried out on the Stanford students, it emerged that parents passed on religious and political behaviour; for instance, the prayer habit came from the mother whereas going to mass - a social act - was transmitted by the father. 'The country of origin' - the cherished country or region - was the place of one's childhood. From these preliminary studies we may provisionally conclude that culture is not genetically transmissible, but that in our childhood all of us pass through a phase of cultural 'impregnation' which is almost biological in nature. The important thing to keep in mind is that this impregnation is difficult to reverse. For it to happen, at least one generation has to go by. Subsequently, any culture can be transmitted to the next generation; we know for instance that anyone can learn any language.

All of us, regardless of our race, can 'assimilate' any culture provided it has been transmitted to us in childhood. A black skinned people or one with a North African genic frequency could fully well imbibe French culture. A genic Chinese can easily become one hundred per cent Japanese just as an African can become one hundred per cent French. One is not born French, Japanese or English, one becomes French, Japanese or English. And it is not as if immigrants come with a clean slate. They too leave their imprint on the host society. Immigration does not spell biological extinction but leads to the inevitable confrontation of cultures. Political, not biological factors determine the outcome of this confrontation and it is these political factors which are going to decide whether there will be a dominant culture or a cultural mix.

10

THE FRENCH EXCEPTION

There is nothing exceptional about immigration in France; what is exceptional is the growing influence of the National Front. Populist xenophobic movements exist elsewhere; but-the National Front alone tries to make people believe that it articulates pan European aspirations and is the harbinger of a nationalist revival in the West. Now this is not true. With the exception of the insignificant Vlaams Blok in Flanders, the parties that the Front claims as allies either do not have much clout, as is the case of its German and Scandinavian partners, or deny any connection with Le Pen, as is the case of the Liberal Party in Austria and the Lombardy League in Italy. The National Front's efforts to internationalise itself should not blind us to its singularity. There are many populist, xenophobic parties but none of them has a leader as charismatic as Le Pen, such a broad electoral base, a doctrine so firmly rooted in national history and such an outrageous programme. No other party save the Front has gone as far as to suggest withdrawing citizenship from naturalised immigrants and deporting them en masse to their countries of origin (which in any case will probably refuse to take them back).

French populism owes its peculiarity to the fact that it took root in circumstances no less peculiar. A doctrinarian left and a spineless right had left the French with little choice. There was general discontent and tension between immigrants and natives had reached an all time high. Besides, France has had a tradition of xenophobia which was used to give legitimacy to National Front rhetoric. In short, the situation was just waiting to be exploited by an 'entrepreneur' of Le Pen's calibre. In such times, the role of the 'entrepreneur' is crucial. Immigration had not been on the national agenda; it only became an issue the day a political 'entrepreneur' decided to make capital out of immigrants very much in the same way as Drumont had done with the Jews in *La France juive*. Both situations were clearly of the politicians making.

Why have politicians chosen this moment in particular to play up the issue of immigration? There is nothing new about immigration nor is it more widespread. The real reasons for bringing it to the fore are ideological. People have had enough time since the Second World War to get over the taboo on xenophobic discourse. The rest of Europe and the United States have not proved any different; it has taken one generation since the end of legal discrimination for people to shed their restraint on the subject of race. In circumstances such as these xenophobic discourse can thrive; but it need not do so. 'Necessity' in this case is purely political, for the traditional opposition between left and right, socialism and liberalism, has been eroded. The rapprochement between the right and the left - the former born out of Enlightenment, the latter of the French Revolution - is not the result of any ideological convergence of views but because the left was compelled by economic necessity to support the market economy and accept the random nature of history. Now that their two hundred year old quarrel had finally petered out, over what were they going to fight?

INVENTING THE IMMIGRANT

Political 'entrepreneurs', bereft of their traditional enemies, had a limited stock of ideologies to turn to; they decided to pick the one which would help them the most to mobilise the masses. In the political market place, immigration emerged as the best bet. Immigration is one thing everyone understands. Its appeal is tremendous as it affects all aspects of life: material (jobs, accommodation), cultural (education, leisure), spiritual (Islam) and passion (sex and violence). So what better enemy than the immigrant? The immigrant is the other par excellence; his otherness is much greater than the differences that separate the left from the right. His otherness makes him stand out immediately, at least this is what we are told. The immigrant is what we are not, providing us with the reason for our own existence. 'As I am not an immigrant, or less of an immigrant than you are, I am more French or more Austrian or more Italian or more Flemish than you are!' The immigrant satisfies the basic need for a scapegoat. In the days of the quarrel between left and right, it was the bourgeois, the capitalists and the Americans who were the scapegoats for the left and the Communists, the proletariat and the Soviets fulfilled the same role for the right. All these categories have vanished and immigrants once again find themselves in their primordial role, one that has been theirs for centuries: they are the outsiders, eternally suspect wherever they go. Their alieness permits the enactment of a whole set of political rituals. They are a potential threat, the likely culprits; woe betide anyone who defends them for he is immediately guilty of betrayal.

How is it that such stale ideas are again beginning to find a place in our so called open, modern society? It does seem as if most people are ill at ease with modernity; they cannot or do not want to enter into the market economy and competition or assume the personal responsibility and solitude modernism implies. These are just the kind of people xenophobia merchants are on the look out for. However, immigration is not merely an individual concern. It upsets modern societies collectively as they fear collectively for their identity. Modernity is breaking down traditional reference points; national identity and culture are becoming extremely fluid, as with cultural contributions poring in from all sides, they are beginning to lose their distinctive character. The barbarian seems all the more menacing as we no longer know who we are, having imbibed so much from outside. In California, which is at the vanguard of multiculturalism, Whites, for the first time in their history, are being forced to ask themselves what it means to be white in a society where the Blacks are in a majority; the Whites have become a tribe like the rest. And it is in times like these that the entrepreneur has a field day.

Where there are no entrepreneurs, as is the case in Great Britain, or they are ineffectual as in Holland, immigration is only one of the many national concerns; it is not the focal point of public debate. Immigration in France is more or less as it used to be fifteen years ago, whether we look at it in terms of numbers, sender countries or visibility. But at that time there was no

Jean-Marie Le Pen to exploit it. The same can be said for Flanders before the advent of Karl Dillen and his nationalist party. In Austria, for years the small liberal party was content with its steady five per cent of the vote. It took a new leader, Jurge Heider, for the party to acquire newly found xenophobic overtones and, much to the embar-rassment of its members, the party's share of the vote shot up from five to twenty-five per cent in the 91 Viennese elections. It was the same story in the United States. Take the case of David Duke: he managed to get the Republican party nomination in 91 for the office of Louisiana's Governor by daring to raise the black issue after thirty years of enforced silence. Or that of Patrick Buchanan, the xenophobic candidate who ran for the Republican presidential nomination in 1992.

Populist resurgence does not occur anywhere and everywhere. France, Vienna, the American South, Flanders, Northern Italy, all have been the breeding grounds of fascism and racism. Ideologies, like dormant volcanoes, suddenly erupt after periods of inactivity. Underground cliques and coteries - the new right in France, War Veterans' associations in Germany, the Ku Klux Klan in the U.S. among others - kept alive xenophobic myths and discourse as well as the cult of national identity. On the other hand, those places where such a tradition did not take root in the heady years between the two wars have not witnessed such a resurgence. Holland has no Le Pen and England no Heider. Germany too has no real equivalent - the Germans are still weighed down by their past. Or could it be that Germany has changed?

However, we are not living a replay of the thirties. Fascism is dated; it belonged to a specific time and place. To brand fascist all the movements riding the current wave of populism is to underestimate their originality. They are all using the same theme, but each comes out with a different tune. Race has ceased to be an issue; today's entrepreneur springs to the defense of national culture at a time when just about anything and everything passes off as 'culture'.

THE ANGELS OF ANTI-RACISM

To counter the xenophobia entrepreneurs, activists - anti-racist, champions of multiculturalism and human rights - have in turn jumped on to the bandwagon of political showbiz. Their working capital is otherworldliness and the nobility of the soul. 'Anti-racist movements,' observed Claude Levi-Strauss, 'are dangerous, but they are not just that.' A typical Levi-Strauss formulation, which has to be read carefully for the full import to be understood.

Anti-racist movements are dangerous because they conceal the fact that xenophobic feelings are natural. Wherever different groups coexist, each group keeps its distance from the other. 'Savages,' who had fully recognised this fact, kept away from other savages. Strident anti-racist postures have thus given rise inadvertently or through ignorance to widespread feelings of guilt.

The 'they are just not that' expresses a complete refusal to equate on the same moral footing racism and anti-racism. Racism leads to violence; anti-racism does not. Rejecting violence is not the same as inciting people to violence.

Anti-racist methods are completely ineffectual. Activists, like xenophobia 'entrepreneurs', also function within the 'everything is culture' / 'identity' paradigm, which only makes for confused thinking and rhetoric. All in all, neither anti-racist rhetoric nor xenophobia can tell us how to live together in society. Xenophobic we all are, there is no use trying to hide it. The question is how to live in peace in spite of our xenophobia.

If our aim is to defuse the situation, to my mind, we would do better to think in terms of economics rather than in terms of culture or morality. In principle, economic thinking does lead to policies that can be implemented; the same can hardly be said for philosophical speculation. Looking at the problem from an economic perspective is all the more imperative for it is our failure to do so that is making contemporary immigration 'exceptional'. As Alain Touraine pointed out, 'Fifty years ago, immigrants could speak no French, but they worked. Today's immigrants speak French but they do not work!' The new fact about immigration to Europe has less to do with numbers or ethnic and religious origins than with the non integration of immigrants into the workplace. At least this is what I shall endeavour to show.

THE MYSTERY OF THE ORIGINS

We would do well to keep the following facts in mind: in France, fourteen million inhabitants are of foreign origin. One out of four has at least one foreign grand-parent. Ten million of them have already acquired French nationality and most of the others will get it in the next ten years. Very rarely were our ancestors the Gauls. They came from all over: Germany, Flanders, Brittany, Italy, Poland, Judea, the East Atlas mountains or the Volga. But the French refuse to admit that theirs is a land of immigrants. They conveniently forget about their foreign ancestry in a bout of collective amnesia. Like the United States, France too is a machine producing hundred per cent French citizens out of an assortment of diverse peoples. But unlike in the United States, we take no pride in our immigration; on the contrary, we try and hide it. For us there is no glory in rediscovering· our roots. It is not France's diversity that is surprising but her refusal to acknowledge it. Or to put it differently: it is because our origins are blurred that we refuse to acknowledge them. There is no need for collective psychoanalysis; the explanation can be found in our history. France, rather the French state, is like an assembly line, turning out French citizens en masse. The first immigrants, from within, were carefully processed by the state machine so that all traces of provincial language and custom were removed. Slight variations of accent are all that is left today. The machine has not been any kinder to its own - the Brittons and the Basques - than it has been to foreigners.

The idea of France and a French identity has always been part of an unvarying ideological scheme, one that has nonetheless known how to mould itself to the times. First you had France, the eldest daughter of the Church, exterminating the Hugeunots; then came the Revolution with its attack on the aristocracy; finally the Third Republic was content to decimate provincial languages (will the Fifth Republic meet the same fate out to Islam?). With the revocation of the Edict of Nantes, you could only be Catholic; after Jules Ferry, you had to become secular, republican and could speak only one idiom, that of Paris; in today's France, you have to be modern. Ideologies may come and go but they all serve a single master: a powerful centre, a hegemonistic state, in other words the bureaucracy. Without this bureaucracy there would have been no state; without the state there would have been no France; without France there would have been no machine to churn out the French. This is what gave us our history and a certain joy of being French. However, today we hear that the machine has over the last twenty years become flawed; an idea many people believe in, which still doesn't necessarily make it true.

THE INTEGRATING MACHINE

Even if we admit that the integrating machine has developed a snag, who is to blame, the machine or the immigrants? Either the immigrant has become more resistant or the machine has lost some of its teeth! Sociologists tend to subscribe to the second hypothesis, as they lament the near disappearance of old modes of integration: compulsory military service, republican school teachers, Christian or Marxist trade unions, the Communist Party, apprenticeship, the work shop, the factory, the Church... These moulds which shaped perfect French citizens have worn out or broken. But did they ever work as well as it is made out today, not without a certain amount of nostalgia? Now that is not quite so sure.

In the 'glorious period' of integration, even after spending thirty years in France, immigrants had great difficulty in speaking the language, the ultimate test of integration. The old modes of integration may have died, but aren't the new ones just as effective? Today all of French speaking Africa watches French television. In these countries, television serves as an initiation to immigration, coaching students every day about their future country of adoption. Through it, the immigrants know beforehand much more about France than their predecessors did in the first half of the century. When they arrive, their coaching continues, as television has succeeded in homogenising the French, their language, their behaviour in ways a secular school teacher could never do. If this popular media culture is displeasing and encourages aggressiveness rather than good manners, should the blame be attributed to the immigrant or television?

Sport is another very effective mechanism of integration. However very few discuss its role as an integrator as it is culturally unfashionable to do so. Sporting events - football in particular - bring together natives and outsiders in the same way as the military service did in the past.

When all is said and done, the flawed integrating machine hypothesis needs to be qualified if not invalidated altogether. Or perhaps we should reframe the argument. The old cultural, social and religious modes of integration - the school, trade unions and the Church - have been replaced by new modes of integration : the mass media and showbiz. Far from educating, these breed aggressiveness and moral laxity, a reflection of what popular culture in France has become; immigrants just happen to be its most visible manifestation.

What kind of material for integration are the current lot of immigrants? Are the problematic ones - ninety per cent of Algerian origin - really more difficult, by virtue of their origins, race, culture or religion, to gallicise than the Italians, the Jews and the Poles who came before them? Ninety nine per cent of the French will say yes, revealing how little they know about the history of immigration of their own country. Immigrants have never been considered easy to integrate even if they were white, European and Christian, whatever we may say to the contrary today. Around 1850 the French hated Belgian immigrants. Italians are no longer visible in French society, but this was not always the case. Around 1900, anti-Italian riots broke out in the South of France, claiming more victims than any anti-Algerian 'ratonnade'(racist attacks against North Africans) in the last thirty years. The Jews from Central Europe, currently assimilated into the Judeo-Christian family, were not considered part of it before the War. They were the Jews; this was reason enough to discriminate against them, even eliminate them, often with the abetment of the French police. The Poles, who were good Catholics, were not treated any better in the twenties by the native French than the Zairians of today.

The turbulent history of immigration in France remains an untold story for most. Its disclosure is disquieting; the resentment building up between the native French and immigrants, coupled with an overdose of inflammatory rhetoric, could very well turn verbal clashes into violent assaults.

THE ELUSIVE NATIONAL IDENTITY

Have we lost our values and is that why integration is more difficult? After the death of Marx, it became fashionable to view everything as culture. The trendy 'everything is cultural' theory, the fine concept of a national identity and plan are proffered to explain the supposedly successful integration of immigrants in the past. In this 'idyllic' past, France was sure of what she stood for; about her identity, she had not an iota of doubt. To feel secure, the immigrant only had to accept the grand national design and merge himself into the mainstream. But which identity, which national design are we referring to?

Definitions vary depending on whether one belongs to the left or the right. For the rightists, the priest was the symbol of the nation; Christian and family 'values' were its bedrock and the best way to integrate foreigners. It is this France that can face the onslaught of Islam. The leftist view is diametrically opposite. The school teacher, not the priest symbolised France; the national plan was secular and republican. This left harks back to the time when the immigrant just had to step on French soil to learn the Gauls were his ancestors and become a true citizen, free from prejudice, rid of his barbaric superstitions. For the left, the enemy is not Islam but fundamentalism. There is something to be said for both the conservative and republican analysis, but both seem far removed from reality. For how is one going to ordain this return to values - Christian or republican - and who is going to see they are respected? Who is going to draw up this plan for the nation? The way the State imposed its will under the Reign of Terror or at the time of the Vichy government makes one shudder lest history repeat itself.

The same holds true for 'values'. When we say our values are being threatened, it means that we can list them. Now that is just not possible. It is all very well to talk about upholding values as long as we remain vague about the term 'values'. But the minute we begin to list them, there will be utter confusion. Which values are being threatened by the North Africans? The family? Their families are much more cohesive than ours. The virtue of our daughters? They protect their daughters much better than we do. Democracy? It is to escape despots that foreigners flee to France. In truth, we accuse foreigners of threatening our

values because we are unwilling to accept that these
values have changed, if not disappeared under the
impact of modernity; modernity has nothing to do
with immigration.

Culture is no exception - don't the fervent defenders
of culture know that culture is all that changes? True,
the change is faster when there is confrontation with
a foreign culture, but it is this very confrontation
which enriches our own culture, otherwise we would
still be the Gauls. By implication, this means the great.
debate on multiculturalism is really a non issue, for,
ever since the Roman invasion, we are all 'multicultural'.
Besides, just a century ago, hundreds of local dialects,
patois and regional languages were spoken in France;
wasn't France then as multicultural as it is today?
What is the point of denying multiculturalism when
our children our singing American rock and dancing
to African beats, when even the Bicentenary of our
Revolution is staged in such an unFrench way by Jean-
Paul Goude. Rock, which has come to so dominate
French music, is a multicultural music par excellence;
it vehicles behaviour and gestures that have had an
undoubtable impact on our so called basic values.
Sexual and family codes have been turned upside
down. Must we then forbid rock to preserve French
culture? It would have been much simpler to put an
end to immigration but it is a bit too late in the day
for all that. France is de facto a multicultural country,
a fact it cannot get round to acknowledging, just as
it refuses to admit that it is a land of immigration.

There will always be some tribune in search of an
electorate who will try and tell the people that they
cannot be French and something else at the same time,
that they have to choose between Islam and France.
'Dual belonging' has always been viewed with suspicion;

Captain Dreyfus fell a victim in his time. And who knows, a Harki called Slimane might just be the Dreyfus of tomorrow. Dreyfus was Jewish and French; Slimane will probably be Muslim and French. It is possible to be several things at the same time without there being any contradiction. One can even feel European. Multiculturalism or diversity is in fact the common culture of most French, and they have not had any problem living with it. Having several identities has never stopped people from living together in a liberal society in which politics is distinct from morality. It is up to intellectuals and moralists to dwell on issues such as national identity, values, culture and diversity. It is not the politicians job to do so.

But now for the crux of the matter: Islam.

SO MANY ERRORS IN THE NAME OF ISLAM

Is Islam different, intrinsically incompatible with a secular Republic? The answer could have been yes, had Islam been a unified religion, and all North African immigrants identified with this single form of mythical Islam. It so happens that Islam is as varied as Christianity, its practice just as if not more diverse, varying as it does from fundamentalism to detachment. Even more than Christianity, Islam imbibes the culture in which it is followed: a Java Muslim has less in common with a Saudi Wahabite than a Catholic with a Lutherian. The French, partly out of ignorance, partly because they have been incited by tribunes, often confuse Shiaism and Sunnism, Islam and fundamentalism, Arabs and Muslims, Muslim law and the Muslims' status in the West. The Shias, not very common in France, have a clergy; the Sunnis, on the other hand, do not. There are in fact very few Muslims who identify with the extremist positions of Middle Eastern sects. Islam excludes the possibility of a Muslim living in a non-Muslim society from asking for Muslim law. Unfortunately, those who pretend to fear Islam the most in France have the habit of pointing to its most intransigent traits so that their words may carry weight. In this way, fundamentalists who in their own societies would have gone unnoticed are given legitimacy by the tribunes. Paradoxically, the tribunes are helped by some human rights activists who claim to defend 'genuine' Islam.

Which brings us to the following question: are all immigrants from the Maghreb really such pious Muslims? Ninety five per cent of the Beurs choose English, not Arabic as their second language. In point of fact most of them, the Berbers in particular, do not even know Arabic. So we are being paradoxical when we say that Maghrebins are more difficult to integrate than past immigrants; the Maghrebins speak better French and have more secular credentials. To hold the Beurs responsible for all the ills of Islam is all the more illogical as most of them, especially the women, have come to France to escape the more repressive aspects of their religion. It is not because of Islam that Maghrebins are different. The real reason for their difference could perhaps be their family structure.

Many French attribute to Islam behaviour which has nothing to do with religion; this behaviour is more the result of the Maghrebin family organisation and the modest origins of the immigrants. Many Maghrebins carry with them the idea of the extended family in which several generations live together, girls are married off at a young age and fertility is high. When in time, the extended family begins to look more like a French family, it will, for economic reasons, have shed not its Muslim, but 'tribal' character. Now this is a pattern all immigrants seem to follow. Similarly, as immigrants from the Maghreb are often of peasant stock, many urbanised French conclude that all Maghrebins are country bumpkins and wrongly consider peasant behaviour, the same the world over, as being a reflection of the entire country.

That leaves us with racial difference. Very often in xenophobic discourse, religious or cultural difference is just a euphemism for basic racism. To which race do the Maghrebins belong? Berbers and Arabs have very little in common. And of course we often term as racial traits cultural attitudes which will change over time. Didn't the Italians and the Jews seem a little more dark when they first came into France? The same thing is happening today to the Maghrebins. A Maghrebin is swarthy if he is a labourer; however if he has a university degree, his skin automatically becomes much fairer. In the long run, with social mobility and intermarriage, race ceases to become an obstacle to integration.

Since the grounds for differentiating Maghrebin immigrants from traditional European immigrants are neither racial, cultural nor religious, does this suggest that there are no differences at all? It is useless to deny the fact that differences do exist, but they are not of the kind the National Front and public opinion imagine.

The first difference has to do with origins, with Algeria, not with Arabism or Islam. The second difference is Beur unemployment.

The French have not quite forgotten their personal or collective grudge against Algeria. They vacillate between contempt for the former colony and hatred for the enemy. Algeria's development since independence has done little to assuage these feelings. What is more, the eight hundred thousand pieds-noirs repatriated in 1962 were unable to put their painful past behind them, as a result of which their children share their resentment. Often, these anti-Algerian French are less condescending to Moroccans and Tunisians, whose civilisations are recognised as being great and ancient. This recognition, however modest it might be, is reflected on the emigrants from these countries. The immigrants' self-esteem and behaviour are influenced by the host society's attitude towards them. Algeria is looked upon with bitterness and contempt; emigrants from that country are therefore more destabilised by their migration than Tunisians and Moroccans who are held in greater esteem. Their positive identity is further strengthened by the fact that they can keep alive the myth of returning home one day. A myth the Portuguese, the Spanish and the Turks also share. The Algerians on the other hand rarely speak of their origins and for objective reasons do not wish to return to their country, which makes their position vulnerable in the host country.

This brings us to a paradoxical premise: the stronger the sense of identity of immigrants with their country of origin, the easier it is for them to integrate, and the more readily the host society accepts them. Examples to prove this point are legion: the Jews, the Italians and the Portuguese among others. It follows that for the Algerians to integrate more easily in France, the French must have a better image of Algeria or at least get to know something about the country. Now school going children in France know next to nothing about Algeria. They do not even know that Arabs are not the only inhabitants of Algeria, and that most of the immigrants are Berber.

UNEMPLOYMENT : THE REAL DIFFERENCE

And now to Alain Tourraine's aphorism, 'Fifty years ago immigrants could speak no French but they worked; today's immigrants speak French but they do not work'. Herein lies the big difference between the immigrants of yesterday and today. Algerians are not the only ones not to work; most second generation immigrants from the South do not work. France is not an exception in this regard. The children of immigrants are most often than not out of job; their unemployment has distorted the way people perceive immigration as a whole.

What percentage of the Beurs are unemployed? Accurate figures are not available as French law forbids any kind of ethnic consideration at the time of census taking. All we have to go by are partial but reliable sociological studies whose results have been confirmed by personal accounts. In the past immigrants were exotic and rejected as such, but they worked; it is hard to imagine a young Pole, Italian or Jew of the twenties or thirties being jobless for long. The break came when immigrants no longer worked; today young Maghrebins and Beurs are more often than not unemployed. However, in the public mind it is their ethnic origins or religious beliefs which are held to be the factors working against their assimilation. The fact that upper class Muslims, even those who have just arrived, are hardly noticeable because they have integrated economically just goes to show how fallacious this view is. Jean-Claude Barreau, ex Chairman of the Migrations Office, observed, 'There are as many foreigners of Arab origin in Neuilly-Sur-Seine as there are in Argenteuil, and as far as I know, Neuilly-Sur-Seine has never had any immigrant problem.'

Xenophobia, it seems, has more to do with immigrant unemployment and their excessive dependence on welfare than with Islam and race. At least this much is certain - unemployment coupled with Islam, Algeria and Arabism festers xenophobia which would otherwise have remained within limits.

If we accept this hypothesis, it means we have been tackling the issue of immigration from the wrong end. Politicians and the media harp on the need for cultural assimilation, which is taking place and make only a passing reference to economic integration, which is not taking place at all. More than the origin of the immigrants, it is unemployment that is responsible for violence, crime, gangs and even a return to Islamic fundamentalism among the youth; having met with rejection in the workplace, they are on the look out for an alternative identity. Had more second generation immigrants worked, had their economic integration been as successful as their linguistic integration, then there would have been no more than the normal public reaction to immigrants. Nothing could have stopped them from becoming excellent French citizens. An economically integrated Beur would stop being perceived as a barbarian; he would have become modern and no religious extremism has been able to resist modernity for long.

Speculating about the kind of synthesis Islam and modernity would give rise to, the Tunisian theologian Ali Chebbi said that what would be left would be 'the rituals, the moral values and the feeling of solidarity with the Muslim world'. None of this is incompatible with French citizenship. French Muslims, were they to become middle class, would observe the rituals of Islam just as the Jews observe the rituals rather than the tenets of their religion.

My analysis - the new factor about immigration from the Maghreb is unemployment and not culture-may appear to lean too heavily on economics and sociology. But just because Marx has died does not mean that sociology must be buried alongside, and we give in to the 'everything is cultural' vogue. I maintain that the state cannot - nor is it desirable for it to do so — define culture or values. On the other hand, it is the job of the state to avoid tribal wars and concentrate on areas where it has the power to act: improving social housing,'repainting the lifts' and above all changing the rules of the labour market so that immigrants can find work. Unemployment excludes, employment integrates. Any policy seeking to integrate must look to providing employment.

11

THE INTEGRATING MARKET

The analysis: xenophobia is indexed to the rate of unemployment of immigrants be they legal or illegal, French nationals or not. The challenge: reducing Beur[1] unemployment - Beurs are a typical example of second generation immigrants living in France - as this would speed up their integration. The conviction: the liberal doctrine, which advocates a return to market forces, offers possibilities hitherto unexplored to deal with immigration and integration. What has been stated above is not a liberal solution to immigration but a set of propositions that need to be critically examined. Politicians have a habit of speaking in the same breath of legal immigrants, French citizens of foreign origins, current legal and illegal immigration and asylum seekers; I shall try to keep these categories distinct.

BEUR UNEMPLOYMENT

Does Beur unemployment have to do with intrinsic

---

1. Beurs are the children of immigrants from the Maghreb settled in France.

factors such as culture, or with external factors such as economic structure. Unless this question is answered there can be no worthwhile policy. If cultural factors are responsible for unemployment, then Beurs are jobless because they are Beurs who are not culturally predisposed to work. All one can do is wait patiently for them to develop a work ethic. Should we however hold the view that Beurs do not work because they lack the qualifications, it means that education, not the Beurs, has to be reformed. One would have to wait even longer in that case. There also is a third point of view which holds that Beurs do not work as they are victims of discrimination. Then it must be our endeavour to fight against racism. It is easy to say change culture, change education, change society; but these worthy sentiments are of little use when it comes to grappling with immediate problems. For it is in the immediate future that we have to change the objective conditions in which the Beurs live. Which takes us to a fourth policy option, one that is in fact operational: the reform of the labour market.

In the first place let us proceed on the assumption that Beur unemployment is no different from the unemployment of young unqualified French. Beurs share the same behaviour and attitudes as the rest of the French of their generation; it just so happens that because of their underprivileged background, they are often backward at school and have to face unemployment subsequently. The economic outlook does not really affect Beur unemployment. Even in a growth cycle, their level of employment does not rise; in fact it actually fell in the eighties. Beur unemployment therefore has no relationship with Islam nor the Maghreb nor even growth; it is the result, to my mind, of three

'social choices' - the SMIC or minimum wage, the RMI[2]
and the content of our education.

Let us look at education first. Our schools are
dispensing a sub culture which lays more emphasis
on the rights of the citizen and not enough on the
duties of the worker. The old moral science classes
have been replaced by vague archeo-Marxist discourse:
school and even vocational education are, paradoxically,
anti-company, anti-industry and anti-blue collar. Any
degree, no matter how worthless, is considered a
passport to a white collar job; the 'baccalaureat for all'
will only widen the gap between expectations of the
young and economic ground realities.

To a SMIC earner his wages might seem low; but
when you add the social security contributions to it,
the SMIC cost the employer one hundred and twenty
thousand francs a year in 1992. For most companies,
particularly the small ones which would be willing to
recruit young, relatively unskilled labour, such
expenditure is not economically viable. An opinion
poll conducted by SOFRES in March 1992 showed that
companies with less than a hundred people on their
pay rolls were willing to immediately take on *five
hundred thousand under twenty-five year olds* if the social
security contributions were reduced by fifty per cent.
Since 1976, governments have from time to time
agreed to cut down the SMIC and welfare burden. But
these welfare cuts depend on bureaucratic whims;

2. The RMI is a special allowance given to the destitute to enable them
to reintegrate into society. Anyone residing in France over the age
of twenty-five years or who has at least one child to support and
whose total income is less than 2000 Francs per month is eligible to
apply for it. In return, the beneficiary has to participate in any
training programme or activity stipulated in his or her contract.

their cumbersome and ad hoc provisions do nothing
to allay the misgivings of potential employers.

The RMI acts as a disincentive to work. After a
couple of years of half hearted job hunting and a series
of rejections, young unskilled people are happy to fall
back on the RMI; 'unemployed' has become a social
category from which there is no moving out. So the
SMIC and the RMI which at the outset were intended
to protect the weak, have proved to be more of a
hindrance than a help.

The net result of these three social options has been
the creation of a social category which, unable to
integrate into the workplace, is forced to subsist at the
fringe. The labour market is like a citadel that shuts
out unqualified youth. Employers contributions,
collective conventions and complex labour laws protect
those who already have a job, but they do little to help
those who are looking for one. As a result, the working
population is growing older especially in the industrial
sector, where no fresh blood is being recruited. Young
immigrants and immigrants' children from the Maghreb
and Africa are the first to be excluded as they are the
least qualified and the most discriminated against.

How can we open the labour market to these
sections? There are two alternatives: American style
job reservations or deregulation. In other words we
have to choose between a social democratic solution
and a liberal solution.

Quotas along the lines of American affirmative
action or Dutch and British positive action presume
that immigrants' children are identified on the basis
of their ethnic origins; this would run counter to our
national tradition. The French Republic only recognises
individuals equal before the law; as soon as they

acquire French nationality, the law of the land is blind to both their community and their religion. Any legal recognition of ethnic or religious communities, even if there is a good reason for it, would raise the spectre of Vichy and racial discrimination, and cause public indignation. At the same time if you can't name the problem, how can you solve it? Everybody knows that Beurs are idle, the police knows that Beurs are filling the police stations and the prisons, but when it comes to distributing accommodation, seats in schools, or taking on employees, then ethnic distinction ceases to exist. Even if ethnic criteria are sometimes used, this usually happens in an illegal, underhand manner. Ought we then to break with the French tradition and stop being colour blind? Would it be a good idea to adopt the Anglo Saxon principle of division on community lines and reserve quotas? Should de facto discrimination continue, then there is no doubt about it, the minorities will follow the example of the American and British Blacks and demand quotas.

We do have a second alternative which is to deregulate the labour market. In the past, as we have seen, immigrants began to work as soon as they entered France; similarly there were fewer unemployed Blacks in the United States fifty years ago. What has changed since then? We are told that a modern economy only recruits qualified workers and no longer requires blue collar workers. In this way unskilled immigrants are marginalised. The argument sounds plausible enough but is not true; a modern economy rejects unskilled workers only when the cost of their labour is higher than the company's break even point. In Japan, where the cost of unskilled labour is low, neither the young nor the immigrants are unemployed. You just have to walk into a store or drive up to a service station to see for yourself. In truth, the exclusion of poorly qualified wage earners is less the result of modernisation than of the welfare economy. The more regulated the economy is, the greater the number of unemployed among the underprivileged.

How is the labour market to be deregulated? Were the cost of unskilled labour to fall in France, French companies would begin to recruit. This can be done either by removing the minimum wage stipulation for unskilled labour or through an overall reduction in social security contributions. I will no doubt be told that the experiment was tried out in the eighties and it proved to be a failure. That may be so, but deep rooted attitudes cannot be changed with half measures and stop gap arrangements. A reduction in employers' contributions will only be effective when there is a corresponding cut in unemployment allowances so that the young are motivated to work. Finally, the decrease in social security contributions must be matched by a decrease in compulsory social protection. If not, the whole welfare system will go bankrupt. The same analysis holds good for apprenticeship.

Apprenticeship had been part of a French tradition till a coalition of workers and teachers unions managed in the sixties to get it virtually scrapped. In this way, the workers unions were able to strengthen their hold and hike wages; teachers were able to monopolise the training of young minds and eliminate any influence 'capitalist exploiters' could have had. In contrast, apprenticeship remains a standard practice in Germany, involving people from all age groups and thereby limiting the unemployment of unskilled youth, Turkish youth in particular. Every now and then, the government in France makes noises about introducing German style apprenticeship schemes. It seems to forget why apprenticeship was done away with in the first place. As in the case of social security contributions, both the rightist and leftist governments have only taken half hearted, temporary measures. Reestablishing a labour market and apprenticeship would require a time-bound coherent political plan, one which could be spelt out clearly and acceptable to all. We must recognise that companies are sometimes better integrators than the school; as a result, apprenticeship ought to replace the last years of schooling, which in most cases are quite pointless.

No one has dared so far to try this: however, the liberalisation of the work market seems to be the only way for the rapid integration of second integration immigrants. Are there any other suggestions and is any one really interested? Or should we just keep the Beurs unemployed to prove that they can never be integrated? The majority of the French would perhaps prefer to maintain a controlled labour market, but in that case we would do well to take a good look at Los Angeles and reinforce our police protection in suburbs which are becoming increasingly dangerous to live in.

INTEGRATION: A STATE AFFAIR OR A PRIVATE AFFAIR

Why have governments failed till now to control migration and integrate immigrants? Because their policies were flawed? Because there was too much public pressure against change? Or could it be that the State is not qualified to manage integration. This last hypothesis is rarely considered and yet, going by experience, it is clear that modern states are incapable of controlling social policy as they are subject to the dual constraints of voter pressure and bureaucratic inertia. However, is it feasible to privatise immigration and integration? It would indeed be difficult to sub contract the protection of national borders. But why must everything else remain in the hands of the state? For there is nothing as yet to prove that it is more efficient.

For instance, let us look at placement management. Most job seekers are immigrants or belong to immigrant families. Now the *Agence nationale pour l'emploi*, the national employment exchange, with its centralised, inefficient bureaucracy, is not necessarily in the best position to help them find work. In fact we know it is doing a bad job. There is nothing in principle to stop one from subcontracting placement management to private companies. Concessions granted in several public services are working well and the same system could be extended to employment. Private administrators would be far more keen to ensure that their clients get placed properly than government employment exchange officials; in fact it is in the latter's interest to see the number of applications pile up. Interim private placement agencies are more efficient than the *Agence nationale pour l'emploi* for the simple reason that placement is a remunerative activity for the first, not for the second. In the United States - which we should view as a laboratory rather than a model - placement concessions for unqualified youth exist in a number of cities. The system works to the advantage of all parties; job seekers get absorbed faster and the State is freed of a task it is ill equipped to handle. Tax payers too stand to gain as they don't have to bear the burden of so many unemployed youth. Entrusting unemployment management to specialised, private firms is thus a very feasible proposition.

Let us take this privatisation of integration a little further. Scrapping the minimum wage and reducing social security contributions could be made conditional to the employer's commitment to create new jobs for immigrant children. Better still, regional councils could take the initiative and the responsibility for such agreements. This would lead to improved urban planning, reduce unemployment and integrate the immigrants. Though French tradition does not allow for any specific commitment to take on immigrants or Beurs, second generation immigrants would be the natural beneficiaries of such regional and national contracts. In any case there is nothing to stop employers from using their discretion at the time of recruitment. We are of course assuming that employers are conscious of their personal responsibility towards immigrants and have a sense of enlightened self interest. For it is the immigrants who, besides being prospective clients, are going to fulfill most of their manpower needs. If companies rather than the state took on the responsibility of immigrant children, then decentralised private placement could, in the space of just a few years, put an end to ghettos and the ensuing violence.

Am I being utopian? Not in the least, as the scheme I have outlined covers the interest of all concerned parties - the state, regional councils, companies and immigrants. We would do well to recall the very successful precedent of privatising the settlement of industrial disputes. Privatisation put an end to the recurrent strikes that Marxian doctrine considered to be the basic feature of our economies. Today strikes survive only in the public sector. It is to the market, not the state that we owe their near extinction. Why can't the same thing happen in the case of ghettos? In order for the market to integrate, fresh immigration must be managed to ensure that new ghettos do not come up to replace the ones that had dissolved with integration.

12

THE STARTING POINT

Three stag-headed baobabs guard the entrance to the village of Gandiaye. Amid the straw huts, the police station stands out as the only substantial building. That day it was deserted, all its doors wide open. An order of the sub-prefect on the official notice board enjoined the inhabitants not to beat the tam-tam from May 15 to September 15. In Senegal, there is an old saying that the sound of the tam-tam during this period drives the rains away. Women pound millet in wooden mortars - as if straight out of a carving of timeless Africa. The village elders confer under the shade of a kapok tree, though sometimes their conference can prove to be fraught with danger. The Dakar 'Soleil' in an article it ran the day before recounted how the fall of a single branch had killed seven old people in the Thies region. The aged are there, so are the women and children, but where have all the young men gone? They are in France or on their way there - somewhere in Portugal, Spain or Italy: Paris is their ultimate destination. Mahmadou also made the journey and he tells us of his odyssey.

MAHMADOU'S ODYSSEY

Mahmadou did not leave his village until he had consulted the marabout. The marabout promised him great riches and gave him a gris-gris which would make him invisible when he had to cross a border. The gris-gris fulfilled its function. Mahmadou set off for Bamako by train and then he took a bus across Algeria and Tunisia. He stowed away to Sicily in the hold of a rickety old boat, from where he went up to Italy, travelling on foot for the most part. A smuggler helped him cross the Alps. When they got to the top he said, 'Down there is France'. Mahmadou rushed down to the valley and went to Paris where some 'cousins' were waiting to receive him. Like all his countrymen who had made the journey from the bush to Paris, Mahmadou had an address to go to. When he arrived he spoke not a word of French nor did he know how to read or write. But that didn't matter - he was living among his own in a hostel of illegal immigrants. Every Senegalese village has its replica in Paris or Marseille, with its 'elders', marabout, tailor, cobbler and cook.

Mahmadou did not remain idle for long. The Senegalese are good tailors and Mahmadou soon became part of the informal economy, working at night, stitching ready made garments in a cellar at Sentier. You won't find a Mahmadou selling trinkets on the large boulevards; those are the traditional hawkers, the Baol-Baol from the Thies region. Nor will you find him peddling cannabis or heroin. These dangerous but remunerative activities are only meant for 'Dakar intellectuals'; they know Paris much better than the Toucouleurs, Mahmadou's tribe. So he worked by night and slept by day, with little time to acquaint himself with the capital. Though he lived there, Paris still remains a mystery to him. While in France, he kept a low profile and did not move much out of the closed world of his community hostel so as to avoid trouble with the police. This is how enclaves of foreign manpower spring up in some quarters and cities of our national territory. Their inhabitants, however embarrassing they may seem to the French, ask for no more than a job. Mahmadou is paid the equivalent of the minimum wage. He gets no social security benefits. He sends back whatever he earns to his family by money order; the village elders in his hostel in Paris see to it. In Senegal the money goes very far; it is enough to support ten people. Emigrant remittances will finance the construction of a village mosque, a koranic school for the marabout, the installation of some water pumps and tin roofs as well as a few head of cattle. When Mahmadou fell ill in Paris, he got himself treated in hospital, passing off as a 'cousin' whose resident's permit was in order. Africans in Paris know that to the French, all Blacks look alike especially when photographed in Polaroid.

After toiling for three years, Mahmadou grew homesick and decided to return to Gandiaye. He went back by the same route he came. The villagers accorded him a hero's welcome. He had been to France; now he was a real man. In keeping with the village tradition, he sent his mother for a pilgrimage to Mecca and invited the whole village to a feast. He forgot though to keep aside enough money to make one of his dreams come true; he had always wanted to marry a lazy, plump Drianké smelling of amber and henna. A few months is all it will take for Mahmadou to fritter away his savings. And then.... back to France.

There is no question of Mahmadou staying back. The village authorities have neither the will nor the means to keep him - it is not in their interest he stays. For the marabout, Mahmadou is better off in France; then he will get his tithe in hard currency. Without the money orders from France, what will become of the elders, the women and the children? They will probably have to leave the village to join the ranks of Dakar's urban poor. Mahmadou earns much more abroad than he does in Senegal; so social pressure builds up for him to leave again.

This is how two million Senegalese emigrants, scattered in France, the United States and Italy, are supporting the six million left behind. The same is true for other African countries.

ABDOULAYE'S RETURN

Abdoulaye Bâ decided not to go back to France. He was going to stay in his village. Had he taken leave of his senses? His village thinks he's gone mad. Abdoulaye spent ten years in France; he had a steady, well paid job as a quantity surveyor and his papers were in order. But he told me homesickness got the better of him. He wanted to do something for his country, and he didn't want his daughter, who was born in Paris, to become too French. I had been told in Dakar that I would have absolutely no difficulty in finding Abdoulaye. All I had to do was get to the main bus stand in the Medina, near the Colobane market. There I had a pick of 'express buses' to choose from. The 'express bus' is in fact a derelict contraption on wheels; a benevolent patron saint is your only protection against accidents. So choose your patron saint with care - each bus has one whose portrait

covers more than half the windshield. I chose to seek
the protection of the 'Good Mother' with Papa Mc:lo
at the wheel. It was not the best of choices. Even before
we got to Rufisque, the bus broke down. Near Kaolack,
it got stuck in the stand and I had to cover the rest
of the distance in a ramshackle cart drawn by a
donkey. No one had given me Abdoulaye's exact
address but his farm — three hectares of irrigated land
— stood out from a mile. The green patch in an
otherwise red, clayey landscape was impossible to
miss. Abdoulaye, the quantity surveyor, is now striving
to grow, Insh' Allah, beans for the Rungis vegetable
market.

I confess that my meeting with Abdoulaye Bâ was
not a chance one. His name had been warmly
recommended to me in Dakar by the Minister of
Immigration, who is keen on resettling Senegalese
migrants in Senegal, no mean task indeed. The Ministry
can only handle a limited number of cases; these are
then advertised as 'success stories' for the consumption
of the Senegalese living abroad. Accordingly, Abdoulaye
Bâ was shown great consideration so that he could be
projected as a hero; his saga was to be the success
story that would make the rounds of all the Senegalese
haunts in Paris. Unfortunately, the· villagers were
proved right. Abdoulaye Bâ was really mad to have
imagined that he could resettle in Senegal and carry
on an honest, remunerative business. Even though his
project had been cleared by the Minister and the *Office
français de migrations*, he still had to wait seven years
before he could begin. It took him five years to get
the administrative clearance required for the national
bank SONAGA to give him a loan on easy terms. The
SONAGA in turn kept him waiting another two years
before releasing the first installment of the loan. In the

meanwhile, the cost of the agricultural equipment Abdoulaye needed had risen fourfold; but Abdoulaye was not allowed to revise his initial loan application. Why did it take so long? First, the Senegalese administration is what it is. Second, SONAGA, like all local banks, is left with precious little after the state, public enterprises in the red and those who the regime favours have snaffled all the bank's money.

Abdoulaye persevered against all odds. In 1992 his three hectares yielded two six ton harvests of beans - just enough to pay back the bank which is constantly holding out the threat of seizure. But what can it seize? The land Abdoulaye cultivates does not belong to him but is part of a national property managed by a local council which allocates land to the peasants. In principle, the allocation is free of charge. But as Abdoulaye could not or would not give the councillors the usual bribe, the latter refused to give him a piece of land. Once again we have a clear example of how the absence of private property is one of the main factors responsible for the flight of the peasants from the South to the North. To get back to Abdoulaye, he occupied an abandoned, clayey bit of land and irrigated it. If the prices remain stable in Paris this year, he plans to go in for a third harvest.

At some distance from his field are vast mango plantations protected by high fences. To whom do they belong? One is owned by a Supreme Court judge; another by a retired general; the third is the property of a minister's son. These people do not have to go into exile and never have any difficulty getting either a property deed or a bank loan. Why has this foolish Abdoulaye come back to disturb our peace? Why doesn't he go back to France? Mutter the villagers.

Abdoulaye's trials are in no way extraordinary. All the 'resettled immigrants' vetted by the Ministry had the same story to tell. I met a Paris trained driving instructor who had to wait four years before getting permission to set up a driving school in Dakar, a tailor who had to wait three years before his machine which had been confiscated by the customs was restored to him, and many more. The news filters back to the Senegalese diaspora all over the world and deters those who want to come back.

There are several ways of looking at Abdoulaye's story. On the plus side, Africa too has its share of entrepreneurs, capable of putting the experience they gained in France to good use in their own country. This should have been the logical outcome of migration and training abroad, leading to development and jobs in the South. But that has not happened; to set up a business in Senegal in the present circumstances requires a determination verging on madness. But not everyone is a hero; the risks involved in starting any business are simply too high for there to be many takers. And so emigration has become the best bet.

How can you deny Mahmadou and Abdoulaye the right to emigrate?

It is not as if Mahmadou and Abdoulaye do not want to return home. They do. What can we do to help them? The answer is not to repeat the mistakes of the last thirty years.

HOW AID PRODUCES EMIGRANTS

We are on our way to Popenguine where the Senegalese president lives. The motorcycle escort clears the way for the President's Mercedes. Children, lined up on both sides of the street, cheer as our motorcade whizzes past. Women perform dances in their traditional costume and Socialist party supporters wave portraits of Abdou Diouf. We happen to be in Africa's most pluralistic country but democracy does not mean a modest State. In May 1992 Abdou Diouf had told me, 'If you don't help us, our immigrants are going to swamp you.' As if to underscore the imminence of the threat, he went on to say that in 1981 he had done away with the exit visa required under his predecessor Leopold Senghor. The Senegalese government has nothing to gain by keeping back its citizens. 'On what basis am I to stop a Senegalese from leaving the country?' Besides, one can hardly expect the much less motivated African police to prevent people from slipping out when the countries in the North seem to be doing such a poor job of protecting their own borders. Is Diouf suggesting more aid? He is asking for nothing less than a Marshall Plan. Since its independence, Africa has already received the Marshall aid several times over, but there is little to show for it. Worse still, the main beneficiaries of such aid are today among the poorest, Tanzania being a case in point. What is more, it can be proved that aid has a direct bearing on emigration. Let me explain how.

Since the last thirty years, aid to the Third World, when it hasn't been embezzled outright, has been invested in state institutions. The bureaucracies of the South are being financed by the bureaucracies of the North with the money of Northern tax payers and the ravaged peasants of the South. The initial consolidation of the State was justified, as without a State to maintain law and order, development is not possible. But we moved out of the first stage a long time ago; today aid is not consolidating the State, it is fattening the nomenklatura and the army. The bureaucracies of the North and international organisations have supported and financed completely inappropriate development strategies. 'This aid and advice from the North' has led to the decimation of agriculture in the Maghreb and Black Africa; trade has been wiped out and private property destroyed. The uprooted peasants and ruined traders were left with no choice but to emigrate. Finally, aid also brought along a constant stream of Western bureaucrats, officials, military advisors and ministers to Africa. They came to represent for ambitious young Africans the ultimate symbol of social success. Young Africans would much rather be part of this jet setting bureaucracy than captains of industry.

My detractors will tell me I am being trite. Liberalisation is the new catchword in the countries of the South with everybody talking about the need for pruning the public sector, privatising and setting up 'small projects'. The pity is they only talk about it; in reality little has changed. Time and time again I was asked in Africa and the Maghreb, 'You Liberals have won; had you foreseen it?' What we had foreseen was that State controlled development and public aid would make the nomenklaturas grow richer and the poor poorer. Since the so-called 'victory of the liberals', nothing except rhetoric has changed. The very bureaucrats and experts who had advocated state control are now singing a liberal tune; their policies however seldom match their words. The talk about privatisation is a good example of this masquerade. In Morocco for instance, the government declared that there were a hundred and twelve public sector enterprises ready for privatisation; so far not a single one has been privatised. In Algeria, the law allows one hundred per cent foreign equity in all public assets that come up for sale, but nothing has ever come of this. Tunisia is the only country in the Maghreb to have privatised twenty of the fifty companies on the privatisation list. Needless to say, military expenditure has not been cut in any of these countries; in the Maghreb and Black Africa, it still accounts for 15% of public expenditure, three times higher than in Europe. Thus, even though the State's coffers may have been depleted from time to time, the State is still intact and the poor remain where they were. Emigrants have to care for the poor; the aid is for the rich to manage and even pocket.

THE KING'S SUBJECTS

His Majesty is everywhere. Hassan II smiles down at you from all the walls in Morocco. He has been photographed in every conceivable pose and dress: on foot, on horseback, seated on a Louis XV throne, in uniform and in a pinstriped suit. I know of no other nation where the photograph of the sovereign is as prominent. The Moroccan press is full of His Majesty; every word he utters, every speech he makes is faithfully reproduced. There are long articles in praise of the King, and his subjects are told of the many foreign delegations that come daily to pay their homage to him. How the Moroccans react to all this is a moot point: the plight of neighbouring Algeria seems to have quelled any urge to revolt. Perhaps Moroccans feel a surfeit of monarchy is better than anarchy. The West fully endorses this view and plays up to His Majesty. But His Majesty is rich and his country is poor. Incomes are falling and agricultural production is going down. The aristocracy, the upper and moneyed classes live in the lap of luxury; they build palatial houses facing the sea, they drive fancy,

imported cars and have a regular harem. They get by
with foreign aid, phosphate exports and a bit of
tourism. But Morocco as a nation could not survive
if the King's subjects stopped emigrating. Morocco's
growth rate is too slow to create enough jobs for the
coming generations. Unemployment is becoming an
acute problem in all the Maghreb countries; it is far
more visible and dangerous in an urbanised society
than in a rural one. Demographers and economists
agree that it will take thirty years for the situation to
stabilise and economic growth to match the increase
in population. In the meanwhile, the only option left
to Moroccans is to emigrate, a venture which enjoys
the wholehearted approval of his Majesty. Moroccan
remittances from overseas amount to about seventeen
billion dirhams every year, the second largest foreign
exchange earner for the country after tourism. All this
money is remitted through the Central Bank which
keeps the hard currencies and pays the recipients in
dirhams. In this way, emigrants finance not only their
families but the State. The common man is guaranteed
a meagre subsistence whereas the State and the
aristocracy can invest abroad, which they prefer to
domestic investment. For how long can things go on
like this?

His Majesty is worried. With Europe tightening its
borders, emigration has slowed down in spite of the
leakages via Spain. What is worrying his Majesty even
more is that his subjects abroad are beginning to forget
their country and change their nationality. From the
Moroccan point of view a change of nationality makes
no difference. A subject of the King will always be
a subject of the King; his children too, as Moroccan
citizenship cannot be relinquished. That his subjects
join the European mainstream is something the King

cannot abide. A Moroccan must always remain Moroccan; his exile is only temporary but his ultimate destiny is to return to the Kingdom. Hassan II's rejection of immigration and the apologia for an unchanging cultural and religious identity meet favour with conservative Europeans who do not want the 'Arabs' to integrate. These conservatives hold Hassan II in the greatest esteem. They may have a point. However, Moroccan immigrants in Europe do not share this opinion as they have the irritating habit of adopting what Noureddine El Aoufi calls 'the Greek scenario'. He explains that like Greek immigrants, Moroccans take two generations to identify with their host country and forget their country of origin; they stop sending back money and treat their impoverished country with condescension. A young Moroccan born in France does not take long to become a Beur. He identifies far more easily with his peer group from the Maghreb than with his own ancestors. His Majesty would like to stop this deviance towards integration: the Hassan II Foundation, the secular arm of the King for his overseas subjects, has stepped up its cultural, associative and religious activities so that Moroccans do not follow the Greek example and remain true to their country.

What does it mean to be a good Moroccan? El Aoufi's answer is that a good Moroccan is one who sends hard currency back to his country.

THE LIBERAL NORTH SOUTH SOLUTION

It was at Rabat that I saw a blinding light. 'How can you advocate a liberal solution for the North and something else for the South?' The economist, El Aoufi, professor at the University of Rabat, tries to catch me out in my own contradictions. How can a liberal of all people oppose the free movement of men and merchandise? The countries of the EEC have closed their borders to immigrants as well as to goods - textiles and agricultural products - on which quotas have been fixed. El Aoufi's words brought back to mind Friedrich Von Hayek's last public speech. This was in 1984 in Paris when the members of the Association of the Mont-Pèlerin had met to define a liberal approach to migration. Hayek, as intransigent as ever, reminded his so called liberal economist colleagues that though they had every right to oppose migration, they could not do so in the name of liberalism. Nothing in the liberal doctrine could legitimise putting obstacles to free movement.

Many intellectuals from the Maghreb have voiced this demand. They are asking Europe to apply the liberal principles it advocates for itself, sometimes with the same passion with which they defended a Third World approach a few years ago.

The Third World approach has not altogether disappeared. The curators of nationalist ideologies can be found in Tunis at the Alecso (The Arab League for Culture, Education and Science), a museum of ideologies. Abdelwahab Bouhdiba, a sociologist at the University of Tunis and spokesman for this UNESCO of the Arab world, told me how happy he was that Europe had decided to close its borders. For Bouhdiba, immigration was just another word for the exploitation of Arab workers who were treated like beasts and paid a pittance. When Europe speaks loftily about humanitarian principles, it is actually defending its material interests. Today Europe is protecting its cultural identity and its labour market. 'What could be better,' says Abdoulwahab Bouhdiba. The Arab world can now preserve its vital forces - Arab workers are far more useful at home - and its elite. Bouhdiba's only fear is that Europe will go in for a quota system of the kind in Switzerl nd or the United States, as this - perhaps his analysis is not off the mark - is the surest way of creaming off qualified workers and leaving the Maghreb with unskilled youth.

Bouhdiba's closed and aggressive nationalism is certainly not unusual in the Arab world. What is unusual is the outspokenness of the man in a country where academics prefer joining hands with their counterparts from the North to protest against their common enemies, namely xenophobia in Europe and Islamic fundamentalism in the Maghreb. All of a sudden Bouhdiba, realising I was carefully noting down all that he was saying, exploded in anger, for our meeting was not supposed to be an interview. He showed me the door and shouted down the staircase, 'I take back my words.' I did not quite understand what he meant; I therefore leave it to the readers to make what they will of both what he said and what he retracted. I am only relating this incident to give an idea of the potential aggressiveness that exists on both sides of the Mediterranean. Not all French intellectuals are liberals, nor for that matter are all Arab intellectuals. This makes solidarity among the liberals from the North and the South all the more necessary.

Assuming that El Aoufi is right when he says a liberal solution is required for Europe-Maghreb relations, then let us try and carry the argument a little further. Currently, the market for goods and labour is obstructed by protectionism at the borders. We see on the other hand that the effect of such protectionism is being countered by the illegal movement of goods and men:

whenever artificial government constraints are placed on the market, it has the habit of resurfacing unofficially. Had there been no protectionism, the law of comparative advantage between the North and the South would have come into play and benefited both sides. Noureddine El Aoufi feels that a plan for a common market between the Maghreb and the European Community is as realistic as the NAFTA or the free trade zone that Japan has set up with South East Asia. The Maghreb, taking advantage of its favorable climate and cheap labour, would grow more cash crops for the European Community and develop its textile industry. The competition from the South would force the North to adjust to the new circumstances in keeping with capitalist logic. In the long run all parties would stand to gain.

Would this lead to a massive influx of labour from the Maghreb to the European Community? An invasion of immigrants is not very likely, as in point of fact employment opportunities, not borders regulate migration. Besides, a common market with the Maghreb would result in an inflow of capital to the South which would curtail migration. Finally, if illegal immigrants turned legal, they would become more expensive and less attractive for employers. With liberalisation, the North would loose some of its appeal, as the South would offer greater economic opportunities. This is what happened when Spain, Portugal and Greece joined the European Community; integration into Europe provided these three countries with an alternative to emigration.

From my conversation with El Aoufi, a liberal solution emerged which seemed flawless, at least on paper. Its deficiency is that it assumes the tricky question of transition has been resolved. The impact of liberalising relations between Europe and the Maghreb will not be confined to economics alone. Xenophobic reactions in the North are to be expected. The resentment will be greater in sectors most vulnerable to competition from the South, such as agriculture and textiles. Morocco and Tunisia would probably adjust to the market economy as easily as Greece and Portugal. The same does not seem likely for Algeria, at least not in the immediate future.

Liberal thinkers rarely take into account the fact that transition takes time. The liberal critique of bureaucratic societies is usually accurate; so for that matter is its description of a better tomorrow. But how one is to move towards this better tomorrow remains unclear, as the experience of East European economies trying to divest themselves of communism only goes to show. The transition to liberalisation, with the free flow of goods and men between the Maghreb and Europe, will be just as hard to manage as it is in Russia. Be that as it may, a liberal solution to immigration would be just. This must be borne in mind while formulating long term strategies, even though a liberal solution does not provide an immediate answer to the current phase of uncertainty. For the short term, conditional aid is what we suggest.

CONDITIONAL AID

The Japanese experiment of investing in South East Asia and the free trade zone between the United States, Canada and Mexico should help our understanding of the question. We have already had a look at both these schemes but to recapitulate briefly: in Japan immigration is tightly controlled, an annual quota is fixed for the number of trainees who can enter Japan, the trainees are reemployed in the Third World and the goods manufactured by companies set up in the South are exported back to the North. The North American model is less controlled, allowing much more scope for private initiative. American investors set up business' on the Mexican side of the border in the 'maquiladoras'or free trade zones. These enterprises reexport their produce to the United States or to the rest of the world. Everyone stands to gain by the 'maquiladoras'. The Mexicans get good jobs in Mexico itself, the United States is able to control immigration more effectively and companies pay much less in terms of wages than they would in the United States. With the proposed North American common market, free trade would become widespread, a far better prospect than exodus. In both the Japanese and the United States examples, the same principles are at work. The idea is to move goods rather than men, to generate employment in the South so that people can prosper in their own countries without being forced to break traditional family and community ties, to create economic interdependence between North and South, to distribute production in terms of rational economic criteria and finally, to control migratory flows and mitigate the impact of cultural clashes.

It is not as if Japan and the United States have found the magic formula to solve the problems of the North South imbalance and migration; but it is experiments such as these that can help us find an answer. For instance, the 'maquiladoras' could well serve as a model for the Maghreb and Black Africa. The creation of free trade zones would provide European companies with new investment opportunities. Both the North and the South stand to gain from the relocation of economic activity: production in the

South and cheaper goods for the North. The same pattern could well apply to Eastern Europe too. Jobs 'lost' in the North would be replaced by more sophisticated activities; in any case, the loss would be compensated by a lower rate of immigration.

Initially, there is the risk that Europe will be importing both men and merchandise. This is where 'conditional aid' comes in. Conditional aid could help synchronize the free movement of goods with migration control.

Conditional aid would require the governments of the countries of the South and East to allow European entrepreneurs to invest in free trade zones and reexport freely without any tariff or quota barriers. On their part, European entrepreneurs would undertake to create a certain number of jobs and market the goods so produced. Job contracts could be given in the free trade zones to immigrants who agree to return to their country. One could even go a little further and demand that the countries of the South 'hold back' their emigrants in exchange for investment from the North. At first sight, this idea may appear both preposterous and farfetched. Nonetheless, it could be applied to at least contractual employees in the free trade zones; this could even be made one of the conditions of the work contracts freely accepted by the interested parties.

'Conditional aid', in the form of direct private investments, should logically replace state to state aid and all the worthless grants and loans the North has been giving the South for the past thirty years. The countries of the Third World have grown poorer, partially as a result of this aid which was used to finance corrupt regimes and a dubious brand of African and Arab 'socialism'. Conditional aid, by linking aid, investment, employment generation and migration, can only be beneficial to the Third World. The new conditional aid would allow each partner to play the role it is best suited for. The private sector would take care of investment, employment and trade; the State would look after its borders. Such a plan would give substance to the fine speeches politicians make. We are all agreed that developing the Third World is the only real solution to the problem of immigration. But till now, who has put forth any concrete, workable proposal? Conditional aid is workable: in the medium term, it could ease emigration; in the long term, a liberal strategy would stabilise it.

In the meantime, what are we to do? We can't stop immigration, we have to manage it.

13

MANAGING IMMIGRATION

Immigration is not necessary. The example of the Japanese automobile industry proves this point Japan used robots to overcome its shortage of manpower. Europe on the other hand steered a totally different course, choosing instead to take on lowly paid, unskilled workers. At the time it seemed the strategy made good economic sense; in fact it did not, neither for the automobile industry nor for society as a whole. Europe lagged behind in terms of technical innovation, quality suffered and prices were not competitive.The burden of settling immigrants fell upon the taxpayers, without mentioning the fallout immigration has had on the urban environment, transport, security, schools, hospitals and so on and so forth. The example of the automobile industry is not an isolated one; it is the same story in all branches of economic activity where there is a concentration of immigrants - garbage disposal and construction to name a few. It was believed and still is that only immigrants are fit to do mechanical poorly paid jobs. As a result, there has been little or no innovation in these areas. Had there been no cheap immigrant labour, these jobs would have been automated by now. And there would have been no need to call in poorly qualified, poorly paid labour. This analysis clearly invalidates statistical forecasts put out periodically by demographers who explained that if European companies were to continue functioning, Europe needed to import immigrants.

So continuing with immigration doesn't make sense any longer. If it does continue covertly, it means that somewhere along the line someone has an axe to grind. There are certain professional categories which stand to gain directly from closed borders. Smugglers, suppliers of false papers, corrupt officials, employers who exploit illegal immigrants, lawyers who defend them, drug sellers who use illegals as dealers and the police, all have a vested interest in continuing with border restrictions. By holding out the constant threat of arrest, imprisonment and deportation, they have several million illegal immigrants in Europe at their mercy. Paradoxically, illegal immigrants also stand to gain. It is because they are illegal that they can find work easily. Had they not been illegal, they would have been competing with the unemployed labour force whose papers are in order. Take the Senegalese and the Malis for instance. There are thousands of them in France. All of them are gainfully employed. Were they by some miracle to be legalised and covered by the welfare system, the collective conventions and the minimum wage, many of them would loose their jobs immediately.

We are thus functioning outside the rule of law. How do we get back to it? Should we open or close our borders?

It is impossible to close the borders. This is something law abiding citizens will not tolerate. Which French person will accept waiting for two hours at the airport in front of a police counter while the police checks the identity of each and every passenger and each and every passport? Deporting foreigners living illegally in France is equally unfeasible. Which French citizen will accept being rounded up in the metro and waiting for hours for the police to sort out those whose papers are in order and those whose aren't? Lastly, how many French citizens will accept that thousands of refugees be forcibly escorted to the border and left to the mercy of despots? Even that is problematic as illegals often refuse to disclose their country of origin. Can't immigration be checked at the time of issuing visas? Though the consular sections of our embassies in the Maghreb and Africa have the habit of viewing anyone who applies for a visa as a possible delinquent, it has not had the slightest effect on illegal immigrants; they do not apply for a visa or manage to get one easily by other means; on the other hand, I know several francophone and francophile intellectuals who refuse to come to France because they cannot put up with the unbelievingly humiliating treatment our diplomats meet out to them. I have also met several businessmen, traders and entrepreneurs who refuse to work with French companies for the same reasons. Because we are scared of the immigrant invasion we are cutting ourselves away from the elite. We should not be surprised if the younger generation in the Maghreb prefer English to French and business shifts towards Germany or the United States.

National controls which are either impractical or counterproductive will become even more unrealistic with European integration. Isn't there any alternative?

Perhaps what the European Commission is suggesting
- checking employers rather than borders - is an idea
worth looking at.

CHECKING EMPLOYERS

Jacques Delors says that immigrants are flocking to
Europe because they can find jobs; all you have to do
is to check companies so that these jobs are scrapped
and immigrants put off. This simplistic solution, if we
are to go by the recommendations of the Brussels
Commission, could well become the basis for a European immigration policy in the new European social
space. From Salonika to Glasgow and Oporto to
Copenhagen, employers will have to respect the
Community norms for minimum wages and welfare
subscriptions. It will no longer be possible to call in
illegal immigrants nor for that matter will it be in the
employers interest to do so. Instead of checking
borders, the company will be inspected. The argument
sounds logical enough. But is it really that much easier
to check companies than borders? To put it bluntly,
policing the market is no more tolerable than policing
foreigners.

In reality, 'the European solution' is impractical
though it is politically expedient as governments will
be able to shift the blame on the companies and make
them a convenient scapegoat. The heavy demand for
immigrant labour cannot only be explained in terms
of higher returns; with social security contributions
being as high as they are, if companies were to recruit
legally they would go bankrupt. They have to take
on moonlighters for their survival. For companies
(particularly those in the construction and service
sector) to stop recruiting illegal immigrants, welfare

costs must fall and immigrant labour supply be regulated - through quotas for instance - so that investment in technical upgradation replaces cheap labour. It is the job of the State not of the employers to create these preconditions.

Finally, the bid to put an end to the parallel labour market might just have the opposite effect. Currently, the unofficial labour market absorbs a relatively high proportion of illegal immigrants who would otherwise have been jobless. Now what is worse, immigrants working on the side or immigrants who do not work at all? If, as we believe, xenophobia is proportionate to the rate of unemployment, then the 'European solution' is hardly the right answer, assuming that it can be applied in the first place.

QUOTAS TO PROTECT THE BORDERS

How are borders as porous and long as those of the European Community to be controlled? And how is one to put an end to special favours, legal loopholes, corruption and employers' connivance, all working if favour of illegal immigration?

Quotas of the kind that exist in Switzerland are what we suggest. In Switzerland, immigration quotas are negotiated every year at the level of the cantons with officials, employers and union representatives taking part in the negotiations. Quotas are fixed by consensus and vary according to economic needs, the infrastructure available, the degree of unemploy-ment and the likely reactions of the local population. Foreign workers thus taken in are given permanent resident permits and they have the right to bring in their families. Henceforth, this will be the only way immigrants can enter Switzerland. There is of course the problem of asylum seekers which is no different in Switzerland than in the rest of Europe.

In France, we must have two types of quotas, one for permanent residents and another for limited duration stay, depending on the nature and origin of the immigrants (Switzerland had a seasonal workers quota which had to be scrapped under pressure from human rights associations).

The limited duration stay quota may help resolve the problem of the growing number of African immigrants. Poles, Italians and even Algerians could think in terms of permanently settling down in France and the French could think of assimilating them. Can the same be said for immigrants from Black Africa? The French do not want to assimilate them. But neither do the Africans want to be assimilated. Africans travel to France for two reasons. First, there are the economic considerations, and then a journey to France is looked upon as an initiatory rite. This is something that is hardly ever mentioned. For a young Senegalese or Mali, going to France is a sign that he has finally become a man. For him, a trip to Paris means acquiring a bit of dash and, with a little luck, returning home with a small fortune. The desire to know and experience is as compelling as economic necessity. However, the desire to go back home is just as strong. As a way out, we are suggesting limited duration stay quotas.

Quotas would allow the State to control the influx and to pick and choose. A public debate every year, or better still, one every four or five years, would force people to soften their stands and get down to brass tacks. We could then decide upon the number of new entrants and their composition, on the assumption that some people are easier to integrate than others and that every country has the right to shape its future.

Let parliament and the media thrash out the issue in the knowledge that a zero quota is absurd; it is an open invitation to violation. Quotas will settle the issue of the nationality code. Only immigrants who have been taken in as permanent residents and their children will in time be given French citizenship. On the other hand, no reform of the nationality code will ever have any impact on migration as citizenship is not really a motivating factor for migrants.

We could also think in terms of a European quota which would be the natural corollary to common borders and a European response to immigration, whereby immigrants would get distributed evenly among all member countries. Quotas will become a contract that Europe will conclude with the rest of the world. It is not as if illegal immigration would disappear overnight - we have the U.S. and Swiss examples before us - but quotas would nonetheless provide us with an instrument to manage border control and the labour market, thereby reducing the dichotomy between the law and reality.

REFUGEES: A LIBERAL DEFINITION

By introducing quotas we would, in principle, be in a position to resolve the question of legal immigration. However, the problem of asylum seekers still remains. We know that a large percentage of the immigrants coming in are asylum seekers and this situation has arisen from the abuse of the Geneva Convention on political refugees. The word abuse has been used deliberately, as on an average eighty-six percent of all asylum applications are ultimately turned down after a long drawn out legal and administrative procedure.

How do we avoid becoming prisoners of our own laws? Should we amend the Geneva Convention?

Given the current functioning of the United Nations, that seems a faint possibility. Can't we speed up the scrutiny of asylum applications? This was done in France in 1991-92. But speeding up procedures did not stop people from crossing borders. In fact, it has given rise to certain anomalies: illegal immigrants who know their cases are going to be decided soon stop coming to the *Office d'accueil des réfugiés*; they just vanish leaving the administration with no way to identify them. Besides, as the French administration is extremely tough about giving stay permits, a thriving counterfeit racket has come up, as in the United States. Asylum applications must be disposed of quickly and applicants turned down must be deported from our soil. But who will deport them, how and where to? Should all the Blacks be rounded up because many Africans are living without papers? Most of the 'solutions' offered on the subject are either unrealistic, preposterous or smack of populism.

A catch-22 situation? Not really; a scrutiny of asylum applications shows that ninety per cent of asylum seekers are not political refugees. Some are looking for work; some want welfare protection. The limited duration stay quota meets the needs of those who want to work as well those of the employers who want to take them on. Replacing the theoretical ban on immigration with quotas will ease the pressure on asylum seekers and employers recruiting them. That leaves us with asylum seekers who are only on the lookout for social security and allowances. It would be a good idea to scrap welfare protection and allowances, however modest they might be at the present moment; there is nothing in the Geneva Convention against this. The number of fake applicants will fall, though there still will be some because fraud is still widespread. This can be countered by making non falsifiable identification papers, European ones if possible. However these restrictions will never dissuade genuine political refugees who fear for their lives from coming to Europe; humanitarian associations are sufficiently active to take care of them.

Does a market based approach to immigration offend human rights? It all depends on what we understand by human rights. Are human rights there to provide us with intellectual consolation? In that case, let there be a flood of asylum seekers; never mind if we are giving fuel to xenophobic movements without in any way ensuring the happiness of fake refugees. What satisfaction can an illegal immigrant derive from living in a hostile, precarious environment with the threat of deportation constantly looming large? Anything is better than dying of hunger in Zaire, you may say. Quite true, but asylum seekers rarely die of hunger. Those who manage to reach Europe are among the most enterprising; their departure only aggravates the situation in their own countries. It would thus make more sense to help them use their energies back home, as had been suggested when we dealt with conditional aid. Real humanitarianism to my mind is allowing asylum seekers to live well in their own countries rather than badly in ours.

Obviously all these solutions are far from being perfect. But then being liberal in regard to major social issues is to admit that there is no perfect solution. Universal trends are far beyond the scope of the State; were the State to become too efficient, freedom would disappear.

LET'S DREAM

"Fellow citizens, there are some among you who are

xenophobic; a few might even be racist; and then there are
the many who are neither xenophobic nor racist. Xenophobia
as such is not serious, it is the normal reflex of different
populations living together on the same soil. Some among
you are of French extract; some, immigrants or descendants
of immigrants; some of you might even be illegal immigrants.
But all of us together make up this unique country which
is France, a country in constant quest of its identity. No
other people in the world have asked themselves so persistently
who they are and where they are going to. Our traditions
have made us what we are but that should not stop us from
living together. We have to organise ourselves better so that
coexistence is easier and violence eradicated. My role as
President is not to look into your soul or preach morality
but to suggest policies that can be put into practice.

"I see that the issue which divides the French and
incites hatred of foreigners is not so much race or religion
as work, rather the absence of it. For some, there is security
and relative comfort; for others, there is nothing but worry
and the life of a marginal. Very often, unemployment,
menial jobs and illegal work are the lot of immigrants and
their children. This only heightens their difference in the
eyes of the other French. We could wait for the school to
carry on its historic task of merging differences; within a
generation or two, North Africans will become as French
as the rest of us and Islam a religion like the others. The
question is are we willing to wait that long. The answer
is no; that would only mean more violence. Today we are
talking violent; tomorrow we will be violent.

``There is shorter way out, one that I shall call
integration through employment. Let me spell it out for you.

``For its part, the State shall allow children of fourteen
years and above, with the consent of their families, to leave
school and complete their education as apprentices in
private companies. For all sixteen year olds who do not

continue their studies, apprenticeship shall become the normal channel for joining the labour force. Apprenticeship may even become compulsory for them. Small and large companies shall have to make some sacrifices, as they shall have to take on a large number of unskilled youth. However, this shall give them an opportunity to fulfill a national duty - integration, a task they alone are capable of performing. In return, employers' obligations shall be lowered and obstacles to the recruitment and training of young people in companies removed. Social security benefits and State concessions for companies will be all the more if their efforts are quantified and made public.

``Our policy of integration calls upon those who already have a job - the wage earners - to make a personal effort to welcome into their companies new workers who till now have had no experience of work. This is already happening in large industries; small and medium enterprises must follow suit.

``Young people too must make a special effort. The jobs they will do in the first few years of their working lives will be badly paid. They must view this as a means to facilitate their own integration into their community and as an investment for their future.

``The task of managing this vast enterprise shall be handed over neither to the State nor to the state employment exchange, as neither are qualified to do so, but to the Mayors who shall work in collaboration with the Chambers of Industry and Commerce. The Mayors shall decide how much welfare assistance is to be given in place of the RMI which is being handed out indiscriminately. It is the duty of the Mayor to ensure that in return for welfare assistance - which could be a minimum wage - the beneficiaries are made to participate in activities useful for the community as this alone can bring about genuine integration. The Mayor must also ensure that everybody has the freedom

of religion and the right to practice it - Islam is no exception - in appropriate places of worship. Lastly, the Mayor shall see to it that there is a fair distribution in social housing and schools, keeping in mind the objective cultural differences that may exist between the French already living in France and those who have just entered.

``Entry on our national soil shall henceforth be regulated by means other than ineffective identity checks and dubious family gatherings. Every year, Parliament shall determine the composition and strength of the limited duration stay quota. We shall welcome all those who enter under the quota system and be uncompromising with those who try to enter clandestinely. Full welfare protection shall be guaranteed to those who enter legally and denied to those who come in illegally.

``Lastly, we shall have to completely redefine our relations with poor countries and Eastern Europe: we shall stop financing their leaders and see to it that henceforth the only aid given is direct, employment generating investment in the private sector. In return, we shall ask their governments to guarantee that our immigration laws are respected in their countries. Thus, with less State and more enterprise, we are for the first time laying down the principles of a genuine minority integration policy. In this way I shall be discharging my duties to the State, defining at the same time the limits to what a President can do. The rest is not for politicians but philosophers to decide."

Thus ends a speech in search of a speaker.

14

A FUNNY KIND OF WAR

Addicts, like immigrants, are the other; they are different, barbaric. Opium helps them escape from bourgeois society; cocaine and amphetamines allow them to bypass its rules; with hallucinogenics, they can reject them altogether. Drug addiction is the ingestion of a foreign substance. But the relationship between drugs and immigration is not merely metaphoric; drug related offences and crimes account for half the prison population of the West, almost all offenders being illegal immigrants.

But what is a drug? The State decides: a drug is any substance the State has defined as such. In 1620, Louis XIII banned the consumption of Nicot's weed in public places. Did it threaten law and order, was it perceived as being dangerous, or was it banned because it came from outside, who can tell. Since then, tobacco started being cultivated, became an industry and a major source of revenue for the State. So it was no longer a drug. Neither is alcohol, which intoxicates and kills. Marijuana, though milder and not in the least lethal, is a drug, because it is forbidden. The alcoholic is one of us, we can laugh at him or take pity on him; on the other hand, the opium addict comes from elsewhere, he arouses in us the fear of the unknown, hatred and repression. In the nineteenth century, opium was sold freely in Europe and the United States. For a long time, amphetamines were legal stimulants, before being declared drugs. Ethiopians, Indians and Bolivians legally consume what in our country are prohibited drugs and in theirs just ordinary stimulants. What a drug is changes from place to place and time to time. In what way are drugs dangerous? Are they a threat to law and order, and health, or is it the State itself which is in jeopardy?

Drugs are condemned and banned not just because they are harmful, but because they are foreign. It was only when Chinese immigrants started selling opium, not before, that the American government prohibited it. Marijuana was banned because Mexicans brought it in; cocaine was banned in the twenties because it made Blacks turn violent. In the thirties, the French government came down on heroin, as it came from Germany (to begin with, it was a German cough remedy); heroin, it was said, was the Boche. The Chinese Emperor banned opium as soon as the British began to sell it in China; before that, it was freely produced and sold there. The Japanese government clamped down on opium because it was foreign. That did not stop it, in 1940, from manufacturing and distributing a *made in Japan* amphetamine as a stimulant for soldiers.

The ban on drugs therefore has more to do with politics than health. This is not an apologia for drugs, the intention is to find the most effective ways to resist them. Western governments have chosen to wage a war against drugs. What began as an American war, gradually spread across the rest of the world with the

U.S. government imposing a supposedly new drug free world order. This has now become the new moral order. There can be no compromise on drugs. Any discussion on the subject is dangerous unless you don't come out strongly against them. Failure to do so is interpreted as proof of a personal stake or preference. The experts have been bought off. Specialists on drugs, teachers and civil servants are all dependent on public money; it is difficult for them to take a stand against official policy. Leon Schwarzenberg, a French minister, was sent packing in 1988 after he made a modest attempt to liberalise drugs. Transnational ideology brooks no argument.

To question this ideology, one would have to be independent of the State, indifferent to power and very courageous indeed. For me, who neither smokes nor drinks, my concern is primarily that of a father for his children. As a liberal intellectual, I cannot fail to be stunned by this funny kind of war against drugs. After having gone to all the places where the war is on, in both producer and consumer countries - hospitals, asylums, de-addiction centres, customs, police, psychiatric wards - I saw they were fighting a losing battle. Worse still, the study showed the war against drugs claimed more victims than drugs themselves. Violence, prison, disgrace, marginalism and exclusion are more the consequences of prohibition than of drug abuse. The war against drugs is not a rational war but a war of ideology and passion; it is not being waged to lighten the sufferings of the addict but to satisfy the state's craving for war. A war that has no end, as every day sees a new Sedan. With each passing day, violence and addiction are on the rise. Western governments carry on notwithstanding. Why? Because with this war, the State acquires a semblance of legitimacy - medical, moral, almost scientific. Doesn't the war against drugs enjoy public support? Yes, it does. Ill informed and misled, the public is incapable of distinguishing between prohibition and war, and an effective anti-drug strategy.

Is there any alternative to this war? As it is not possible to eliminate drugs or the desire to take them, I shall not discuss any liberal 'solution'. However, a liberal approach to drugs would do less harm than aggressive prohibition. The following pages, I think, will bring this out clearly. A case is not being made for the liberalisation of all drugs, but for a respite in the war against drugs. Only this can ensure a genuine appraisal of the various drugs. Unlike those champions of the war against drugs who claim to be the sole custodians of the truth, I shall content myself to raising a few questions, questions which have no ready made answers.

15

THE GOOD EMPIRE

Bob Martinez has blue eyes and wears a red tie for effect. The American press refers to him as the 'Drug Czar.' His colleagues prefer calling him 'Governor' - he was in fact the Governor of Florida till 1990. Martinez now rules over a far bigger empire, with George Bush appointing him Director of the Drug Enforcement Agency. The United States annually spends twelve billion dollars on its war against drugs, an amount that far exceeds the budget of several African and Latin American countries. The Czar has thousands of policemen, soldiers and advisors working for him, and troops stationed in all drug producing countries. He can also call upon a legion of judges, jailers and doctors. Martinez's good empire is a thousand times more powerful than its evil enemy, the narcotraffic empire. The war against drugs pits David against Goliath, guerrillas and the Mafioso against the might of the United States. It is a symbolic war, the classic struggle between good and evil.

The Czar is reputed to be handsome, well built, a smooth talker, though not known to shine for his intellect. Is this a fair estimate of the man? It's hard to say, as an interview with Bob Martinez is a completely stage managed affair. In the U.S., everything to do with politics has to come neatly packaged. The Czar's office is very much in the patriotic mould. The walls are covered with flags, medals and photographs of the Czar posing next to George Bush, the Pope, Ronald Reagan, Billy Graham, etc. Our conversation is going to be recorded, to make it seem all the more consequential. In fact, the interview turns out to be a monologue, as Martinez does not hear a word of what I say. He just intonates a much rehearsed speech which he uses every time he talks to the press; the lines never change. His press secretary, who looks like an American footballer and goes by the name of James Banta, often interrupts and prompts the governor whenever he misses his cue. 'Forty minutes is all you have,' announces Banta at the outset; that rules out an indepth discussion. To add to my discomfiture, after every five minutes, Banta tells me how much time I have left; when only five minutes remain, Banta begins a minute to minute countdown. A technician wearing headphones is hovering around to check the quality of the sound - or is he a security agent?

I only half listen to Martinez, my carefully prepared questions forgotten. The forty minutes go by too slowly for my liking, full of hackneyed statements and predictable lies. The inevitable "crack babies" are thrown at me: thousands of children allegedly born too small or deformed because their mothers had taken cocaine. Though the story had figured very prominently in the American press, it had never been really checked out. The facts are painful enough, so why do officials make it sound all the more gruesome? Why this charade? You see, the Americans are at war

or playing at war: a good and just war, it is needless
to say.

'In waging the war against drugs,' declares Martinez,
'we are protecting the weakest, the poor, the Blacks
and the Hispanics; they are the main victims of drug
addiction.' The war against drugs does not kill. It
protects. It is a moral war, one that upholds capitalist
morality. Martinez is particularly distressed about the
production losses incurred by American companies
due to addiction. 'Fighting against drugs,' he explains,
'is raising our productivity.' A strange argument as
most addicts work and are no less functional than the
rest of us.

AN ANTI-LEFT CRUSADE

What does Martinez have to say about those who feel
that he is fighting a losing battle? 'The United States,'
he replies, 'is winning; the anti-drug army is marching
from victory to victory.' At this point, statistics are
hurled at me. Didn't I know that since the outbreak
of hostilities, cocaine consumption was going down by
10% every year? I can't challenge these figures, accessi-
ble only to the government of the United States. And
then to clinch his argument Martinez adds, 'The
handful of intellectuals who refuse to support the anti-
drug war are "leftists"!'

Does he consider Milton Friedman, a conservative
and an abolitionist, a leftist? 'No, but he is an
intellectual.' This is reason enough to discredit him.
What about George Schultz? He too had come out in
favour of legalising drugs. And having served on both
the Nixon and Reagan administrations, he can hardly
be suspected of leftist leanings. Stunned, Martinez
looks at his press attache for advice. 'Hasn't Schultz

retracted?' asks the Czar. 'Yeah, yeah, he retracted,' mumbles a servile Banta. Now that is not true. But then all is fair in love and war.

One of Martinez's priorities is to win allies. 'This has to be an international war, like the one we had in Kuwait.' With Russia all is well. Relations continue to improve. In Latin America, things are getting better and better. Bolivians have started using pineapple instead of coca. 'Pineapple, that's the answer for Bolivia!' exclaims Martinez. However, Europe worries the Czar. Thank God socialist France is practicing repression American style - the war against drugs makes for strange bedfellows indeed. On the other hand, the Dutch have proved to be embarrassing with their tolerance towards marijuana. Martinez sees no difference between hard and soft drugs: marijuana is a stepping stone to hard drugs. 'You can't deny that!' proclaims the Czar. Completely untrue. Alcohol, not marijuana, is the only stimulant that may lead to cocaine.

On the whole Europe is soft, the Czar reckons, because it has yet to feel the full impact of the attack. Wait, he tells his European friends, cocaine is not far off. The battles won on the American continent will divert drug traffic towards Europe. When Europe is hit like America was, the Europeans will react like the Americans; of this Martinez is convinced. 'You persist in believing that drugs only affect some specific, target groups; that is how it begins. Later on, everybody catches the "epidemic." Then public opinion changes.' This may well happen, especially if Martinez and his ilk play on public ignorance and insist war is the only way out. But is it really a war they are fighting?

I personally think the term crusade is more

appropriate. It began with a Protestant bishop, Reverend Brent who demanded prohibition. He managed to get opium banned in the Philippines after American colonisation; then, he spearheaded a campaign for a worldwide prohibition. In 1912, at the Hague Conference, his efforts succeeded. The crusading spirit lives on, even in leftist circles. Mario Cuomo, the secular Democratic governor of New York, declared in 1990, 'those who do not believe in the devil think of drugs'. Can it not be said for the history of the United States that it has been one long crusade? First against the Red Indians, then slavery and communism. For it to be good incarnate, the United States needs an enemy either from within or from without: first it was the Salem witches, then the Bolsheviks and now, the Medlin cartel. Let us go back to 1917 and the Anti-Alcohol league congress held that year. Reverend Sam Small had said, 'When prohibition will have won, our America, victorious and Christian, will be not only a saviour but also a model and guide for a new world civilization.' At the time he was referring to the prohibition of alcohol. Since then, names have changed: drugs have replaced alcohol, the medical corps the priests. Martinez does not claim to defend religion, but the health of all Americans as well as ours; the crusade has been medicalised to acquire a scientific veneer.

Drug addiction is an 'epidemic', the Czar says menacingly. Will I catch it by breathing the Washington air, I wonder. I have no more time to speculate, as my forty minutes are up. Now I can begin my investigation.

DOCTOR PICKENS' MICE

Baltimore. At the Addiction Research Center, the fluffy

pink tailed white mice in Doctor Pickens' laboratory seem innocuous enough. They are in fact V.I.P.'s. On them hangs the scientific or I should say pseudo-scientific rationale of the anti-drug war. I am not exaggerating. On the drugs issue, there are two diametrically opposite schools of thought .

The first, of libertarian inspiration, is epitomized by Milton Friedman. The addict takes drugs out of 'choice'; he gives them up too out of 'choice'. Social, cultural and personal factors condition this choice. In such an analysis, the role of the state is limited to informing addicts about the risks they are running, as has been the case for smoking. The State can also work to mitigate the objective conditions for addiction by improving the dreadful urban environment. Taking this argument to its logical end, addicts being free to choose, must take the consequences for all their acts. An addict who commits a crime or an offense ought to be punished not because he is an addict but for the crime committed. Drugs can in no way absolve him of his responsibility.

On the other hand, there is the prohibitionist school of thought à la Martinez. Addiction is an illness which deprives individuals of their free will. Addicts are no longer in a position to choose; this is their illness. As a result, it is the government's responsibility to protect the population against coming into contact with drugs which spread the disease. Furthermore, patients have to be imprisoned or isolated in order to safeguard the healthy population. Addicts have to be cured forcibly as they are incapable of reaching out for help on their own.

Are addicts free, do they freely decide whether or not to take drugs? The answers to these questions will

- or ought to - determine any policy. And this is how the Baltimore mice come into the picture.

Doctor Pickens' laboratory is State financed; scientific research here is tailored to serve national ideology. Pickens' mice have a catheter inserted in them all the time so that they can inject themselves with drugs whenever they want. They just have to push a pedal with their feet - something animals do easily - for hashish, cocaine, heroin or morphine to flow. After a few intakes - the number varies from mouse to mouse for genetic reasons perhaps - the mice get addicted. Nothing distracts them, they just go on drugging themselves till they die of hunger or an overdose. The mice, Pickens points out, naturally choose the same drugs as humans; 'this proves addiction is chemical and biological in nature' and that we have a lot more in common with mice than we think. There is nonetheless one exception: mice do not take to hallucinogenics; they do not touch LSD and mescaline. Pickens has thus come to the conclusion that once a mouse has tasted drugs, it gets dependent because it has no choice. Its organism gets addicted. Pickens willingly accepts that what holds for mice must hold for men: drug use, he claims, changes the human brain and destroys man's capacity to choose almost irreversibly.

The whole repression rationale is based on this single laboratory finding: never has so great a government owed so much to so small a group of mice.

THE EXCESS GENE

'Martinez obviously hasn't convinced you,' observes Roy Pickens. 'The American government is rather clumsy in explaining its war against drugs and why it rejects any form of legalisation.' Politicians have turned what ought to be a scientific campaign into a war. In addition, the publicity drive was poorly conceived and counterproductive. Take Nancy Reagan's 'Just say no' slogan for example (it was also taken up in Europe). A patently absurd campaign as by definition an addict cannot say no. So let us start again, suggests Pickens.

First of all there can be no distinction between hard and soft drugs, those that can be liberalised and those that can't. All drugs, including alcohol and tobacco, have two characteristics in common: they are more or less disruptive and more or less addictive. All drugs are supposed to have the power to change behaviour and personality to varying degrees. It is true, Pickens acknowledges, that marijuana is neither very disruptive nor very addictive; nonetheless it causes loss of memory. Does one drug lead to another, does one go from tobacco to hashish and from hashish to cocaine? In all likelihood, no. It depends, admits Pickens, on the availability of the drug rather than on any biological 'necessity'.

The second basic distinction to be kept in mind is between drug abuse and drug addiction. Not everyone is tempted to use drugs; the temptation to experiment depends on a variety of factors - personality, circumstances and most importantly according to Pickens, genetic predisposition. But one thing is certain: the greater the availability of a drug, the greater the number of occasional drug users. Now among these users, a certain number are bound to get addicted. What is the percentage? This is hard to tell. In the case of alcohol, 10% become chronic alcoholics. For heroin and cocaine, the proportion could well go up to between 30 and 50%, says Pickens.

When a drug user becomes a drug addict, adds Pickens, his brain undergoes a transformation; given the current state of medical knowledge, it is not possible to reverse this condition. The drug addict is a chronic patient who is a permanent liability to society. At this stage, Pickens feels it is pointless analysing the social or psychological origins of addiction. The illness becomes a biological disease. Psychoanalysis has nothing to offer. It cannot be a cure, it is mere rhetoric. Roy Pickens compares the addict's dependence to schizophrenia. For a century psychoanalysts thought they could cure schizophrenia; all they did in fact was talk about it. Now we 'know' that schizophrenia is genetic in origin (at least this is what Pickens claims though many psychiatrists would dispute this assertion) and so is addiction. The addict, whether under medical supervision (heroin addicts can be cured with methadone; for cocaine addicts there is no comparable substitute treatment) or in prison or a marginal - jobless, criminal, antisocial- becomes a disruptive element and a heavy burden on society.

In a nutshell, Roy Pickens' argument is this: the purpose of the war against drugs is to reduce their availability by making them scarce, expensive and illegal. Scarcity will automatically bring down the number of drug users; this in turn will reduce the number of addicts. On the contrary, the free sale of drugs will increase their availability; they will become cheap, legal and plentiful. This will inevitably lead to an increase in the number of users and addicts. That's simple arithmetic!

Roy Pickens wonders why some people can resist drugs and others can't ? Why do some drug users never get addicted? The answer is probably genetic in nature: some can resist, others can't. There must be an 'addiction gene'. It *has* to exist!

In any case, Pickens is working on genetic predisposition. In his laboratory, mice who have undergone genetic manipulation are exposed to drugs in the hope of discovering a resistant species . Pickens explains that the 'excess gene' is probably not just confined to drug abuse; most likely, it conditions any immoderate tendency: compulsive drinking, use of cocaine, eating, gambling, sexuality, even eating too many salted almonds . Were the gene to be discovered, not only addicts but also gamblers and sex maniacs could be cured of their obsession. One could even think in terms of preventing all excesses through prior genetic manipulation, a kind of vaccination for those who are prone to excess.

But what do we mean by excess? And who will decide, on what basis what is excessive? The State? In the United States, there have been comparable precedents with lobotomy and the compulsory sterilization of the mentally ill.

GI'S VS MICE

Dr. Pickens 'official' mice are very controversial even in the United States. Especially as the experience of American GI's in Vietnam contradicts laboratory findings. Several million Americans went to fight in the Vietnam War in the early seventies; 40% used some form of opium. Once they returned to the U.S., the addiction rate of this group fell automatically. There are still a few heroin addicts among the veterans, but they would have become addicts anyway. If not heroin, they would have found something else. Irreversible dependence has not been as firmly established as

Professor Pickens in the U.S. - or Gabriel Nahas in France - would like people to believe. Besides, the Pickens experiments did not give the same results when repeated by Canadian scientists in Toronto. It is true that the Canadian mice were given a choice between drugs and other distractions. Couldn't Pickens' mice have been conditioned by factors other than drugs, stress or cramped spaced for instance? Furthermore, Pickens' mice did not *choose* drugs, they were thrust upon them by the researcher. Finally, are we mice? We have a free will: initially the addict has a 'choice'. Not the mice.

Suppose the dependence theory is valid; is this enough to warrant a war against drugs? Pickens' reasoning, apparently logical, is not. Let us assume for a minute that the cycle described by Pickens is true (availability equals abuse equals addiction). Then why wage a war against drugs? Criminalisation does not seem to be the best way to break the cycle. Indeed, liberalisation is likely to yield better results; for a start, educating exposed groups seems like a good idea. Legalising a drug does not mean inducing whole scale intoxication; the sharp fall in the number of smokers in recent years amply illustrates this point. The war against drugs is going to cost America twelve billion dollars in 1992, not to mention its repercussions on criminality, corruption, Third World destabilisation, urban fear, and so on and so forth. Suppose they put an end to the war. All this money could be used more profitably to educate people and improve social conditions so that one does not feel the urge to use drugs in the first place.

All this tends to show that a liberal approach and a scientific study of the nature of drug addiction are not incompatible. Doctor Pickens's mice, now part of a crusade, could just as well be used to bring about a rational conciliation.

For there to be a ceasefire in the war against drugs the American government must want peace; something I very much doubt. For then, it will loose the legitimacy that war confers on it; all the Martinez' of this world would be reduced to unemployment and the American world order would loose a powerful alibi. Ever since prohibition, the U.S. government has wanted to impose its repressive ideology on the rest of the world. At it's behest, the Hague Convention which prohibited drug traffic was ratified in 1912. It was also the U.S government which insisted that the ban on opium and cocaine be included in the Versailles Treaty of 1919. Since then, the establishment of a world order and the fight against certain drugs seem, amazingly enough, to be linked. Only one thing has changed: previously moral and religious arguments were employed; now they are supposedly scientific. The American crusade has modernised; it has turned into a scientific ideology and acquired therapeutic overtones. The new world order will be a medicalised one. Must we give in to American ideology?

In the pages to come, we shall see how the French government has caved in.

16

BRING THE
NARCOMANICS

Colonel Kouznetzov has managed to keep alive the theatricality of the happy Breznev days. I had been told to stand at the appointed time in front of the Byelorussia Station, next to the green pastry shop with Byzantine domes. Sure enough, a ramshackle Volga - of undefinable colour - grey, beige, it was hard to say - was waiting for me. It did not have a license plate and the windows were up. I hadn't even closed the door when the driver started the car, blared the siren and over a loudspeaker ordered the traffic to a halt to make way for us. We drove off at top speed from the city centre racing through the traffic lights till we reached what seemed to be one of the northern suburbs. At last we got to our destination; the Volga shot through a drawbridge into what looked like a fortified castle with crenels made of red brick. There it stood, prison no 3, one of the four big prisons in the capital. Any Muscovite could have told me the way and for three dollars, a taxi would have taken me there. But that would have been too flat for Ioury

Kouznetzov, the prison governor. In these democratic times, he wanted the world to know that the Police had still retained its authority.

Prisons are never a pretty sight. Though No.3 with its archaic latches, rusty doors and broken window panes is less forbidding than our functional cells. Provided you can forget the spectre of the Gulag hovering all over the place: the ancient drawbridge we just crossed spelt decline and death for many a Soviet.

'You just cannot imagine how many I have seen go by,' murmurs the Colonel, dreamy all of a sudden. He himself has survived all the purges of the last thirty years. In his office, as uncomfortable and shabbily maintained as the prison, Lenin's portrait remains ubiquitous; he stares at you from wooden frames, canvases and tapestries. The anti-communist revolution has yet to cross these walls. Even more surprising, Dzerjinski's portrait occupies the pride of place. He was the man who founded Tcheka, the secret police later rebaptised KGB. 'Glasnost did not pass us by,' the Colonel hastens to assure me. 'We no longer lock up political dissidents or the enemies of the regime [that remains to be seen]. You can visit any prison cell, speak to whomsoever you please; you can even dispense with the warder if you want. But there is one condition [I am waiting for the catch], after you have seen all you want, you must let us offer you a stirrup cup.'

The Colonel bursts out laughing. So does his staff. Every one is happy. No wonder I was so warmly received; my visit has provided them the opportunity to polish off a few bottles of cognac. I cannot refuse. So Russian cognac and sausage it is at ten o'clock in the morning!

ADDICT OR DISSIDENT

Twenty bare chested young men - it is extremely hot-
are crowded in a cell meant for four. There is nothing
particularly Russian about such promiscuity. Some of
the prisoners pretend to be sleeping. Others take
refuge behind their blankets. A group of four ·is
absorbed in a game of chess, using bread crumbs as
pawns - something that could only happen in Russia.
'Bring the narcomanics!'shouts the Colonel. This is the
legal name given to delinquents, as opposed to addicts
who limit themselves to the harmful but not forbidden
pleasure of inhaling glue or benzene. Two scrawny,
young inmates - their cheeks sunken in, heads shaved
and eyes red for lack of sleep - slowly heave themselves
out of their mean bed; they seem to come straight out
of a Dostoevsky novel. Vladimir refuses to talk. His
case is being heard and he doesn't want to take any
chances. But Andreï has much to say.

Andreï is twenty-eight years old; his scars and
tattoos suggest he is no angel. He has a funny look.
Is he stoned? Cynical is more like it. He was found
with twenty grams of hashish, for which he has to
serve a 12 to 18 month prison term. Did he use drugs
often? 'Yes, but I am not a peddler.' The court, he
claims, sentenced him on the charge of taking drugs;
that was enough to put him behind bars. How did
they find and arrest him? His parents informed the
police. His father, a ʻcommunist worker', could not
tolerate his son's idleness nor the company he kept.
'What is the point of working in this perestroikan
madhouse?' he tries to justify himself. 'Boris Yeltsin
is demoralising the youth; everyone is smoking; our
Russia is adrift.' After his parents reported him,
Andreï was not arrested immediately. Instead, on the

recommendation of a doctor, his name was put on police record as a narcomanic. He was told that according to the law, he had a year's grace period in which to give up smoking or get treated. He saw no reason to do so. 'Hashish,' he explains, 'is not harmful and does not lead to dependence. I read this in Moscow News. In any case, there isn't any hospital in Russia to take care of addicts. There is only the prison.' 'That's not true!' exclaims the interpreter. A greying official, provided by the Ministry of Interior, he had been content till now to do a word to word translation. But this was too much for him, 'Who says there aren't any deaddiction centres.' 'You mean the prophylactoriums,' retorts Andreï. 'Let me tell you, your compulsory deaddiction centres are worse than prison. I'd much rather remain where I am.'

Andreï continues his confession. 'I am talking only because the Colonel promised to let me move on earlier to the next stage if I did.'

- Next stage?
- Labour camp. Release when you compare it to prison.

Why was Andreï in prison? Because he took hashish or because he went against his parents and society? Before 'democratisation', narcomania was not a punishable offense. But Andreï would probably have been accused of dissidence or mental illness, interned in the Gulag or a psychiatric hospital. In the ruins of communism, cannabis is the new way young people express their dissent. And for die-hard nomenklaturists, the war against drugs has become the modern day alibi for continuing with social repression.

The Colonel keeps opening the cell door to look in. He is getting impatient and reminds me about the stirrup cup awaiting us. As we go, I hold my hand

out to Andreï. Startled, he hesitates awhile before
shaking it. He then recovers his aplomb and lets me
know how well versed he is in things French, 'Give
my love to Alain Delon and Patricia Kaas.'

At last the Colonel can open his bottle. After a
generous helping of garlic sausage and downing
several glasses of cognac it is time for confidences.
'Our profession is shameful. We dare not let our
children know what we do,' confides the Colonel. The
officers add, 'We tell the others we are in the Army.
But the Army despises us.' Tears run down their
cheeks. We toast to a new Russia. I try to raise their
morale by praising their cognac, smuggled in from
Armenia. Illicit no doubt but not a drug. There is the
usual hugging and kissing and then I leave. The pilot
car once again hurtles across the draw bridge. The
siren blares and the Colonel orders passers-by to move
to the side for our cavalcade. Ten minutes, and I find
myself back at the Byelorussia station. Tomorrow at
the 'interpreter's' suggestion, we are going to visit a
deaddiction centre.

THE POTEMKIN CURE

What do they do with drug users in Russia, look after
them or put them behind bars? It is difficult to tell
when rhetoric, reality and rhetoric about reality overlap
each other to such an extent: we are after all in the
land of Potemkin. A minister under Catherine II, he
kept the Empress in a state of happy illusion by
having prosperous looking cardboard villages built
along the route she was to travel. More recently, Stalin
and his successors updated the Potemkin method;
model kolkhozes and workers heroes were put on
display for the Russian people and wonder struck

foreign 'observers' alike. The technique did not die out; in fact, it was honed and sharpened to perfection. When Nancy Reagan visited Moscow with Ronald in 1990, the Soviets who knew all about her commitment to the war against drugs took her to a deaddiction clinic built specially for the occasion. It would have been a pity to use the sets only once; so two years after the Reagans, I had the honour of visiting psychiatric hospital No. 13.

'The purpose of our hospital,' explains Doctor Kaplan - he claims to be a psychiatrist by training - 'is to isolate the patients to protect society... But patients come here of their free will.' So narcomania is a disease, not an offense. I remark that today there seem to be no patients in his hospital. 'It's their walk time' is his answer. I can't see anybody in the courtyard. We continue with our inspection. The rooms are small but clean; the beds are made with quilts neatly tucked in. The place has a near deserted look. In the corridors, we cross three or four oldish ladies who seem more like the inmates of an old people's home than a deaddiction centre.

- They are alcoholics, my host stammers. We treat alcoholics too.

- But the hospital is empty, doctor!

- We are reorganising everything. Democratisation, you know. And then, adds Kaplan, narcomanics are still not used to the idea of coming in freely and getting themselves treated in an open establishment.

As we run out of conversation, I ask how many narcomanics have AIDS.

- There was one case.

- One case in the whole of Russia?

- No, in the whole of the former USSR.

Did Dr. Kaplan detect a note of sarcasm. 'Well,

right now there is only one but this is just the beginning,' he corrects himself.

SHADOW BOXING

Double speak, fake dispensaries, projecting drugs as an offense - the embers of a despotism on its last legs, proof that this chapter of history is coming to a close? Since the summer of 1991 when free debate was allowed in the Russian Parliament, some liberal deputies formed a human rights committee and have been fighting against the administrative internment of narcomanics in prophylactoriums; they have the support of the International Commission on the Helsinki Agreements for the respect of freedom in Europe. In the autumn of 1991 the latter informed the Russian government that the labour medical prophylactoriums (LTP in Russian) violated human rights as in reality internment was not on medical but administrative grounds. The Russian Ministry of Interior, overseeing the LTP's immediately responded by renaming them; from LTP's they became 'institutions of social reform'. The inmates were restored their civil rights and their forced labour was remunerated at a meagre fifty roubles a month. Colonel Rudolf Voljenine, the man in charge of all prophylactoriums (now renamed reformatoriums) in Russia, says without batting an eyelid that his patients are henceforth free to do anything ...except leave without being fully cured. In other words, they have to stay there for at least two years.

During my visit to prophylactorium No.2 in Moscow in June 1991, Voljenine regretfully admitted that discipline had become lax; under pressure from deputies and the press, he had been forced to release a few hundred narcomanics as the grounds for their internment seemed too flimsy. It upset the Colonel to speak about these patients, 'Do you realise, soon they'll be demanding a lawyer!' The unhappy colonel and the votaries of repression have another reason to be distressed. The Russian parliament's human rights committee has succeeded in getting a law voted by which taking drugs is no longer an offense. In the prevailing parliamentary chaos, the abolitionists scored this unexpected though inconsequential victory as using drugs may no longer be illegal but having them in one's possession is. Impossible to implement, this symbolic piece of legislation will probably be repealed. Comments Igor Nikiforov, narcotics expert with the Ministry of Health, 'The fight against narcomanics is far too serious to be left to politicians. All professionals are in favour of the repression of all drugs, without distinction. With Russia going through a period of transition, this is hardly the time to go about legalising drugs.'

A transition to what? In all likelihood, to status quo.

And so in the tumultuous aftermath of communism, we have yet another example of Potemkinism. This seems to be the fate of all reforms debated in Russia. Speech is free, but that does not change the facts. Call it whatever you like - prophylactorium or reformatorium - it still remains a labour camp where those who disturb social order are interned. Using drugs is not a crime, but users are put behind bars for having drugs in their possession. As far as the repression and treatment of narcomanics is concerned, the militia not the medical corps still calls the shots. Loquacious parliamentarians and verbose journalists discuss ad infinitum 'vast transition strategies' in Moscow while the Nomenklatura still intact holds on to power. In Russia, everything has changed and nothing has changed. Especially not the KGB.

THE KGB SAVED!

'That you can enter the KGB is proof that democratisation is under way!' Even more extra-ordinary, I think to myself, is my being able to leave the place alive. The USSR is no more and things have really changed in Russia. For one, the KGB has changed its name. Since January 1992, it has been rechristened the Ministry of Public Security of Russia. Though everyone in Moscow continues to say KGB and perhaps they are not wrong. General Nikolaï Ermakov is delighted with his little welcome ploy, one he has undoubtedly tested on earlier visitors. Is Ermakov his real name? Chubby, pink cheeked and blue eyed, he has a tuft of blond hair brushed up above his forehead. Dressed in a grey suit and white shirt, he has an air of elegance hard to find in Russia. We sit on opposite sides of a long narrow table. Next to me is the interpreter; facing me, the General with his two aides, Iouri Motsak and Dyourabek Arminov. Pseudonyms, I presume. The aids too are dressed in grey. They seem to stick together as if part of an inseparable trio. Today, it is my turn to do the questioning. The decor is neutral, the furniture down to a minimum with the inevitable green imitation leather so dear to Russian bureaucracy. The trio before me is in charge of the 'repression of contraband and narcotics' for the whole of Russia.

Why on earth has the Russian Secret Service opened its doors to me? The reason is simple: thanks to the fight against drugs, the KGB is trying to refurbish its image. The General starts speaking, 'The

Russian intelligence service, conscious of its obligations to mankind as a whole, is fighting with all its might against the universal scourge of drugs. We are a completely disinterested party, we are fighting first and foremost against the "Afghan transit".' The Afghan transit is carrying drugs produced in Afghanistan and Pakistan to West European consumers; the General insists the canabis is 'produced and consumed outside Russia'. Fifteen tons of 'grass' had been seized in 1991. I point out that it was only cannabis. 'Afghan grass is very dangerous because its highly concentrated,' retorts Ermakov. 'Russia is acting in a true spirit of abnegation. All the peoples of the world must unite to resist "white death".' This happens to be a favorite expression of the General, one he often repeats.

From Moscow's point of view, the 'international war against drugs' has a positive side. The General could certainly not have bought his suit in Russia. Ermakov makes it a point to attend any conference or seminar on drugs, wherever it be held. He shows great alacrity in signing agreements with foreign governments and intelligence agencies. He has an 'excellent' professional rapport with his American colleagues; his exchange of information with the Scandinavians is 'excellent' too. In short, thanks to the war against drugs, the KGB is back in business, this time as an almost respectable, legitimate partner.

The war against drugs is also proving useful as a means to survive 'democratisation' in Russia. In the new Republics of the ex-USSR most attached to their independence cooperation with the authorities in the fight against drugs is excellent, says the General. 'We are fighting against the separatists!' In Central Asia where grass and poppy grow in abundance the 'separatists' are trying with the help of the mafia to create drug manufacturing and processing enclaves. So the KGB is protecting the virtue of its citizens, the health of its young people, the West against narcomanics and ... whatever remains of the Empire. What will become of Russia without her four hundred thousand reconverted KGB agents? And what will become of her mammoth bureaucracy without such a noble international cause?

I cannot leave this 'great establishment' without one last toast. The cognac here is much better that the one I got in Prison No 3. As for the drug addicts, they have become the pawns in a game they do not understand. A game the Americans are playing to extend their 'world order.' For the Russians it provides the proverbial scapegoat and serves as an alibi to perpetuate 'internal order.'

17

THE OPIUM WARS

A slight breeze caused the waters of the Pearl River
to swell. As the first rays of the sun filtered through
a blackbird began to sing. It was five o'clock in the
morning and Zhao Lei, the commissioner of police,
leapt out of bed. The rains had stopped for a while;
Canton was hot and sticky. A southerly wind was
blowing towards Hong Kong. Just what we were
waiting for, said Zhao Lei to himself.

At five thirty Zhao Lei was already in his office.
He called his superior Xigong; the old sage told him
the stars were propitious.

Six o'clock. A hundred policemen began loading
traditional wooden casks - of the kind used to carry
and measure opium in the past - on covered lorries.
Where did Zhao Lei get these ancient relics from? Or
did he have them made specially for the occasion?
When the convoy reached the banks of the Pearl River,
the policemen unloaded their cargo opposite Shiamen
island - an old French concession. The casks were
arranged in a pyramid. A second convoy brought
more policemen in full costume complete with white
gloves and visors.

Zhao Lei was jubilant though the wind still worried him. Were it to change its direction and blow over the city, the whole operation would turn into a fiasco. At this stage Zhao Lei could not afford any mistakes; he had staked his career on the success of this operation, having received the green signal to go ahead a few days ago from none less·than the Prime Minister, Li Peng.

At six o'clock that morning, Canton's inhabitants awoke to the news of the coming event, broadcast in Cantonese and Pekinese over the local radio stations. Loud speakers placed strategically at all the cross roads imperiously enjoined the people to collect on the banks of the Pearl River at three o'clock in the afternoon.

At the appointed time, at least one million Chinese had gathered along the banks of the river. Zhao Lei himself lit the oil cans placed at the foot of the pyramid. And in this manner, reenacted, down to the minutest detail, the historic exploits of his far off predecessor, Lin Zexu, the Emperor's police chief in Canton.

In March 1839, Lin Zexu had destroyed twenty thousand crates of opium, confiscated from British merchants. Zhao Lei, though, was more modest. On the 20th of July, 1991, he was content burning ten tons of opium and a hundred kilos of pure heroin, seized at Yunnan on the Burma border. This was the best his men could do in spite of his orders to seize the maximum possible. It had not been easy convincing the Prime Minister about the need to burn the drugs. Some of Li Peng's advisors felt opium and heroin had both medicinal and commercial value. It would be a pity to destroy what could be sold. Nevertheless, Zhao Lei managed to get his way; he got the better of his tolerant detractors just as Lin Zexu had done in the past. 'The government,' Zhao Lei told me, 'had to show the people it would not tolerate drugs. A grand gesture was required. Fire would purify the nation.'

The wind did not change its direction. So the crowd was spared the noxious fumes of burning opium. As people watched, some were reminded of the time when opium was smoked freely; some, who had never smelt the drug before, developed a taste for it. That day marked the beginning of a new opium war. Radiating confidence, Zhao Lei told me, 'We will win this war in two years.'

THE BANQUET

Commissioner Zhao Lei has the smooth, fresh complexion and authority that age and endurance seem to confer in China. Like all communist leaders, he is a survivor. Only he knows how he lived through the 1949 'liberation', the 'Great Leap Forward', the smashing of the Gang of Four, the Tiananmen massacre and countless other Chinese tragedies; this is a secret he will never part with. Before Zhao was put in charge of the war against drugs, he had never been abroad. Now he has started travelling. In China, that means a lot. He loves 'to consult and cooperate with others engaged in the international war against drugs.' After Tiananmen, the war against drugs is China's way of bringing herself back into the comity of nations.

Zhao has even been to Lyon to meet his colleagues from the Interpol. However, French food did not agree with him. Perhaps the twenty four course banquet he threw in my honour was his form of subtle revenge; the only delicacies I could recognise were live prawns, holothurians, eels and glutinous rice! In China, any

foreign guest is reason enough for a banquet. As
communist morality forbids serving alcohol at an all
Chinese gathering, such occasions are never missed.
The commissioner downed one glass after another of
rice wine, rounding off each with a resounding *kampei*
(bottom's up), after which he would display the empty
glass to all the guests seated around the table. A drink
with a sixty five percent alcohol content is not considered
a drug in China. Zhao Lei, his face aglow with alcohol,
expounded warmly on Sino-French amity, our past
alliance against fascism and our future struggle against
heroin traffickers. 'We are fighting the third opium
war of Chinese history.' China lost the first war, won
the second and will win the third 'in two years', for
so it has been decreed from the top.

Lin Zexu's auto-da-fé sparked of the first opium
war. The Chinese army and navy were ill equipped
to resist the English. In 1842, they compelled the
Empire to accept opium imported from India, open its
ports to Western traders and transfer Hong Kong to
the English. The war was very much a real one, but
it came, in time, to assume mythical proportions. In
Chinese imagination and ideology, the war symbolises
the clash of a decadent Empire with Western imperialism;
Lin Zexu emerged from all this as a sort of local
Vercingétorix.

Zhao Lei recollects the second opium war perfectly.
He had taken part in it. The Communist Party had
just stepped into power in 1949 and one of its first
resolutions was to wipe out opium and opium addicts
as well as prostitution. 'In the space of just two years
(already!), there was not a single opium addict left in
China', Zhao Lei informs me. Which just goes to show
that a nation can eradicate drugs, if it so chooses. But
at what cost? The commissioner recalls that the task

was much easier then as 'the Communist Party had mobilised the entire population to rally around this great cause'. No one had to go out and search for drug addicts, peddlers or producers. The people would denounce them. The methods used were expeditious: factories were destroyed, stocks burnt and traffickers executed. How many were executed? Zhao doesn't seem to recall the exact figures - 'a few thousand perhaps'. What happened to the drug addicts? In 1950, China supposedly had twenty million addicts. 'We did not have any medicine, but with ideological reeducation and forced labour, all the addicts were cured.' - or they died. In the thirty years that followed, drug addiction was unheard of in China. Zhao Lei says, 'Policeman under fifty were incapable of identifying an addict as they had never seen one and doctors under fifty had never come across a case of venereal disease.' Till the dragon reared its head again.

In 1980, Zhao Lei, an opium war veteran, was called back to duty and became a commissioner. To what does he attribute this sudden outbreak of drugs? 'To liberalism'. In 1980, Deng Xiaoping's government opened the country to Western influence. He had to do so to attract foreign technology and capital; this meant that some evil genies would inevitably find their way back into China. The Yunnan province, situated at the border of the Golden Triangle, thus become a transit point for heroin from Burma to Canton and Hong Kong. Opium is now a thing of the past. Heroin, easier to transport, more expensive and more potent is the new scourge afflicting Chinese society. The use of the drug is still however not very widespread; Zhao Lei informs me that seventy thousand addicts were arrested in 1991. Even he finds the figure to be somewhat on the low side. Statistics in China are always doctored - everyone knows that. Still seventy thousand is a far cry from the twenty million in 1950. Punishment remains what it used to be: death for traffickers and forced de-addiction for addicts.

Who are the addicts? 'Independent shopkeepers and cooperative bosses for the most part,' replies Zhao Lei. In short, capitalist entrepreneurs. 'They want to be fashionable and end up becoming heroin addicts.' These sections of the population are particularly vulnerable because they are 'individualistic'; on the other hand, workers in the public sector, who share a feeling of' community solidarity' and participate collectively in 'building socialism,' are immune to temptation. Somewhat farfetched, you may say. Nevertheless this is how the Chinese express themselves, in a language that has remained impervious to time and outside influences. The new opium war is thus an ideological war to defend socialism against the perils of opening out to the world and against the temptation to individualism.

THE CURE

Traffickers get a bullet in the back of their neck and drug addicts, forced de-addiction. One can ascertain the number of executions; finding out how effective the treatment is another thing altogether. Executions are public; a collective affair, they usually take place in a stadium. Treatment centres are a carefully guarded secret. One sometimes wonders whether they really exist. I had to wait for months before I was given permission to visit one at Kunming in Yunnan. Obviously, it is a model centre, the kind of which is used for propaganda. Propaganda is an important part of the war strategy against opium - in communist

China, rhetoric about reality is more important than reality itself. The centre was a prison; I met warders, but could not spy a single doctor.

Wang Yugong, the centre's director, explains the three simple principles on which the cure is based: suffering, ideological education and manual labour. During the first fortnight, addicts are severed from their drug and forced, under the constant supervision of a jailer, to study the history of the opium wars. This way they see the link between their own suffering and the suffering of the Chinese people, victims of British imperialism. Once they become historically aware, the addicts are rehabilitated through manual labour. The director introduces me to Miss Mei; she is twenty years old and has almost been cured. 'A pusher lured me into trying heroin,' she intones. 'Soon I became lazy and stopped working. I started losing weight at an alarming rate and my parents went bankrupt buying me drugs.' The mother, an 'individual shopkeeper', gave her daughter away to the police to help her out. 'When I came to the Centre, I weighed only forty kilos.' But Miss Mei did not take long to recover. The director explains obligingly, 'Here we serve four meals a day, and Miss Mei has two bowls of rice with each meal.' Miss Mei, suddenly all excited, chips in, ' We take a bath every day and our bed sheets are changed once a week.' After three months of treatment, Miss Mei will be declared fully cured; in China, all de-addiction cures always succeed in three months.

That heroin addiction could be an illness not just a symptom of guilt is an idea that has never once crossed the minds of my Chinese interlocutors. For them, there is no such thing as drug dependence. They do however acknowledge that a certain number of addicts, after having been treated once, go back to their former ways. What is the rate of failure? Wang Yuguong replies, 'In Kunming, we have a cent per cent success rate.' Yuan Yongyuan, the extremely competent director of the fight against narcotics in Peking, had in fact told me that the rate of failure is eighty per cent. 'The same as in the West', he hastened to clarify. But that is where the comparison with the West ends. For in China, an incurable drug addict is not treated as a sick person who has had a relapse; he immediately becomes a habitual offender. In the case of the first arrest, addicts are treated as victims whom the State must look after, provided they are not traffickers and provided they do not have more than five grams of heroin or fifty grams of opium in their possession. However if they fall back on their former habits after the cure, they become criminals. Then there is absolutely no question of rehabilitating them; they are punished and sent off for two years to a labour camp. Till date, not a single non Chinese has been able to enter these camps where Aids it seems is playing havoc.

IN TOUCH WITH THE MASSES

Commissioner Zhao Lei is never tired of repeating that two years is all they need to win the war against drugs, just like in 1950. I voice my misgivings, citing the failure of the European and American governments. 'Yes, but China has one big advantage over the West: the communist party.' The Party is in touch with masses, and the masses abhor drugs. The police never has to look for drug traffickers, there is always someone to denounce them. The Party listens to the masses but educates them at the same time. Zhao Lei has had 'dazibaos' put up all over China to explain to people how to recognise drugs and drug users. The police is holding an increasing number of street meetings on the subject in the large cities of the South. The Canton auto-da-fé, intended for the edification of the masses, will be repeated elsewhere, with 'traffickers' being publicly executed. School children are now studying the history of the opium wars in great detail and the Party's propaganda machinery is vigorously projecting Lin Zexu as a national hero. The Chinese word for propaganda   has no pejorative connotation: it is the education of the masses so that they can rise to 'socialist modernisation.'

Can one argue with a Chinese commissioner of police? As my interlocutors are great respecters of authority, I was rather wary. Besides, it would be discourteous, considering I had just been feted with a twenty-four course meal. I decided to yield to the urge notwithstanding.

'Opium, you say, comes from Burma; in the 19th century, it came from India. But didn't the Chinese smoke opium much before the British imported it? All the travellers accounts of the last century tell us the use of opium was a common practice before the English had anything to do with it.'

Was the Commissioner going to choke or was he going to have my head chopped off? The Commissioner did neither; instead he gave me a broad smile.

'There were a few Central Asian minorities which did smoke hashish, and some degenerate mandarins and traders took to opium. But when the British started importing it, the nature of the problem changed. It lead to the systematic intoxication of the entire Chinese population.'

What the truth is, no one can tell. The opium war has become more of a myth than historical fact, both in China and in the West. For China, English opium revealed the demonic nature of the West; for Western intellectuals, this war confirmed that capitalism, especially British capitalism, was immoral. The Chinese attitude towards drugs is a reflection of our own. In China, drugs are abhorrent because they come from elsewhere; in the West, they are abhorrent because we consider opium to be an Asian vice; the American government in fact banned opium because it was supposed to come from China. Drugs, as we can see, are always from elsewhere.

To continue with our argument, I asked Zhao Lei whether he knew the ban on opium in 1836 had been preceded by a lively debate in the court of Emperor Daogouang on the possibility of legalising the drug? The mandarins spent two years discussing the issue. A hundred and fifty years ago, they used exactly the same arguments as we do today. The ministers who favoured legalisation emphasized that the Chinese had always smoked opium and nothing would stop them from continuing to do so. They said the opium produced in China was cheaper and of better quality than the opium imported by the English. They concluded that legislation, by encouraging local production, would eliminate English opium from the market; and opium so cultivated could be taxed by the Emperor whose coffers were in any case empty. But it was the votaries of prohibition who had the last word. Their argument had a moral authority which pleased the sovereign: 'the Chinese do not need to take drugs'. The rest is history. The English army intervened and the Emperor submitted; he no longer had the means to win his war against drugs and the Chinese got used to English opium. It does seem that they did need the drug after all.

Zhao Lei obviously knew all about the 1836 debate which took place in the Chinese court. However, he interprets it differently. The Emperor, he says, was defeatist and those ministers who favoured legislation were traitors. Fortunately, commissioner Lin Zexu had saved China's honour. For Zhao Lei, there is only one way to contain drugs: the choice is between war and capitulation, and Lin Zexu is his spiritual mentor.

Unlike in 1839, the Chinese government did not have to fear international reprisals after the 1991 auto-da-fé. In point of fact, the ban on drugs - which put China at the fringe of the international community one hundred and fifty years ago - has today allowed her to take her place in the comity of nations. It is also a convenient way to forget that a regime so concerned for the health of its people was the same that fired on the students at Tiananmen Square, that night in June, 1989. How many traffickers will Zhao's men execute for China to win the new war against opium and avenge the defeat she met at the hands of the British? No one will ever get to know how many were hanged and how many reeducated through ideology.

DRUGS AND TOTALITARIANISM

In China, the war against drugs seems to be all the more a pretext for repression as opium cannot be dissociated from her memories of the past, and her present ideology. Opium addicts are particularly obnoxious to the Marxist regime because 'they do not contribute to the edification of socialism, as they are lazy or traders who have become rich.' At least this is what we are told. The existence of opium addicts negates not just the world's last communist regime, but also national unity, a concept much older than

Maoism. For centuries, Peking has tried to force unity on a heterogeneous people - political unity on diverse nations, a common language in place of the many local dialects and uniformity of thought in the name of Confucianism or Marxism. China's past and present are based on this constant tension between centrifugal provinces and Manchu or Marxist despots; the latter through sheer force of propaganda have never let up their efforts to impose a mythical union. 'China has to be united if she wants progress' is a slogan oft repeated in communist China. The facts however have never borne this out.

I had a taste of this abhorrence for duality when I applied for a visa to pursue my enquiry on drugs in China in February 1992. Getting the visa was by no means easy. In my visa application I had stated that I was both a journalist and an economist. The Chinese consul had some difficulty with that; he finally explained to me when the visa was granted after much waiting that 'one cannot be two things at the same time'. In Chinese official thinking, duality is not understood: that an individual can function in different capacities, have a multifaceted personality or express opinions which are different from the norm is just not accepted.

As a result, there can be no one more intolerable or dangerous for a totalitarian regime than opium addicts. Apart from their personal pathology, they represent duality and the possibility to escape society's norms. By treating drug addicts as deviants who have to be rehabilitated or criminals who have to be sentenced to forced labour, the Chinese government only reveals its innermost nature and its rejection of any form of dissidence; it does not treat addiction.

18

THE SAMURAI BETRAYAL

In principle, governments are not averse to the use
of drugs; sometimes, they even distribute them. During
the war against the United States, the Japanese
government prescribed a heavy dose of meta-
amphetamine for their suicide-pilots, the Kamikaze, in
order to boost their morale before they flew off on
their death missions. Was this powerful 'stimulant'
discovered in Japan in the forties more potent than
the patriotic mix of ether and red wine given to French
soldiers who fought the First World War, one wonders.
But to get back to our story, while meta-amphetamine
was being prescribed at home, the Japanese authorities
in China were distributing opium to the Chinese to
sap their will to resist. So amphetamine it was for the
colonisers and opium for the colonised; the former
were administered a stimulant, the latter a sedative.
Towards the end of the war, Japanese arms factory
workers too got their daily dose of amphetamine. The
fact that the drug was made in Japan - a national drug,
if you will - is not immaterial, as what follows will
reveal.

Once the war was over, large stocks of meta-amphetamine lay rotting in military depots. Chemists decided to grab them and sold amphetamine under the brand name of *Philopon*, attributing to it all kinds of beneficial properties, fatigue relief in particular. There is no doubt about it, in the post war 'zero years', Japan's citizens were fatigued. As a result, *Philopon* became a national passion, consumed by all sections of the people; writers would idealise it and fall in love with their syringes. This ardour continued till 1953, 'the year of national recovery'; thereafter began a phase of high economic growth. In the same year, a Tokyo schoolgirl was killed by a psychopath, 'under the influence of *Philopon*,' - that at least was the verdict of the press. Public opinion turned against meta-amphetamine. One simplistic explanation for the about turn in public opinion could be that the Japanese had taken to a new intoxicant - workaholism. Whatever be the case, the schoolgirl's murder was the reason given for banning *Philopon*.

Curiously enough, exactly the same thing happened in 1982 when *Philopon* addiction was once again on the rise. A certain Fukugawa committed a heinous crime similar to the one in 1953. Once again, the crime was attributed to the fact that its perpetrator was under the influence of drugs. The Fukugawa affair sparked off a wave of denunciations against drug addicts, making the use of repression all the more easy. It came at a convenient moment, as it nipped in the bud whatever vague desire for tolerance some Japanese psychiatrists began to show. The Fukugawa affair, explained journalists, psychiatrists and policemen in a rare show of unity, proved that drugs were not harmless and that each and every addict was a potential criminal.

Since 1953, *Philopon* has thus been banned: producing, selling or using even minute quantities constitute a crime liable to several years of imprisonment - at the time of the first arrest, the sentence could be anything from one to three years. Thanks to these harsh measures, I was told, the police needed only one year to eradicate the *Philopon* epidemic from Japanese society. This is the 'Japanese model' and the official story of the victorious struggle against drugs as recounted to me forty years later by Yoichi Furuya, the Director of the anti-drug squad of the national police.

PRISON IS THE ONLY CURE

Furuya looks like a modern day Samurai; forty years old, crew cut, white shirt, a sober bureaucrat not given to introspection, he is the perfect cog in the apparently smoothly turning wheel of Japanese society. The Tokyo national police headquarters are just like any other office in Japan: overcrowded, dilapidated and disorderly. 'The only possible response to drugs is zero tolerance, police repression and prison,' says Furuya. The most repressive countries of South East Asia, Singapore and Malaysia, have drawn their inspiration from the Japanese model, except that in Japan there is no death penalty for traffickers. Public opinion does not demand it, internment is enough in Furuya's view. All the rest is literature. In Japan, sociologists and psychoanalysts do not speak about drugs; psychiatrists rarely refer to them; addiction is first and foremost a matter for the police.

In 1957, Japan had to face a new epidemic; this time it was heroin. It was quelled 'through harsh measures' and was, according to Furuya, totally eradicated in 1963. In Japan, there is nothing subtle

about the war against drugs. Addicts are not sick, but
criminals. Unlike in the West, what addicts have to
say is of little interest. In fact if Furuya is to be
believed, most addicts are 'truck drivers who do not
want to fall asleep at night, bar girls, pimps, blue
collar workers and the jobless' - nothing romantic
about them.

- How does the police recognise them?

- *Philopon* users are restless; they have sunken
cheeks and scrawny legs, and the needle marks are
visible.

However, usually there is no need to hunt for
addicts; more often than not, someone gives them
away to the area police station, the *koban*. A *koban* is
really a tiny sentry box for policemen on beat; by
extension, the word has come to mean the policemen
who patrol the city, look after neighbourhood security
and check deviance with the help of idle matrons.
Addicts can also be reported by doctors who are
required by law to declare all addicts coming to them
for treatment to the police authorities. The police then
has the right either to have patients imprisoned or to
make them undergo a forced cure in one of the few
specialised treatment centres. A treatment centre is not
very different from a prison. The treatment given is
immediate severing from the drug, group therapy of
some kind (this is a recent innovation) and nothing
more. In Japan, there is no question of maintenance,
methadone or harm reduction, as is the case in
England or the Netherlands.

It is hardly surprising then that drug addicts stay
clear of doctors and do not for the most part want
to do anything to get deaddicted. The statistics published
by the Ministry of Health speak volumes: in 1990 the
number of addicts who went in for voluntary deaddiction

to treatment centres was two heroin addicts and five hundred and eighty-seven *Philopon* users. On the other hand, fifteen thousand people were imprisoned in 1991 for *Philopon* mania, one thousand five hundred for using hashish and about a hundred for using cocaine. The Japanese have shown themselves to be patriotic and protectionist even in their choice of drugs - they are faithful to the national drug and wary of exotic ones.

IN THE NAME OF HARMONY

Takemitsu Hemmi is a psychiatrist, one of the few in Japan to take an interest in drug addiction; he is also very well known in the country because of his frequent television appearances to talk about drugs. What does Hemmi feel about the police monopoly over the treatment of drug addiction. He can live with it; he too thinks that addiction is not an illness but an offense. It does seem as if, in today's world, the objective alliance between psychiatrists and the State is more common than confrontation.

To get back to Hemmi, drug addiction is not an illness but a 'reversible behavioural pattern'. Until now Hemmi's analysis is similar to that of the votaries of drug liberalisation. But the similarity ends here. For he says that such lamentable behaviour must be treated, Japanese style. Because addicts are responsible for their addiction, all that is required for them to be treated - note that Hemmi says treated and not cured - is to sever the drug by putting addicts in a drug free environment such as a prison cell or a specialised psychiatric hospital. The psychiatrist is not only refusing to make a distinction between hospital and prison but also sees imprisonment as the beginning, and very often the end, of therapy and rehabilitation. Is there anything to attenuate the disorders and suffering of withdrawal? *Philopon*, explains Hemmi, does not cause any dependence. He supplies me with statistical proof: in 1991 for the whole of Japan only seven really dependent addicts were treated. Only seven, no more no less! And all of them had returned from abroad, where they had developed a taste for LSD and heroin. Concepts such as dependence and withdrawal are absent in medical colleges in Japan, adds Hemmi. They do not exist for the Japanese. The only Western contribution in Japan which Hemmi was instrumental in bringing in was group discussions among former drug addicts. He was the man to have introduced group discussions in psychiatric hospitals but has yet to extend them to the prison. For Hemmi, there is no need for a special dispensation for drug addicts in prison. Besides, the results of imprisonment are remarkable - 'all drug addicts leave prison cured.' This proves the reversible and non pathological character of *Philopon*. Some relapses have been observed but these are 'habitual criminals' and not pathological cases. One factor which contributes greatly to reestablishing drug addicts is the social environment. The repressive attitude of Japanese society towards drugs contributes to the addict's return towards normalcy.

How does Hemmi explain the different approaches to treating addiction in Japan, France and the United States? It is a matter of culture, replies the psychiatrist. From times immemorial, Japan has been a tribal society where individual will has been subordinated to the harmony of the group. Addicts, because they disturb harmony, must immediately be removed from society or isolated. They must be made to feel guilty for having broken the harmony; the role of the policeman or the psychiatrist is to make them understand this. Once they have been made to understand where their responsibility lies, they will of their own accord stop using drugs. Besides, adds Hemmi, Japanese society as a whole is agreed upon these principles. What better proof of this than the fact that most drug addicts are reported to the police by their parents, neighbours or friends.

Then what is the point in having psychiatrists if they say the same things as the police? For Hemmi, the role of the psychiatrist is to fulfill the role of the sociologist. The psychiatrist draws the attention of Japanese media to the relationship that may exist between addiction and social conditions. It is no accident that the Japanese have a predilection for a drug that is a stimulant not a sedative. *Philopon* induces higher levels of activity; it is a productive drug, a reflection of Japanese society as a whole. Japanese addicts are not out of consonance with modern society; they are in fact an advanced caricature of capitalism. The truck driver and the Guinza hostess inject *Philopon* to work harder; they do not seek to be different, nor are they on the look out for thrills. Their behaviour is very much like that of the cocaine sniffing businessmen on Wall Street; it is the very antithesis of the peaceful opium addicts or hashish smokers of Asia. Drug addiction and alcoholism, Hemmi tells us, are fairly new to Japan and represent a break with national tradition. Alcoholism, which is widely prevalent in Japan, started as recently as in the seventies. Westernisation is supposedly responsi-ble for drug abuse in Japan; in the past, the Japanese did not need drugs.

We have just been given a wonderful illustration of scientific and cultural relativism. If Japanese style deaddiction upsets all generally accepted ideas in the West, it is because the effect of a drug is hard to define without referring to the culture in which it is consumed. Drugs are dangerous or innocuous not just because of their chemical composition; a lot has to do with how they are perceived, how the addict is perceived and what is being said about addiction in general.

This eulogy of repression founded on the 'eternal Japan' will thus find favour with those who uphold the 'everything is cultural' hypothesis. I myself was ready to go along with it, when as a precautionary measure, I decided to meet a second psychiatrist who was also an addiction specialist at the Chiba hospital. The second interview made me change my mind. Dr Kiohey Konuma repeated word for word what Hemmi had said; I heard the same arguments, the same statistics, even the same example about the seven dependents who had returned from abroad. Two psychiatrists in such complete agreement could not be just a coincidence; I had been dealing all along with a national ideology.

After I visited the Chiba hospital where addicts are locked up in barred cells next to the mentally ill, I was convinced that it was not social harmony but something else that the police-psychiatrist alliance was trying to preserve in Japan. This something else had little to do with eternal culture and was closely connected with the current policies of the State.

AN IMPERIAL IDEOLOGY

How is it that in Japan only the police talks about drugs? Psychiatrists collude with the police, medical treatment is unheard of, sociologists keep silent and philosophers look the other way; in short the subject is simply not discussed. The only time the issue is raised in the press is to denounce crimes committed under the influence of drugs; intellectuals avoid the question altogether. Why is the drug most commonly used a Japanese one? Why do exotic substances never enter Japan? Though *Philopon* is often made in Taiwanese laboratories, safer than even Japanese ones, it is as Japanese as a Toyota or a Sony assem-bled in South East Asia. Why is protectionism the rule here, be it drugs or the economy? Culture, says Hemmi. Or could it be that the modern State has invented a new national ideology?

It so happens that the repression of drugs in Japan began with the creation of the central State by the emperor Meiji in 1868. This is not a mere coincidence. At the time, Japanese leaders feared that like China their country too would be invaded by English opium. They concluded that a strong centre alone could prevent the import of the drug. Accordingly, the new emperor Meiji did away with the traditional *shoguns* in Kyoto, partly because he suspected they were not doing enough to fight against opium. As soon as he came to the throne, Meiji whipped up a national hysteria against opium through a concerted propaganda campaign; all wild cannabis and poppy which grew naturally in the archipelago was destroyed. This still happens. As there was no word for drug in Japanese, a new word had to be coined, *mayaku*. A translation of 'narcotic', it was first used to designate opium, then opium by-products till finally it came to cover all drugs including cocaine, even though cocaine has a very different effect from opiates. Anything termed as *mayaku* was made out to be diabolical. Since Meiji, the government has considered drug addiction to be a sign of 'Chinese decadence', an attack on the integrity of the Japanese nation, an insult to the imperial system, a betrayal. In this exclusion strategy, it was and still is important to make people believe that drugs come from elsewhere. Actually, the expression 'drunk on hemp' refers to a centuries old tradition. There hasn't been a time when opium wasn't grown in the north of the archipelago and consumed in the pleasure haunts of Edo, the old Tokyo. Meiji banned the drug not because it was an intoxicant but because it could have been imported. What was abhorrent was not so much the drug itself as its possible import; this is true even today. During that period, the State designated several other enemies in exactly the same way: the mentally ill, Korean immigrants and the *Burakumin*, the untouchables, all of whom, like drug addicts, were not 'modern'. They negated Meiji's national vision, they had to be excluded and marked as scapegoats.

Today's criminalisation of drug addicts is the result of pursuing more or less consciously this initial scheme of modernisation and of the State protecting national interests. In Japan, the origin of a drug rather than its toxicity decides whether it should be banned or not. Hemmi says doctors who come in contact with addicts should denounce them. But it is not so straightforward. If the addict is under the influence of opium or marijuana, the doctor is obliged to report the patient to the local dispensary, in other words the police. On the other hand, doctors are free to treat meta-amphetamine users. They can either treat them themselves or refer them to a psychiatric hospital. But they do not have the right to report them to the police, as this would be a breach of medical ethic. Is there any basis for this distinction between opium and marijuana on the one hand and meta-amphetamine on the other? None whatsoever. In fact, marijuana is less potent than meta-ampheta-mine; Japanese doctors know that. But opium and marijuana come from elsewhere, they are *alien*, whereas good old *Philopon* - even when imported from Taiwan - is a completely *made in Japan* product. The ideological nature of the prohibition of drugs explains this hostility of the Japanese towards drug addicts even when they are cured. Criminals who come out of jail are able rejoin the mainstream easily, they have repaid their debt to society. But the drug addict is always a potential traitor.

The modernising State, the imperial system and national identity, these are what the police and psychiatrists are protecting from the temptation of drugs. 'Social harmony' becomes the pretext for imposing uniformity on a society which is as diverse and individualistic as any other. The proof being   that repression has not solved anything. Since the beginning of the nineties, the use of *Philopon* has become more widespread than ever before and Japan is being threatened by a new 'epidemic.' The police commissioner Furuya estimates that the number of *Philopon* users has gone up to a hundred and fifty thousand. And a large number of Japanese schoolchildren have taken to inhaling solvents. 'With it' youngsters are on the look out for their own drug- *Philopon* is too associated with the seedy parts of town to appeal to *yuppies*. Is it going to be cocaine or a new *designer drug made in Japan*? This is the question the *Yazukas* are asking themselves.

The Japanese are in a hurry to become inter-national and enter modernity. Will they succeed beyond expectation, give up their Japaneseness and come closer to the American model of drug addiction?

THE IMPORTANCE OF THE JAPANESE MODEL

The extremely complex relationship the Japanese have
with drugs has given rise to varying interpretations.
Gabriel Nahas, professor of medicine and France's
staunchest advocate of drug prohibition, is convinced
that we should follow the Japanese model. Incidentally,
he happened to be Nancy Reagan's closest advisor on
the subject. Nahas says all the major empires were
destroyed by drugs: opium destroyed India and China,
hashish Islam. Drugs necessarily lead to the decline
of a civilization; drug addiction spreads in the same
way as an epidemic. And epidemics have to be wiped
out. This is one thing the Japanese understood. Thrice
the Japanese government managed to contain and
finally eradicate the evil; amphetamine in the first two
instances, and cocaine in the third.

But how does Nahas explain Japan's inability to
get rid of *Philopon* - whose usage is on the increase
- as well as other drugs that are sneaking in such as
cocaine? The Japanese are becoming prone to moodiness,
he replies; repression has become less systematic and
society is falling apart under the effect of the West.
If Japan is no longer a perfect model for die hard
prohibitionists, where should they turn to? Singapore,
says Nahas: it is the Japanese model with the death
penalty thrown in for good measure.

The much vaunted Japanese experience can be
used by abolitionists too. They could turn around and
say that even an extreme form of repression was
unable to eradicate drug addiction. They could reveal
to what extent national ideologies rather than science
influence rhetoric and shape policies on drugs. They
could show how quickly ideas widely accepted in the
West - biological or psychological dependence,

irreversibility of addiction - crumble when put to the test of comparison.

Policies are justified depending on how the Japanese experience is viewed. The abolitionists say, 'If there is no such thing as dependence, why ban drugs? The decision to take drugs is a personal one; doctors or psychiatrists have nothing to do with it.' The prohibitionists argue, 'If dependence does not exist, it means drugs are a social disorder, for which prison not medical treatment is the correct remedy.'

Every argument, as we can see, has two sides. And, given our current level of knowledge, science cannot help us in determining which is the right policy.

19

THE STATE UNDER THE INFLUENCE OF ...

Where have I gone wrong? For months on end, I   have been looking for a 'French Model' - both the Government and the Interministerial Mission for the Fight against Drug Addiction (MILT) claim it exists - but I just can't seem to find it. The reason is simple: there is no such model. What passes off as the French model is really a toned down version of the American model, couched in socio-psycho-cultural discourse. What we have to analyse is the discourse; perhaps deconstructing à la Derrida is the right way to go about understanding what lies hidden behind the civilian face of a State at war. By deconstructing State discourse on drugs, we are, in point of fact, getting at the essential nature of bureaucracy, in other words the social group which appropriates the State and conceals its corporative interests behind a screen of morality.

Let us now move to the scene of action. Whenever the State intervenes, the locale is of paramount importance. The American drug Czar has his office near the White House. The French Czarina Georgina Dufoix is at a stone's throw from the Elysee Palace; the Interministerial Mission for the Fight against Drugs which she heads since 1992 is located in a private mansion on the Faubourg Saint-Honoré. In the State's hierarchic symbolism, location is indicative of rank. In Paris as in Washington, a private mansion raises the fight against drugs to the level of a national priority. I am not exaggerating. The choice of the location has a story behind it. In 1990, a vague report on drug addiction was hastily drawn up and signed by the Mayor of Strasbourg, Catherine Trautmann. As usual, the report made a series of recommenda-tions - the ENA had taught us that all reports must contain some recommendations at the end. The most concrete conclusion of this report was that the MILT should be shifted to a prestigious locality to show the utmost importance the French government attached to the fight against addiction. The State readily provided the money required. And thus the bureaucrats in charge of the fight against addiction, including those who had drawn up the report, left their make-shift office on rue Saint Dominique to move into the private mansion on the Faubourg Saint-Honoré. The war against drugs does not only claim victims: the men fighting the war are housed in style.

However, in this case, it so happens that most of the men are women. Though most drug addicts in France are men, all the top government positions in the war against drugs have gone to women. In 1974, Monique Pelletier called for a certain amount of discretion in regard to cannabis. Then in 1987, Michèle Barzach liberalised the sale of syringes. Rightist governments have on the whole shown greater tolerance for drugs than the present day leftist government. In 1990, we saw the advent of Georgina Dufoix; with her, the socialists fell in line with the American model. All Georgina Dufoix

has to say on the subject of addiction is that it is very
sad. We can thus give her the go-bye and turn our
attention to what Geneviève C., a sociologist who founded
the Mission and later shaped its course of action, has
to say. Is it by coincidence that there are so many women?
Coincidence or not, the French model is much less martial
than its American counterpart. The State may be waging
a war on drugs but the rhetoric, far from being warrior-
like, is 'social'.

A NATIONAL IDEOLOGY

According to Geneviève C., there is a French way to
resist drugs. So we are resistants and we are French.
Very much in the same vein, a Lyon magistrate who
has specialised in narcotics told me, 'Abandoning the
war against drugs is like the Munich pact, giving in
to the Nazis.' The metaphor is misplaced; drugs are
not a new Nazi creation, they are just plants. But such
metaphors are dangerous for they have a strong emotional
appeal: those who don't support the MILT and it's war
against drugs are traitors. The MILT, I am told, is following
a truly French path, which makes it non American.
A little anti-American rhetoric for effect does no harm,
especially when one has aligned oneself with the United
States. But isn't our policy a copy of the American model?
'It only looks that way.' replies Genviève C. 'Don't think
Washington can dictate our laws to us.' As I still can't
see why the French war against drugs is different from
the American one, she explains for my benefit.

First, and this is significant, she feels drugs can never
really be totally eradicated. All that can be done is
to contain their effect and protect the most vulnerable
sections, teenagers in particular.

That is all very well, but how is the State the best

placed to protect teenagers? What are parents for? And from what and whom are we protecting our children? The enemy is never named, but some obscure malefic force is always hinted at.

The second characteristic of the French war on drugs is prevention. In the classical trilogy - prevention, care, repression - the French method stresses the importance of the first - at least in principle. But actual figures show that the Ministry of Health allocated to drug addiction just the amount needed to run a small provincial hospital. This when thirty thousand cases of addiction have been recorded. But then reality is of no consequence; we are living in an age of State showmanship. Prevention is a positive, reassuring theme; it is very much in conformity with the secular image of the French citizen and the Republican state. Besides, Geneviève C. is appealing to the citizen's sense of duty. If citizens are not behaving in a responsible fashion, it is undoubtedly because 'the State has not educated them enough', she says. The policeman or the soldier represent the American government in its war against drugs; in France, we look to the schoolteacher. Drugs are viewed as some kind of malevolent enemy whose harmful effects education can undo. Geneviève C. says teachers and young people have to be made aware of the need to refuse drugs. An aware French person or one who has been made aware will never take drugs. Their conscience will not permit it.

Am I supposed to conclude from this that abolitionists have no conscience? I seem to have hit the nail on the head. Geneviève C. brings home to me the fact that the votaries of liberalisation are economists (Milton Friedman in the United States) and jurists (Francis Caballero in France), all of whom work in soulless, cold, non emotive disciplines. That may very well be, but how can we assume that it behoves a republican, secular state to assume the responsibility of administering our souls just as schoolteachers had been given charge of our upbringing? Obviously the times have changed and so has the rhetoric. We no longer talk in terms of moral science or civic instruction. Geneviève C. speaks of norms and prohibitions without which society cannot function. The State has taken to using a strange brand of psychoanalytic mumbo jumbo; it is no longer content to just educate, now it also cures. Assuming society does require a certain number of prohibitions to function, how and on what basis must the State decide them? Just because we no longer have priests does not mean bureaucrats should start looking after public morality.

Am I getting carried away by deconstructionism? I don't think so; in fact, we have come to the heart of the matter: the war against drugs is a means to relegitimise - consciously or unconsciously - the modern state. The government has created a 'problem', drug addiction, which has been described as a 'social plague'. A problem calls for a solution, which means the State has to intervene. State intervention in turn needs funds and a policy - in short a leadership. Once all these factors come together, the State can begin it's show. In France, we happen to have a leftist State and the socialists have shown themselves to be far more repressive than the right. What makes the war against drugs a specifically left war? Geneviève C.'s answer ('this is the activist in me speaking' - *sic*): 'Drugs are a symptom of an individual malaise no doubt, but also, and more significantly, of a society obsessed with performance.' Drug addiction is not what it was in 1968 (at the time the left was in favour of liberalisation). Then it meant withdrawing from society, now it shows a desire to integrate into the capitalist system and succeed. So capitalism and competition are the reasons for the new wave of addiction! If this is true, why is it that everyone living in a competitive society is not addicted to drugs? And why are those in non-competitive societies such as Russia taking to drugs in such a big way?

Another leftist argument often heard is this: 'Our publicity campaign is leftist. The right is trying to create a fear psychosis, but leftist publicity is based on solidarity and is sensitive to public opinion, Sensitive to public opinion? According to a study financed by the MILT to justify it's existence, the French fear addiction even more than they do unemployment, immigrants and pollution. Solidarity? MILT's slogan is 'Help them to say no!' with a phone number at the bottom. The calls on this number get relayed to various associations with a view to create 'horizontality' and 'social bonds'... Leftist anti-drug rhetoric is abounding in woolly headed sociological considerations where new words mask ignorance. Shibboleths like 'society', 'social' and so on and so forth are perhaps the left's way of avoiding the use of the term socialism.

In 1991, the 'leftist campaign' is estimated to have cost millions of francs. It accounted for the lion's share of the MILT's budget, leaving little for more beds in deaddiction centres. The main aim of the campaign was to remind the public that the State does exist and that it is there to protect the public not from danger but the fear of danger. In the early eighties Holland had, much before other European countries, tried out an anti-drug publicity campaign with disastrous results. Many people were frightened unnecessarily whereas the most vulnerable sections were drawn irresistibly to experiment with the forbidden fruit. Much wiser from their campaign, the Dutch decided there was absolutely no point alarming the public at large about a risk which only concerned one per cent of the total population. They felt it would be a better idea to train teachers to deal with addicts in schools. But how can mighty France accept that it has something to learn from a small country like Holland.

To continue this exercise in deconstructionism; all this while we have been looking at the basic premises on which state intervention is based. Now we shall turn our attention to the State's modus operandi, as this will shed further light on the French 'style' of functioning.

THE CONSULTATION THEATRE

French civil servants have a phobia about showing their authoritarian side. As far as possible, they avoid confronting issues and decision making is a positive anathema for them. That does not stop them from being convinced of the superiority of public intervention. How do they reconcile a Jacobine tradition with their reluctance to tackle issues squarely? Administrations have a time tested formula for this - *consultations*. Civil servants spend most of their time consulting with and mobilising elusive allies. In the best of cases, they get their policies implemented by those who stand to gain from them, leading to a system of corporative management of the State. The war against drugs is part and parcel of this tradition. But with whom is the State to liaise?

In Holland, an addicts union interacts with municipal authorities. This is not the case in France; our civil servants liaising with drug addicts is taxing the imagination too far. French administrations are happiest dealing with associations. Anything with a vaguely associative character immediately receives the blessings of the French government - and funds too. As the MILT does not really have the means to come into contact with the sections most vulnerable to drugs, it liaises with youth and popular education associations such as the Fédération Léo Lagrange, the Fédération de l'Education nationale, the Jeunesses ouvrières et chrétiennes - associations close to the Socialist Party.

Geneviève C. who also happens to be the secretary general of the Fédération Léo Lagrange - a breeding ground for activists and a sinecure for the socialist party - has thus signed a charter with eight major associations (one of them being her own of course) to carry on the 'Fight for life', a massive battle waged against drugs at the 'grassroots'. Five hundred thousand people, she tells me, have been mobilised. Five hundred thousand people chasing an addict or peddler, the thought is enough to frighten anyone. But we may rest assured, 'the fight for life' is in name only as the major 'popular' associations are associations on paper. Youth and social work associations have fallen into decay over the last years; the number of activists and member subscriptions have virtually dried up. 'Mobilisation' in the war against drugs is a myth. However it is music to the ears of those in charge of these dying associations who, thanks to the State, get funds and a fresh lease of life.

Where does all the money go? In 1991, a group of young people, as they are called at the MILT, were given fifty thousand francs to put up a rap show at Bagneux. Another group of young people in Toulouse were given ten thousand francs to set up a boxing ring in the basement of a building where youngsters congregate. All jointly managed projects are similar in nature - modest and empathetic. However what does all this have to do with drugs? The relationship, I am told, is obvious. Boxing and rap give 'meaning' to the existence of these youngsters, who without them, would have been tempted to try out drugs. Which bring to mind the cold showers and exercise recommended at the beginning of the century to protect teenagers against the evils of orgasm.

In point of fact these schemes never reach the addicts; nor do the publicity campaigns reassure their parents. There is nothing surprising about that considering the MILT doesn't have a clue as to who the addicts could be. I am not making this up, it is quite true. According to the MILT's director, there are about a million drug addicts in France. This is an approximate figure arrived at by cross-checking the number of patients visiting specialised centres with the number of people charged by the police. However other statistics indicate that eighty per cent of drug addicts have never come into contact with a public institution. In other words the MILT does not know who the addicts are. Another one of those wonderful bureaucratic edifices built on non existent foundations. Our sociologists know more about Touaregs or Amazonian Indians than they do about our suburbs.

Geneviève C.'s answer is to create a 'national observatory for addiction'- one that could acquire a bit of glamour and more funds if it were given a European character. We know that the State cannot set up a new institution without commissioning a feasibility study; so a six hundred page report has been duly drawn up recommending the immediate establishment of the laboratory. The budget has been discreetly tucked away in an appendix; so drug addicts too have their uses.

Suppose we concede that Geneviève C. has a point: prevention is necessary, collaborating with associations is for the best and financing rap and boxing in the suburbs is not entirely useless. Let us concede with her that public opinion wants the State to play an active role. Even then, aren't we running the risk of criminalising drugs. To my mind, prevention would be all the more effective if the State stopped trying to be educator, mentor and jailer all at the same time.

Why then must the war go on? The answer perhaps lies in the fact that professionals of the war against drugs have no desire to see it stop.

THE AFFABLE COMMISSIONER

The MILT is the civilian, intellectual face of the war against drugs that is projected in the media. But the seat of real power lies elsewhere - the Ministry of Interior. Here warlords hungry for inside information mastermind strategies. Here the French administration reveals its true colours - closed, opaque and above the law. It is the best equipped bureaucracy in the world to stonewall investigation. Meeting even a minor civil servant requires months of patient waiting and several politicians to intercede on one's behalf. The only other example of such a closed, brahmanical and arrogant bureaucracy is the Chinese bureaucracy. Even so, it is easier to get an appointment with a high level dignitary in China than with some obscure deputy director in Paris. The French bureaucracy is out of bounds for journalists; even parliament has no control over it. We have the striking example of how in 1992 the Ministry in charge of War Veterans had kept from even the minister a secret file on the Jews - the handiwork of several generations of bureaucrats united by a common passion for secrecy. It can be said in the defense of this bureaucracy so busy keeping everyone in the dark that when it

comes to itself, it is equally in the dark: it is utterly
incapable of assessing its own success and failure and
the economics of its own interventions. But then, French
civil servants are not accountants, they are philosophers,
which absolves them of all responsibility and preserves
their mystique.

Predictably enough, the two hours I spent with
Commissioner D., one of the men in charge of the anti-
drug war, did not reveal much more than what I already
knew. On the other hand, the man philosophised at
length on addiction. I tried to learn from D. the cost
of the war against drugs in France to see how we compared
with the U.S.. D. could give me no answers because
such figures do not exist. The whole idea is to ensure
they do not exist, for if they did it would be clear as
crystal that the amounts being spent were not commensurate
with the results achieved. In France, in the war against
drugs, cost is of no consequence. State thinking cannot
be reduced to mere figures. Mobilising as many as possible
is what counts; petty calculations are meant for traders.
When I asked D. how many were employed and what
the fight against addiction cost the police, the only answer
I got was, 'The traffic policeman who controls traffic
also controls drug addicts, it is one and the same thing.'
I tried again, 'Should a legal distinction be made between
hard and soft drugs so as to concentrate on the more
dangerous narcotraffic operations, as in the Netherlands?'
D.'s reply, ' There is no sense in doing so; the police
is perfectly well equipped to tell the difference between
affluent youngsters who use drugs for the occasional
kicks - let off with a warning - and those who are
so far gone they need treatment.' What he is saying
in other words is that you have to trust the police for
they know best.

But does the police really know best? Going by the meagre quantities of drugs seized, the answer seems to be no. 'Well, it is true that till now only small amounts have been seized; in any case we do not know exactly what is coming into France.' The amounts seized are more indicative of the level of police activity than the size of the market. There is no way of finding out what the total number of drug users is, as hardly any complaints are filed. In any seizure, the important thing is not the amounts seized but the arrest of the dealer. Dealers can easily replace the drugs seized, as supplies are unlimited. On the other hand, men are scarce and are worth much more to cartels than the product being sold.

D. clinches his case for repression with the argument that 'prohibition is necessary'. France seems to be - though why is unknown - a potential market for hard drugs, heroin in particular. We have in France, according to D., a large high risk group in the guise of second generation immigrants; more often than not unemployed, living in ghettos, they have the same social profile as black Americans. Now in spite of all this the figure for heroin addicts in France is relatively low - a hundred thousand or so. Is it because heroin is hard to come by? In the commissioner's own words, 'You can find the stuff all over the place.' However because of prohibition, police repression and stiff legal punishment, potential users are dissuaded from consuming the drug. Fear, not high prices, will keep the addiction explosion at bay.

The commissioner's arguments sound convincing enough, but they are not corroborated by experience outside France. In the United States repression is just as strong but the fear of repression has not deterred users. Whereas in Holland and Great Britain, both more tolerant than France, the number of addicts has not grown.

Isn't the number of potential addicts relatively stable? Repression or tolerance do not seem have much of an impact. The commissioner is embarrassed and comes out with a psycho-cultural explanation, 'The French are different. They are not as rational as the Dutch, who know how to exercise self restraint, but are more law abiding than the Americans'. Accordingly, comparisons are not possible as attitudes towards drugs are determined by national culture. Couldn't it be the other way round? The opposite may well be true. For lack of information on the subject, just about anything will do.

The ultimate reason given for banning drugs and police repression is to protect the French from themselves and the temptation of drugs. We must thank the police for their consideration. Commissioner D. is all affability. Why not just accept what he says and allow the police to interpret the laws as they choose to for our security. In this way we will become passive citizens of a cocoon State and let hardened police officers allow despotism with a human face to flourish. The idea is extremely tempting indeed.

As we part company in front of the gate of the Ministry of Interior, D. decides that it is time for some calculated off the record confidences. For a second, there is a look of panic in the Commissioner's eyes, 'I just hope Europe stays united and the Dutch don't impose their system on us.' The very idea makes the Commissioner shudder. May the police protect us from the epidemic of Dutch tolerance. In order to confer legitimacy on the French war against drugs, Holland has to be the devil incarnate.

THE SUPERCOPS

Roissy airport, 10 o'clock in the morning. Custom officials await the daily flight from Rio eagerly. Every day every flight brings in its haul of cocaine. The officials have scrutinised all the flight lists well in advance; they know who bought their ticket in cash, who paid by cheque; they know which passengers fly too often to be above board, which passengers have funny flight schedules and which passengers are between twenty-five and thirty-five, the care-free age to carry drugs. Very often, the victim's fate has been sealed even before he has stepped down from the plane. As soon as his baggage has been identified, it is sent through an X-ray scanner and the false bottom or hidden compact is immediately detected. He is booked there and then and will be a guest of the Republic of France for the next four years - in prison of course.

What purpose does this game of cops and robbers serve? The customs in France (and this is true in most European countries) seizes a meagre ten to twenty per cent of the total volume of drugs entering the country. The percentage has been going down steadily; today the containers used to pack drugs are impossible to check without jeopardizing international trade. No one is prepared to do this, not even for the war against drugs.

What is the point of having customs checks if eighty per cent of the drugs finally do come in? The official reply I got from a director was this, 'Controls make drugs a risky proposition for dealers; this raises their price. When the market price goes up, sales fall.' This sounds plausible enough but it is not quite as plausible as it sounds. In spite of customs checks, prices do not go up as traffickers simply dilute the drugs to maintain price stability. As a result, sellers' profits rise, drug use remains the same or increases and health hazards are even greater because of the spurious drugs on the market. That is why I had to look for reasons other than the fight against addiction to see why the customs adopt such stringent checks and vest in themselves so much power. They have to safeguard their jobs.

With the European unification in sight and the concomitant free trade, customs officers were faced with massive retrenchment. But thanks to the war against drugs, the Ministry of Finance can justifiably continue to keep them on its rolls. Better still, the war against drugs has given the customs the kind of prestige it had never enjoyed before. The traditional customs officer was a ludicrous figure who chased smugglers. Now, with the war against drugs, he has become the custodian of our mental and physical health, a supercop fighting the Medlin cartel. The customs officer of the future is no longer simply going to search bags. To detect heroin in closed containers, he will be equipped with X ray scanners worth five million francs a piece. These will be delivered in 1993. Like his American colleagues and the police, he will have the right to pose as a fake drug dealer in order to trap the real ones. Adventure at last for the new incorruptible cop.

But how sound are our laws? A law enacted on the 19th of December, 1991 allows customs officers and policemen to actually sell drugs (thereby increasing the number of users) so that they can catch dealers red handed. The bill was passed in a routine manner with no questions asked, showing how effectively debate on the issue has been silenced. At the time, Claude Olievenstein had rightly pointed out that it was a law guaranteed to stifle freedom.

Some twenty thousand civil servants, whose jobs were threatened by economic liberalism, suddenly found themselves back in business, even promoted thanks to prohibition. Is the fervour displayed by the anti-drug professionals - the police and customs - in this dubious war part of a calculated strategy? Whenever I asked about the tangible achievements of the operation, I was told by officials that they had not given it a thought. They were incapable of imagining that there could be another way for they had truly become prisoners of the national anti-drug ideology.

THE JUDGE IS ABOVE THE LAW

Judge Didier L. sits in a cramped office in the Law Courts. A large hand written sheet of paper divided into two columns has been pasted on the door facing him; on one side the Judge has recorded all the abolitionist arguments and on the other his counter arguments. Judge L. is a specialist in the fight against addiction. Who are his enemies - drug addicts, traffickers or the votaries of decriminalisation? For Judge L. abolitionists are hypocrites, especially if they happen to be Dutch. Their tolerance towards marijuana and distribution of methadone are tantamount to sacrificing the addict at the alter of bourgeois peace. Quite true, but does that mean our learned friend prefers the addict to the bourgeois? 'Addicts not the bourgeois society are the real sufferers.' Moreover, the Judge goes on, doesn't bourgeois society have only itself to blame, what with parents abdicating. Suppose we concede that parents and bourgeois society are to blame. In what way does that justify prohibition? Prohibition, the Judge admits, is not the perfect answer, but it still has its merits. Most importantly, prohibition is what addicts want.

Did I hear correctly? The Judge turns psychoanalytical: he says addicts need restrictions. Addicts feel a sense of relief when they are taken into custody or sent to a deaddiction centre. But the argument which really clinches the issue in favour of prohibition is that it buys time - the epidemic is kept in check till it finally subsides of its own accord.

The Judge maintains that abolitionists reveal their ignorance of history when they overlook the fact that the drug menace, even though it exists in an endemic form in all societies, only explodes for specific reasons in specific circumstances. The origins of the current drug epidemic in the West can traced back to the post sixty-eight generation. The disease first appeared in the mid sixties in the United States, then later on in Europe after the cultural destabilisation of our post-industrial societies. In Central Europe and in Russia, it was the collapse of the communist system which brought about the current wave of amphetamines and heroin. In Africa and Latin America the fall in the price of traditional cash crops forced peasants to cultivate the poppy. The war against drugs, for Judge L., is only a policy of containment, so that the epidemic may subside. Any form of liberalisation will only prolong the epidemic. We do not need to win the war, if we can hold out as at Verdun, it is enough. Those who desert are abdicators.

'Are my arguments convincing?' asks the Judge, a little worried. I tell him that his conclusion is, provided one accepts his basic assumptions and epidemic metaphor.

Setting aside strategic considerations of the international war against drugs, we get back to France. Judge L. feels that French abolitionists have, out of ignorance, picked the wrong battle to fight. They do not seem to understand that what they are asking for is already being practiced. 'Nowadays no drug user is ever sent to prison. ' No French judge is going to sentence a hashish user. Heroin users are sent to deaddiction centres; cocaine addicts, in any case, are not likely to stray near the Law Courts. So what we have in point of fact is de facto legalisation at the behest of the public prosecutor and the Law Courts. Laws are just being given the go-bye. Should the abolitionists rejoice over their tacit victory?

We have been told that nobody is sent to prison for using drugs. True, provided one only uses drugs. But most people who use drugs need money to buy drugs; so they become dealers and start selling. So now addicts can be divided into two categories: those who have the money to buy drugs and those who do not. If they have the money, they have nothing to worry about. If they don't, they are caught on charges of drug trafficking. No one ever goes to jail for having used a drug but several tens of thousands of offenders are behind bars for trafficking drugs. The distinction seems fair enough. Those who inflict harm on others are punished, whereas those who harm only themselves are let off. A specious argument, since by pushing up prices it is prohibition which makes the consumer an offender in the first place. The distinction the courts make between users and peddler users has little to do with their capacity to inflict harm on society; it is more a social distinction between those who can afford to buy drugs and those who have to take to crime to buy them. It is also another form of racial discrimination. The Judge confirms this, 'As soon as an addict enters my office, I know exactly whom I am dealing with: an affluent hashish smoker, a small dealer or a big trafficker.'

- Is the dealer more often than not Beur, from the Maghreb or African?
- Yes, ninety percent of the time.

The arms of the law do not extend to drug barons-they live abroad - and users. French justice only seems to be dealing with middlemen who are crowding our courts and prisons. Dealers, illegal immigrants for the most part, are made to pay heavily for the ones never caught. Thousands of illegal immigrants live off peddling in France only because drugs are expensive, and they are expensive because they are forbidden. Which brings us to a paradoxical situation in which the prohibition of drugs actually encourages illegal immigration. Were we to liberalise drugs and sell them at government outlets at a relatively low price, illegal immigrants would no longer have this convenient source of income to bank on.

We should thank the Judge for not implementing the penal code; otherwise a marijuana user could end up serving a ten year sentence. Our laws have become defunct; it is indeed a sad commentary on our times that today we have to depend on the mercy of a benevolent commissioner or judge who can in one look tell the good guys from the bad. This is exactly what happened in the seventies with abortion. Though banned by the law, it was so widespread that both the police and the judges turned a blind eye. But from time to time, a judge would take it into his head to apply the law stringently for reasons more subjective than legal. How much longer do we have to wait for the law to catch up with the times? When will this legal arbitrariness come to an end? And who is opposing change?

The police, the judges will tell you with one voice. A ban not enforced by judges is the surest way of strengthening the power of the police who can in this way use its discretionary powers to hold out a permanent threat against those it wants to keep an eye on. Judge L admits that addicts have been forgotten in this debate as they are but insignificant pawns.

THE STATE'S PSYCHOANALYST

The anti-drug war, as we have seen, employs a host of professionals. We have heard the police and the judges; what do psychoanalysts - indispensable allies of the State - have to say? Among the tribe of psychoanalysists who have latched on to drug addiction, Francis C. seems to have been singled out for State patronage. He happens to be a chain smoker. Doesn't tobacco claim more lives than drugs? 'No doubt about it,' C. acknowledges, 'but tobacco is a drug that has been assimilated by Western culture.' Each civilisation, he explains, generates an indigenous drug which it knows how to handle. The Indians have their coca and the Laos their opium, drugs which are no more disturbing than tobacco is for us. But when drugs from the South find their way to the North, it is 'chemical and cultural invasion' which can only give rise to chaos. That is why opium, which in South East Asia allows opium addicts to integrate into society, is a sign of rejection in our society. By choosing marginal rather than mainstream drugs the Western addict is telling society, 'I do not want to be like you.' Drug addiction, for C., is like a coded message that addicts are sending to adult society. Now who could be better placed than a psychoanalyst to decode this message? 'I treat addicts by restoring to them their right to speak', says C.

This is how the psychoanalyst like the customs officer, the policeman and the judge arrogates the role of the inexorable mediator between bourgeois society and the drug addict. Do psychoanalysts need prohibition to justify themselves? Of course they do, replies C. Had there been no social sanctions addicts would lose their bearings. 'Addicts, like children, need sanctions. Sanctions are part of the education-reeducation cycle; they enable individuals to find their moorings in reality. Laws, decrees C., have a therapeutic value. Moreover, prohibition is morally correct; legalising drugs would mean abandoning addicts to the consequences of a bad choice. Legalising drugs is tantamount to telling the addict, 'You can drug yourself silly if you want to, who cares!' Now most addicts are capable of leaving drugs if they get a patient hearing. In C.'s logic, drug addicts are far more interesting to listen to than non addicts.

C., a psychoanalyst and a representative of the law? Things are not that simple. This prohibitionist psychoanalyst who is paid by the State is in point of fact questioning the established order. The addict is telling us through C. 'I do not like progress.' And C. too believes that progress is detestable. He is therefore suggesting a cure for both the addict and society; he goes all out to condemn mass culture, third world exploitation, the cult of success and performance, individualism, machoism and the fascination for money and power. 'Mankind has to be taken care of through sensitisation!' This is C.'s grand design, financed by the State.

The Association founded by C., the 'Grande Oreille' (Big Ear), receives a couple of million francs from the State. Now why on earth should the State finance such a muddle headed scheme? It is standard practice for democratic States to maintain soft dissidence; mild revolutionary discourse gives the State a semblance of tolerance for which it is willing to pay. C. is evidently not going to change the world. But his championing of prohibition provides national ideology with a 'medical' alibi. Addiction professionals can say and do just about what they want provided they do not question national ideology. In this context, let us not forget the Leon Schwartzenbergincident.Schwartzenbergwasimmediately excluded from the Socialist government in 1988 when he made his reservations about prohibition public. Schwartzenberg had entertained the idea of the State distributing heroin to incurable heroin addicts like in Great Britain. In France, one cannot trifle with the war against drugs.

THE INTOXICATED STATE

We know drug addicts cannot do without drugs but can anti-drug professionals do without the war against drugs? It is hard to say, as the war against drugs seems to have created two kinds of addicts: addicts under the influence of their drug and bureaucrats under the influence of their war. In both cases, their lives seem to revolve around drugs. Addicts think they are helping themselves and bureaucrats think they are helping society. Both seem oblivious to the harm they are doing to themselves and to society. Addicts are ruining their health and bureaucracy is generating violence. Both just go on falling deeper into the trap while pursuing ever elusive goals. Bureaucrats in quest of a nebulous victory continue to stretch the frontiers of their war, deploying a considerable financial, human and military effort. The State then becomes dependent on its war. And so both bureaucrats and addicts are in a chronic State of intoxication - the addict's intoxication being individual whereas that of the State is collective. The deaddiction of the addict is laborious but not impossible. Most addicts willingly give up drugs as they grow older. Deaddicting the State is not that simple: there is far too much social and organisational pressure, there are far too many political, administrative and scientific careers at stake. The State is no longer just a drug user. It has become addicted. Last but not least, both addicts and bureaucrats are governed by emotion; an appeal for reason falls on deaf ears. At the individual level, such behaviour can be tolerated. But when the State starts behaving like this it is a matter for concern.

The best cure for the intoxicated State is called tolerance.

20

THE TOLERANCE
ARCHIPELAGO

Sensitive souls are advised against visiting the Drug Centre on Hope Street in Liverpool. It is located in one of the 'bombarded' quarters of the city. Buildings falling apart, broken windows, unweeded gardens, broken down cars and shady pubs are all reminders of the brutal transition from an industrial economy to the services era. The deserted urban landscape in Liverpool - a victim of its labour traditions - is no different from its counterparts in the United States: Baltimore and Detroit for instance. Liverpool, the Labour party says, has been destroyed by Thatcherism. In fact, it had been ruined much before Thatcherism, just as Detroit had been destroyed before Reaganism, as both these cities were just not able to keep up with the pace of industrial change. Unemployment, boredom and a complete break down of social bonds are the city's chief characteristics - in brief, you have all the prerequisites for drug abuse.

It is eight o'clock in the morning and Doctor Patrick O'Hara gets ready to inject a dose of heroin to his first client. Consultation is free, so too is the heroin. For years on end, the patient - a forty year old white middle class male - has been coming to the clinic every day. After his shot, he will go to work, for he has a steady job. Next client please. This one doesn't seem so far gone. He is happy with a dose of liquid methadone. As a bonus, he is told how to inject himself so that he does not damage his veins. The whole day will be spent distributing drugs to people who seem more or less 'normal' - they are neither coloured nor marginals. Addicts in this part of the world are a far cry from the hagard Surinamiens you find in Amsterdam hanging around buses which distribute methadone.

DRUGS, A FACT OF LIFE

'Don't think,' says O'Hara,'that anyone can just enter my dispensary and ask for a dose of heroin.' What we just witnessed was the culmination of a maintenance programme for those considered incurable. Besides, Liverpool is the most tolerant of all the English cities. And as we are in England, where everything administrative has to be complicated, Liverpool's harm reduction programme is in direct contrast with the British government's national policy of prohibition. As a result, the Liverpool police, which tries to distinguish 'as best as it can' between drug addicts who need to be imprisoned and those who can be handed over to Patrick O'Hara, enjoys an amazing degree of discretionary power in a state of law.

In the presence of a heroin addict being administered his dose O'Hara tells me this is not routine. Drug addicts have to prove their dependence; only after a lengthy legal procedure and endless medical tests are they entitled to get treated as incurable drug addicts. The maintenance programme covers three thousand odd patients. Their average age is high, about forty years; they are white, British and come from either the middle or working class; most of them have some regular professional activity. Those who do not fall under the maintenance scheme are sent to deaddiction camps, as is the practice elsewhere. Like everywhere else, the success rate is poor.

In keeping with the 'drugs, a fact of life logic', Liverpool chemists have always distributed or sold syringes. They themselves arrange to have used syringes collected so as to prevent reuse and accidents. By cooperating with the Drug Centre, chemists hope to silence popular protest, as most people do not like to see syringes scattered all over the place. How different from the United States where syringes cannot be bought without a medical prescription and France where their sale is legal but chemists resist selling them. I confront Patrick O'Hara with all the usual arguments. By giving maintenance doses of heroin, morphine or methadone to addicts isn't one taking the easy way out, accepting that addiction cannot be cured ? For O'Hara, the war against drugs seems meaningless as he feels that addiction is not an illness but a natural tendancy and therefore cannot be cured. The doctor can only watch his patients to reduce harm and wait till they shake off the habit themselves. The proof is that very few addicts continue taking drugs after they cross forty. Most addicts get fed up of drugs and go back to leading normal lives. Studies carried out in Liverpool reveal that the average addiction span is anything from ten to twelve years. Addiction can therefore not be considered as an irreversible or genetic disorder. The Liverpool experience does not corroborate American laboratory findings.

IN THE NAME OF PRAGMATISM

As it is neither possible to eradicate drugs or to cure addiction all one can do is reduce the harm done. This is the rationale behind the Liverpool experiment. The title of the programme - Harm Reduction Programme- is self explanatory. The attempt is to reduce the harm addicts inflict upon themselves and society. That is why in Patrick O'Hara's centre, doctors and nurses teach addicts how to inject themselves so as to avoid abcess formation and above all AIDS.

Paradoxically enough, it was AIDS that saved the Liverpool maintenance programme. In the early eighties, it seemed clear enough that the programme was to be wound up by the government in London as it was not in consonance with the spirit of the times - international repression had been let loose by the American government. And then came AIDS and the addiction-AIDS link. O'Hara, like most of his countrymen, asked which was the greater of the two evils, AIDS or drugs? Addiction is chronic but AIDS is fatal. A drug addict doesn't cost National Health Care much but on the contrary an AIDS patient costs a fortune to the taxpayer who finances the National Health Scheme. The Liverpool deaddiction programme was thus conveniently transformed into a fight against AIDS. Let us distribute syringes, heroin and methadone, says O'Hara, not because this has always happened in Great Britain, not because we believe that drug addiction is an illness, not because we think the war against drugs is absurd, but simply as a means to combat AIDS. In Liverpool, the number of AIDS infected drug addicts is the lowest in Great Britain and among the lowest in Europe. Is this really because of the Maintenance programme? Patrick O'Hara is honest enough to admit that he does not really know. There could be other reasons such as the social class Liverpool addicts belong to.

One positive result of the harm reduction strategy is that there are very few criminals among the addicts. As addicts are being looked after by the Centre, they no longer need turn violent to buy drugs. They can lead normal lives and socialise without any stigma. Once again, statistics, though hard to interpret, seem to indicate that the number of drug related offenses is lower in Liverpool than in the rest of the country.

Patrick O'Hara did not use the legalisation of drugs argument to defend his programme. As he is a government employee, it is not easy to do so; even in Great Britain censorship and autocensorship are the norm. O'Hara nevertheless feels that a harm reduction programme is viable whether the drug is legalised or not. 'My approach is a pragmatic one, it has little to do with the theoretical debate on legalisation.' Even if drugs were legalised, the programme would carry on in the same way.

MEMOIRS OF AN OPIUM ADDICT

Had it not been for the longstanding relationship between the English and drugs, the Liverpool programme would have been inconceivable. Tobacco and opium addiction were both introduced in Europe by the English. Thomas de Quincey, an English aesthete, was the first to write the biography of a drug addict. Similarly, anyone who has read the unabridged works of Arthur Conan Doyle knows that Sherlock Holmes could not resist morphine in spite of all Doctor Watson's remonstrances. English literature reveals to what extent writers had understood the corrosive effect of drugs on the human personality. The most revealing document in this regard is undoubtedly Stephenson's Dr. Jekyll and Mr Hyde. The good Jekyll becomes the bad Hyde after giving himself a potion of his own making and dies of an overdose of his own medicine while vainly attempting to rediscover his ego. The allegory is obvious and gives us an insight into other texts. Like Jekyll and Hyde, Sherlock Holmes and Watson are perhaps one and the same person. The first time the magical dual personality was described in literature was as early as 1818 with Mary Shelley's Dr Frankenstein and his monster. Without such a cultural background, the liberal experiment in Liverpool, the only one of its kind in the world, could not have taken place. O'Hara's programme is socially acceptable only because English GPs, particularly the provincial ones, have for a long time prescribed opium or morphine when they thought their patients could not break the habit. More often than not, the GPs themselves used drugs, a practice not confined to Britain alone. Any drug policy reflects the culture of a people and the nature of the State.

What are the lessons that we can draw from the Liverpool experience?

Abolitionists can argue that drugs when dissociated from the ghetto claim very few addicts. There is less of a chance of AIDS, spurious drugs and overdose. As one no longer has to steal to buy drugs, fewer crimes are committed against non addicts.

Prohibitionists can counter this by saying the easy availability of drugs in Liverpool - distributed to some free of charge - has increased the number of drug addicts. Intellectual integrity does not allow Patrick O'Hara to rule out this possibility. There is no way of gauging the effect of the Liverpool programme on drug use. In all probability, the distribution of methadone, heroin and syringes does not matter one way or the other. Patrick O'Hara is of the view that it is impossible to counter prohibitionist arguments in the absence of conclusive sociological data; such data does not and cannot exist. There is no way of comparing Liverpool with prohibition to Liverpool without prohibition: the choice between liberalisation and prohibition is a philosphical one.

INVENTING TOLERANCE

Rumour: Amsterdam is purgatory where one walks on syringes. Another rumour: the Dutch have found the answer to addiction. What both the votaries and the opponents of the Dutch model share in common is that neither have ever been to Holland to see for themselves. Or if they do go, then it is usually to select those facts which best fit their preconceived notions.

What does Amsterdam's mayor, Edouard Van Tijn have to say?

'Our policies are neither totally repressive, nor totally tolerant. We are looking for a middle path.' Unlike in France or the United States, in Holland drugs are not a subject of ideological controversy. This is because issues such as repression and depenalisation have already been thrashed out. The debate lasted thirty years, now it is over. Dirk Korf, director of the Centre for Criminology at the University of Amsterdam says this, 'In the choice of probable approaches to drugs, Dutch leaders have turn by turn tried out all the options available. In the sixties, the American model predominated: taking drugs was a crime. In the seventies, the psychoanalytical model gained ascendance: drugs meant personality disorders. In the eighties, socio-logists took over with their drugs are a manifestation of social pathology, non conformist behaviour and a young culture. The young had to be brought back to the social mainstream and it was best to avoid saying anything to them as their critique of the established order was well founded.' Acrimonious debate continued till it finally dawned on all parties that there was no single truth about addiction. The contending schools thus put an end to their quarrel in a true Dutch spirit of compromise.

Passions cooled down in Holland only because the Dutch State is of very modest dimensions. Citizens do not look to the government for moral science instruction; all they expect of it is to safeguard their security. In this country extremely wary of authority, the government is judged for its efficiency more than anything else.

Addiction experts and politicians thus decided that there was no need for a full fledged war against drugs but that the enemy had to be fought with cunning. They chose pragmatism as their ideology. So Dutch tolerance of soft drugs is not a spontaneous off shoot of Dutch culture. The strategy did not just happen, it had to be invented. And the man who invented it was Eddy Engelsman, a sociologist by training. In Holland, addiction is a matter for sociologists; psychoanalysts deal with it in France, biologists and geneticians in the U.S., psychiatrists in Great Britain and Austria, the police in Japan and the KGB in Russia.

When Engelsman joined the ministry of Health in 1972, the standard practice, like everywhere else, was repression. The tougher the Dutch police got, the deeper Dutch youth went into a subculture of drugs. Engelsman broke the spiral by suggesting what he called the 'normalisation' of drugs. By asking politicians to treat drugs like any other problem, he succeeded in depoliticising the debate so that no party could make political capital out of drugs. Thereafter dispassionate analysis was possible. 'Do not think,' says Engelsman, 'that normalisation was an easy job. I have to constantly prove that American style absolute repression in the war against drugs is a failure. The Dutch, like any other people, do not tolerate social deviance easily. Now drug addiction happens to be barbarism in its extreme form.' Engelsman's skill lies in his ability to reintegrate deviants through what he calls 'negotiation'. 'For example, when drug addicts formed their unions in Amsterdam we had little in common with them but we thought the best way of 'surrounding' them would be to negotiate and ask them to participate in our syringe exchange programme among others.' The Dutch, a mosaic of cultures and religions, know all too well that to preserve social peace it is better to negotiate with the minorities rather than marginalise them.

DIFFERENTIATING BETWEEN SOFT AND HARD DRUGS

The unique feature of the Dutch model is the distinction made between soft drugs such as marijuana and hashish, and hard drugs such as cocaine and heroin. This is a sore point with other Western governments, in particular the French government, which comes down very harshly on hashish. It is not difficult to understand French outrage: pragmatism is an insult to the French national ideology on drugs. But everyone in Holland - experts, sociologists, doctors and psychiatrists - are categoric: it is patently absurd to bracket hard and soft drugs in the same category. This just goes to prove to what extent scientific expertise is governed by ideological considerations. Dirk Korf explains, 'Cannabis is not habit forming and does not lead to drug dependance. The contention that soft drugs are a stepping stone to hard drugs is not based on any scientifically observed phenomenon.'

According to Engelsman, the risk of graduating from one drug to another - cannabis to cocaine or heroin - is linked neither to the substance nor to dependence but to a marketing strategy. In the United States and France, the same dealer offers hard drugs to clients on the pretext that soft ones are in short supply. This is why the Dutch govern-ment decided to make soft drugs commonplace so it could concentrate on fighting against hard drugs. In Amsterdam, every effort is made to keep the occasional cannabis smoker and hard drug suppliers apart. There are two distinct channels of supply. A cannabis dealer does not run much of a risk and has no desire to get mixed up in the sale of heroin or cocaine which is liable to stiff punishment. A cannabis user runs no risk at all. On the other hand, hard drug users have to go through sinister channels to buy their supplies which usually acts as a deterrent. Hashish is sold openly or to be precise 'tolerated' in coffee-shops, provided the quantities involved are small - thirty grams at the most. No one knows where it comes from and the police do not even want to know. Coffee-shop managers, when questioned, reply they have their contacts. Many grow cannabis in hothouses. In strictly legal terms these are offenses; however the police is not interested in such minor offenses, and for all intents and purposes, the sale of cannabis is legal. Similarly, the police turns a blind eye to those who use ecstasy and cocaine in small quantities. On the other hand, reselling grass is prohibited and a coffee-shop which offers cocaine or heroin is immediately closed down by the police. More often than not, coffee-shop owners see to it that order is maintained in their establishments and hard drug users are thrown out of the premises, often with the help of clients . There are a few exceptions, but for the most part grass - marijuana and hashish - has become part of Amsterdam's coffee-shop culture; tobacco is usually forbidden (it is considered too toxic); so is alcohol and coffee. The typical marijuana smoker is often an ecologist and sometimes vegetarian.

What have the results of this experiment been? According to all Dutch statistics, tolerance towards cannabis has not led to any appreciable increase in the number of soft drug users. On the contrary, by allowing them to be sold openly, the demand seems to have stabilised. In 1991, 1.8% of the Dutch used soft drugs occasionally and one per cent used them regularly; figures comparable if not lower than those in other European countries. They also include a sizeable number of 'drug tourists' many of whom are German. Everything in this country has been tested, measured and quantified. The Dutch government strives to be as functional as possible; it is all the more forthcoming with statistics as its policies are criticised at home and abroad, so unlike the French authorities who are loath to part with even the most innocuous statistics. French bureaucracy does not feel the slightest need to justify itself. French bureaucrats in charge of the fight against drugs are of the considered opinion that Dutch statistics are all fallacious, making comparisons meaningless. The Italians think the same way. As Emanuele Marotta, the chief of the antinarcotics squad said in Rome, 'We are combatting Dutch statistics with Latin rhetoric.' We are not just dealing with two different attitudes towards drugs: we are dealing with two cultures, two conflicting conceptions of what the State should be.

Judging by the Dutch experience of liberalising cannabis, it does not seem that an increase in the supply of soft drugs leads to a substantial increase in the number of users. According to Engelsman, the population likely to use drugs remains more or less constant. If they cannot get one drug they will just take to another. Now this remark - based on empirical observation - knocks the bottom out of the case being made for reducing supplies.

Is the repression of drugs more harmful than drugs themselves? This is exactly what Engelsman is trying to prove. Take the case of ecstasy whose effects are far from ecstatic; Engelsman does not deny the psychic danger of the drug. It first came into circulation in Amsterdam in the early eighties, supplied by small local manufacturers at low prices. Its use was confined to a closed circle of rock concert lovers: the whole business was carried out under the watchful eye of the police. The drug hardly created a stir and claimed no victims. Till the day the British representative in the United Nations Programme for Drug Abuse Control decreed that ecstasy be included in the list of internationally banned drugs. Why ? The answer is simple enough: the bureaucrats in charge of the war against drugs can only justify their salaries by making rules and regulations even more unwieldy and complex. Engelsman had tried his best to see that the ban was restricted to substances harmful to public health which was not the case of ecstasy. His efforts proved futile. For the British government, it was a matter of principle; medical and social considerations did not come into the picture at all. Weary, the Dutch government just gave in. From that moment, ecstasy ceased to be an innocuous drug. Small producers stopped making it as it was too risky to do so and professional gangs took over. Banning the drug just made it more attractive and the number of users rose. The moral of the story according to Engelsman is that banning a drug is far more harmful than the drug itself.

GETTING ADDICTS TO COME OUT OF THE GHETTO

Everyday between eleven o'clock and noon a huge white bus can be seen standing in front of the Amsterdam station. It is here that heroin addicts flock to get daily supplies of the drug. A nurse gives each one a paper cup and then proceeds to exchange used syringes for new ones. This is step two of the Dutch experiment: maintenance of drug addicts most affected by heroin through the visible distribution of methadone. There are about one thousand two hundred drug addicts on the whole who are covered by the programme: of these, at least one third are foreigners (German and French). Most of the Dutch 'clients' are Surinamian immigrants. Instead of leaving the addicts to their fate and letting them commit all kinds of crimes to buy heroin or relegating them to the suburbs, the Amsterdam town hall brings them out in the open so as to 'surround' them. Generally speaking, Dutch society tries to 'reintegrate difference'; we had already seen this in the case of immigrants. However, it is not as if all Dutch are models of tolerance: the visibility of drug addicts disturbs them. They do not like deviance but at least they are aware it exists. Visibility is the price that has to be paid to overcome the social hazards of drug addiction. The contact with social workers when methadone is distributed could be the beginning of a deaddiction cure. Dutch motives are not entirely altruistic: fifty years ago, the Dutch colonial administration used to distribute opium to the Chinese in Java to 'stabilise' them; now they distribute methadone to the Surinamians.

It is hard to evaluate such a disconcerting experiment. The total number of heroin addicts seems to have stabilised over the years. The percentage of AIDS cases in the Netherlands is the lowest in the whole of Europe and death by overdose is rare. It may be argued that the distribution of methadone is tantamount to making addicts prisoners of their habit so that they do not bother society. Many French psychiatrists hold this view. It is true that both in the Netherlands and Great Britain, maintenance programmes are viewed as a means to preserve security and social harmony. But then isn't society entitled to some protection, or are addicts the only ones to need protection? Doctors and psychoanalysts only seem to care for addicts. Fortunately , psychoanalysis is a little known discipline in Holland.

No one in Holland, be it Eddy Engelsman, a politician or an expert, claims to have a comprehensive solution to drug addiction. The Dutch model is still very much at the experimental stage. The use of grass has more or less been contained; heroin abuse is under control but the use of amphetamine is on the rise and cocaine is finding its way into the market. In the Netherlands as elsewhere, fifty per cent of the prisoners are behind bars for drug related offenses. Most of them happen to be immigrants or underpriviledged; the social factors are the same as elsewhere. Eddy Engelsman has an extraordinary explanation to offer, 'The large number of prisoners does not prove that drugs lead to crime; it only proves that drugs are expensive. The prison population is directly proportional to the market price of drugs. Consequently, if all drugs were sold freely, prices would fall and so would the number of drug related offenses.'

Complete liberalisation is something Dutch public opinion is not likely to accept in the near future. Nor for that matter will the American government allow such a thing to happen. However, I do think this is an idea which could help us understand drug addiction better.

THE ZURICH AFFAIR

A small state and tolerance towards drug addicts go hand in hand. The size of the state can be measured by its attitude towards drugs. In Europe, France is the undoubted champion of prohibition; on the other hand, countries like the Netherlands, Austria and Switzerland have adopted an empirical approach to drugs. The Vienna town hall supervises methadone distribution through chemists; the reasons for doing so are the same as in Amsterdam though the Viennese are more discrete. In Geneva, magistrates find it convenient to overlook marijuana related offenses. This tolerance is often misunderstood and perhaps deliberabtely misinterpreted. In France, tolerance is considered a crime; that is why the French condemned outright the famous Zurich Platzpitz experiment without having bothered to study it.

For about ten years till it was evacuated in 1992, the Platzpitz park was a public platform for addicts;

three to four thousand heroin addicts would come every day to inject themselves and get their daily dose. Some lived there; some would stop by before going to their office or on their way back home. A team of doctors was present round the clock to distribute syringes, give advice and take care of emergencies. Competition among heroin dealers was so fierce that prices fell to an all time low. This had heroin addicts from all over Europe flocking to the park. The first few years of the experiment went off peacefully. But since 1990, rivalry among suppliers led to brawls and scuffles; the police, which till then had turned a blind eye, started taking action. In early 1992, the Zurich town hall, which financed the doctors and the syringes, decided to call it a day and the park was closed to addicts. The votaries of repression had gained the upper hand, or so it seemed. In reality, the lessons to be drawn from this experience are more complex.

First of all, as the Geneva psychiastrist Miguel Del Rio explains, 'no one invented the Platzpitz'; drug addicts congregated there spontaneously, not by municipal decree. Earlier, they used to loiter on the city streets, especially in middle class localities and would make it a point to shoot in public. More often than not, says Del Rio, drug addicts played the clown to attract attention. When neighbours complained, the police would chase them away, driving them from one locality to the next, till finally they all landed up in the deserted Platzpitz park. As there were no neighbours to complain, the police decided to leave them alone.

Platzpitz shook the inhabitants of Zurich out of their complacency. Switzerland was not what they believed it to be; their affluent country was secretly nursing a significant minority of marginal 'barbarians'. They also discovered that heroin addicts were not necessarily poor or foreign; many 'normal' citizens like themselves combined drugs with a regular job, a home and a family. After this, the Zurich municipality gave up repression and concentrated instead on trying to contain the damage. A referendum was held and it was decided that funds be made available for a medical team at Platzpitz. The doctor who took the initiative, Arthur Grob, effectively brought home the economic advantages of the operation so that Swiss public opinion ultimately veered around to his point of view. His argument was this, 'The cost of treating an AIDS patient is so high that even if every year a single addict is spared the virus, it would cover the annual budget of the health team at Platzpitz.' The argument hit home; as in Great Britian, the fight against AIDS legitimised a more tolerant approach towards drug addiction.

Eventually Platzpitz had to be closed down because of the rush of foreigners. The Zurich town hall was ready to pay for its own citizens even if they were drug addicts; it was even willing to pay for the Swiss from less liberal cantons; but it was not prepared to shoulder the burden for all of Europe's drug addicts. As in Amsterdam and Vienna, tolerance only led to addicts and dealers pouring in from all over Europe, which just goes to prove how difficult it is for isolated cases of liberalisation to survive in an open European space.

After Platzpitz what? Drug addicts are back to wandering the city streets, driven from one locality to the next by the police. In a bid to put an end to this stray wandering - disturbing for the inhabitants and dangerous for the addicts themselves - the city has opened *Fixer-Raümes* of the kind that exist in Bal and Berne, where addicts can find what they need to inject themselves 'cleanly'. The funny thing is that the addicts who go these *Fixer-Raümes* are later arrested by the police, in spite of the fact that *Fixer-Raümes* are financed by the municipal authorities. In Geneva too, one can find many such instances of discrepancies between police action and municipal decisions. Policemen arrest and judges punish addicts who use methadone distributed by canton authorities.

The Platzpitz, concludes Miguel Del Rio, was not intended to be a model; no one ever claimed it was one. It's only achievement was to make people realise that drug addiction was not a crime but a social phenomenon which could affect 'normal' citizens. People have now understood that repression is not the answer.

And so you have Zurich, Amsterdam and Liverpool, isles of compassion in an otherwise raging sea.

21

THE ABOLITIONISTS

The year 1974: Richard Nixon launched the first major offensive of the present war against drugs. One man alone, Milton Friedman, spoke out against the war and compared it to the disastrous prohibition of alcohol in the twenties, asking for the immediate legalisation of all drugs. Friedman was a pathbreaker. He was the first to take on causes as varied as tight liquidity to combat inflation, privatising schools and social security. All his social utopias are based on the axiom that individual choice is superior to state decreed order. For Milton Friedman, what one calls the state has always been an organised crime syndicate to plunder nations: the state legitimises its operations with the help of ideological discourse. The war against drugs is no exception, it is governed by the same power rationale.

The ideas that Milton Friedman has constantly put forth have been developed and elaborated upon by anti-prohibition movements the world over. However, Friedman remains the uncontested master and at eighty years old he is a live wire, tireless and unshakable. We hail his independence. In the war against drugs, the kind of pressure exerted by the American government on academic and political circles as well as on the press has been considerable. Many professors have lost their jobs for having criticized the national ideology of repression.

Sitting in front of a log fire at his California ranch which faces the Pacific, Friedman tells me of his long struggle. As we get talking, we both observe that neither of us smokes nor drinks. A minor detail, except that almost all abolitionist intellectuals are in point of fact remarkably sober human beings. What could be the relationship between sobriety and our stand?

I ask Friedman to classify his arguments which seem to move out in all directions. He finds my method somewhat French to say the least but thinks it's worth a try.

AN ECONOMIC ASSESSMENT

To begin with, a 'cost-benefit' analysis of the American war against drugs. On the expenditure side, first there are the twelve billion dollars earmarked for the war. But the indirect costs are even higher. For instance, drug prohibition leads to increased criminality just as the prohibition of alcohol did in its time. It is estimated that in the United States, ten thousand cases of homicide are directly linked to drug trafficking especially as dealers settle their scores through gang wars. By raising the price of drugs, prohibition gives dealers considerable profit margins. This is how drug trafficking has become the most profitable job for young unqualified Americans. According to Friedman, the war against drugs has claimed far more victims than the drugs themselves, especially among the groups the state claims to protect. It is the war against drugs and not drugs themselves that has become the main reason for urban ghettos ravaged by violence, illness and unemployment. Similarly, it is not drugs but the increase in drug prices and the risk premium that comes along with prohibition which have allowed the Mafia and other cartels to thrive.

What is Friedman's answer to Roy Pickens argument that legalisation would lead to greater use and eventually more incurable addicts? Friedman points out that this does not explain the motivations but is an *a posteriori* rationalisation of the war against drugs. Just suppose Pickens is right. In that case, were drugs to be sold on the open market, would there be more users? The few experiments at hand tell us that tolerance of marijuana - we have the examples of Holland, Alaska and Oregon in the seventies - has not led to an increase in drug users. When these drugs were legalised, some people might simply have switched over from one drug, say alcohol, to marijuana, whereas others may have given up marijuana precisely because it was no longer forbidden. Even if Roy Pickens' was right, Friedman would still not budge an inch. Just suppose that in a regime where drugs are openly sold the number of drug addicts does increase in comparison to the prohibition regime. They would, says Friedman, be better treated, better cared for and better respected than in the present regime where they spend most of their time in prison. Legalisation, Friedman adds, would control other far more serious illnesses such as AIDS and accidents caused by spurious drugs, offshoots of prohibition. Finally, the funds currently earmarked for the war against drugs could be put to much better use; we could build more schools instead of prisons, and the police could catch the real criminals instead of running after hashish smokers.

THE SUBSTITUTION EFFECT

If Bob Martinez is to be believed - the war against drugs is moving towards victory - then Friedman's analysis is irrelevant. Friedman retorts, 'If this is the way they are going to win the war, heaven knows what it would be like if they lost it.' Cocaine abuse does seem to have fallen among American youth since 1989, but can this be attributed to the war against drugs? It probably has more to do with changing fashions or greater concern for health; this has been the case with smoking which is on the decline. No one ever launched a war against tobacco as it is not an illegal drug. On the other hand, the number of drug related crimes and murders, far from declining, has in fact gone up since the war against drugs. Finally, alcoholism seems to be more widespread among the youth which could be the result of the prohibition of hashish. We should never, while on the subject of drugs, forget the substitution factor.

The entire history of prohibition brings out the importance of the substitution factor. When the English government prohibited gin in 1732, British workers turned to beer. Towards 1840, the Irish stopped consuming alcohol at the behest of Rev. Theobald Matthew. Instead they just took massive quantities of ether. An old adage would have it that you could tell a Catholic from a Protestant from their breath. A Protestant smelt of beer, a Catholic of ether. It would be naive to believe that drug addicts deprived of drugs would automatically turn into honest, hardworking citizens. More likely than not if addicts were criminals before taking drugs they will remain criminals even after dropping the habit. By talking about the war against drugs as if drugs were the real enemy, one forgets that drugs are nothing more than mere plants. Drugs only bring to the fore urges which existed even without them. Making a drug scarce or even eradicating it will not remove the urge for drugs. The idea that the war against hashish in the United States has led to increased alcoholism or cocaine use cannot be excluded. The question to ask then is which is more dangerous: the substitute or the original?

Friedman's economic arguments seem unas-sailable, but are economic arguments enough to sway public opinion when it comes to such a complex issue ?

DRUGS: THE NEW THOUGHT CONTROL

Milton Friedman continues, 'Even if my economic arguments are unsound, the war against drugs would still be unacceptable because it destroys the legal foundations of American democracy.' How can one describe as a 'crime' an act where there is no victim, where the culprit is also the victim? In the name of which principle can the State condemn individuals who harm no one but themselves; in what way is the State in a better position to decide what is good or bad for individuals than the individuals themselves? Criminalising drug use is totally alien to the liberal philosophy of justice; it is an infringement of the right to hold an opinion, characteristic of totalitarian societies. When drug addicts commit a crime they must be punished for the crime committed and not for having used drugs. In any case, the link between drug use and crime is dubious; in fact it seems that drug users are less prone to crime. All American prison statistics show that most prisoners took to criminal activity before they took to drugs and not after. Anti-drug laws tend to confuse cause with effect. Corrupt laws inevitably lead to a corrupt police force and judiciary. As there is no victim, no third party interest at stake, the representatives of the law would have to be saints not to be affected by the peculiar nature of their dealings with traffickers. We know for a fact that no one has gone unscathed. Another thing to remember is that the American police force has a personal stake in the war against drugs as it gets to keep the assets confiscated from traffickers. (This is also true in Italy.) With corrupt laws and a corrupt police force, public values get distorted. For instance, a poster in Anderson municipality in South Carolina asked young people to turn informers: 'Do you need money? All you have to do is denounce a dealer!'

HOW TO GO ABOUT LEGALISING

How can legalisation be made to work? Incapable of countering the legalisation rationale, prohibitionists try to show that legalisation is not feasible in practice. They have a ready stock of questions: Which drugs are you going to sell? Who will sell them? At what price? In what concentration? Will you sell drugs to children? Good questions you may say, except that they are based on the assumption that the current state of affairs is ideal, which it is not - we all know that teenagers are the first to fall victim to prohibition. We have to prove that legalisation is less harmful than prohibition, not that it is perfect. Friedman suggests drawing up a legal regime for drugs along the lines of the tobacco or alcohol laws. In the United States, every state has its own rules and regulations which are applicable to private companies as regards their sale and advertising.

If drugs were to be sold on the open market, the prices would fall by one hundred per cent. Currently, this is the difference in price between contraband morphine and morphine legally sold at chemist shops. As a result, the black market would loose much of its attraction for the mafia. Medlin cartels would crumble. Does this mean that organised crime would disappear? In all likelihood, criminals would take on some other criminal activity. Legalisation is certainly not going to make saints out of criminals; nor is the urge to cross the line - after all that is what drug abuse is all about - going to vanish. Legalisation will not work miracles, but it will claim fewer victims than the war against drugs. Legalisation, will, all in all, be less harmful than prohibition.

As for the 'Will you sell drugs to children?', children are anyway not allowed to do many things. It would be up to the police to ensure that drugs are not sold to them. And parents could once again begin to assert some of the authority they have relinquished to the State under prohibition.

THE BUREAUCRATIC LOGIC

Having got this far in the discussion it is hard not to get carried away. For two reasons. First, Friedman's arguments seem unassailable. Second because the American government seems to be pursuing a policy which contradicts all the tenets of good sense.

Is the government acting in response to public demand? Milton Friedman does not believe for a minute that the war is on because society demands it. The 'society demanding the war' logic seems to be orchestrated by the government to legitimise its war *a posteriori*. He feels that on the subject of drugs public opinion has been manipulated. The bureaucracy alone has the facts and the funds. It uses both to sustain the war and create a climate of intellectual and moral terror. Only the very strong or small, independent research organisations - the Drug Policy foundation in Washington for instance which has problem finding sponsors - can resist the onslaught. Is the bureaucracy really so perverse as to drag the whole nation into a useless war? Milton Friedman has a different analysis to offer, one that he applies to the bureaucratic phenomenon in general.

The State bureaucracy has invented an enemy and declared a war on it because it has a stake in it. It stands to gain materially and does so under the cover of moral legitimacy. Will the war be lost? In that case, the bureaucracy will just shrug its shoulders and say that it was short of funds and promptly increase its budget. All modern states seem to move in this direction. They invent welfare programmes in the name of social justice, or equality or health, become more and more interventionist and legitimise this through the 'welfare demand' ideology. Milton Friedman asks me to cite one instance of contemporary democracy where a government has given up an interventionist programme because the programme failed. You don't have to look very far for the answer, such a thing has never happened even when Ronald Reagan was President.

It remains to be seen why the public does not protest and revolt. Undoubtedly because the cost of state intervention is spread over a large number of tax payers and as a result the expense is not perceived at the individual level. This asymmetry, typical of modern democracy, allows public spending to go on increasing. In the case of the war against drugs, the

twelve billion budget benefits a limited group of
bureaucrats and costs the tax payer about fifty dollars
a year. Now no one is going to revolt against that.

On the face of it, Milton Friedman's demonstration
seems not only convincing but conclusive. There is
however one serious flaw. He is erring on the side of
optimism. Rational arguments have no place in a war
that is anything but rational. The bureaucracy has
invented an enemy; but isn't an enemy just what the
public wants?

This is what Thomas Szasz, who has another point
of view in the American abolitionist movement, is
going to tell us. He is one hundred per cent pessimist.

PROHIBITION: A RELIGION

A debate with Szasz is more difficult than with Milton
Friedman. Could this have something to do with his
being a psychiatrist? Or is it just that the man is a
natural misanthrope? How can anyone live alone in
the middle of the woods to the north of New York
State in a village as isolated as Manlius? Every time
I put a question to him, he tells me that the questions
are too stupid to warrant an answer; and then his habit
of looking at me fixedly through his thick lenses as
if I were an insect makes me feel uncomfortable, to
say the least.

My first question sounded reasonable enough to
me: 'If we are agreed on the logical necessity for
abolition, how do we get on with it and overcome the
resistance of prohibitionist interest groups and popular
mistrust?'

Szasz's reply is this, 'It is absolutely useless to
suggest solutions as they will never amount to anything.
The war against drugs is a religious crusade; as a

result rational arguments simply won't cut any ice. Wanting to liberalise the drug regime would be like wanting to introduce freedom of thought in Islam: totalitarian thought cannot be reformed, it can only be analysed.' That is just what Szasz is doing and he explains why it is impossible to move away from a totalitarian system.

Szasz's argument about the mystical nature of prohibition is this: in the first place, the distinction between substances which are harmful and those that are not, drugs and non drugs, has no logical foundation. Then what separates a non drug from a drug? Many legal products are fatal: rat poison or bleach for instance. As for prohibited drugs, they are rarely fatal. Szasz says no substance is dangerous in itself; all you have to do is avoid consuming it. Drug use, not drugs, is harmful. Drugs are not banned for their intrinsic properties; prohibition is the means of wielding quasi religious power: 'I forbid you to touch this substance (which in itself is neutral) because such is my will.' Otherwise in the name of which principle, asks Szasz, can you prohibit hallucinogenic mushrooms and not truffles? In truth, the aim of prohibition is to make people believe in the expertise of those who prohibit: 'I know, the doctor or the priest will tell you, that truffles are good for you but hallucinogenic mushrooms are not, and I alone possess this knowledge.' Prohibition is thus a dogma. Anyone who transgresses is called an ignoramus, a madman, sinner or witch. Anyone who dares to transgress must be imprisoned or cured.

THE MAGICAL POWER OF THE MEDICS

Should one not make a distinction between hard and

soft drugs and ask for the legalisation of soft drugs even if this is not possible for hard drugs? Certainly not, says Szasz. The debate on the legalisation of some drugs considered less dangerous than others only serves to strengthen the power of medical experts who decide whether a drug is dangerous or not. They tell you one drug is harmful while the other is not when all they have to say is that nothing is dangerous as long as you don't take it. In other words, it would be enough to inform the public about the effects of each substance as in the case of food products: everyone could then decide to consume what they liked, fully apprised of the consequences. But such responsibility claims two victims, the expert and the user. Experts, doctors and psychiatrists would stand to loose their socio-magical authority. Doctors need prohibition without which they loose their power to prescribe. Prohibiting the consumption of bad drugs such as opium or cocaine legitimises the prescription of 'good drugs' by the medical clergy. Everything hangs together; by lifting the ban on some drugs or medicines, one would be calling into question the doctor's right to prescribe, the very basis of his authority. Besides, consumers would have to assume their own responsibility, something they generally wish to avoid.

Is Szasz advocating a society without doctors and medicine? Once again Szasz thinks my question is naive. In his scheme of things, all products would be sold freely in the market. If Szasz is to be believed, the market is the perfect instrument for ensuring freedom; he says there must be complete transparency of information about all products, be they drugs medicines or frozen food. Then it is up to the consumers/ citizens/ responsible patients to medicate themselves;

ninety per cent of illnesses, Szasz emphasizes, are a matter of primary health care, greater hygiene or self-medication. The need for a doctor only arises in case of a complication. However no one, neither patients nor doctors, wants to demystify health, medicine and medical power. That is why the authority principle will continue to hold sway and medical and psychiatric power will be strengthened in modern society. And in order to maintain their legitimacy, doctors and psychiatrists need to perpetuate taboos; without them, society cannot be subjugated. People like to be subjugated, very few appreciate freedom.

FEAR OF FREEDOM

Man in society, says Szasz, does not want to be made responsible; he is afraid of freedom and runs away from it. That is why he needs religion, it organises the transference of his anguish. Priests may be a vanishing breed but doctors have rushed in to take their place. Health is the religion of our times; doctors are the new priests and medicines have taken the place of icons or magic reliquaries - they are even displayed in the same way! In this new religious dispensation, heaven has descended on earth, 'The medicalisation of our lives is the secularisation of heaven.'

I think I have found a flaw in Szasz' reasoning. When he considers all substances value neutral and puts hallucinogenic mushrooms on the same footing as truffles, isn't he closing his eyes to the fact that drug dependence can completely crush the will of the user? Once again my question seems to irk him. 'Drug addiction is not an illness, but a "behaviour".' Of course, priests and doctors do their best to make us believe it is a sin or an illness. The same was true of

masturbation at the beginning of the century, or of
schizophrenia which psychiatrists persist in calling an
illness though it is only a behaviour.

Unfortunately, drug addicts and their families
welcome this medicalisation of behaviour, as it exonerates
them of their responsibility. Addiction is no longer the
fault of the addict, it is for the doctor or the police
to take care of it. The family too is reassured; it can
shut out the fact that the addict took drugs *out of
choice*. We do not want to know human beings are
capable of choosing evil deliberately, says Szasz, we
want humans to be good. When we take drug addicts
to be criminals or sick people, the inference is that
'normal' humans are essentially good. Hallelujah!

Isn't Szasz confusing freedom with isolation? I
leave him to write his twenty-fifth book in solitude-
or is it his thirtieth - and enjoy this gentle form of
self-intoxication. Szasz's views may seem excessive but
this should not detract from their basic merit. Freedom
is not palatable to most people; nor is the truth, for
that matter. One is always looking for it, secure in the
knowledge that it will never be found.

Szasz's parting shot, 'If drugs were not prohibited,
how would children defy their parents? They would
have to invent some other form of prohibition.' Young
addicts are barbarians; they do not go as far as killing
their fathers; they are content to defy him. So perhaps
it is not such a bad idea after all to prohibit drugs
to ensure that only this edict is transgressed and
nothing worse.

LIVING WITH THE SACRED

For Milton Friedman, the prohibition of drugs is a
bureaucratic necessity. Szasz says it has to do with

people's fear of freedom, whereas Henri Atlan feels prohibition stems from a fear of the sacred. Now why should Henri Atlan, a famous chemist and philosopher who teaches in both Paris and Jerusalem, feel the need to speak about drugs? Is he qualified to do so? At least Friedman is an economist and Szasz a psychiatrist. Atlan says, 'Drug addiction is beyond the realm of specialists.' As specialists have been unable to provide any convincing answer, the police, jurists and politicians all decided to jump onto the bandwagon. So why should philosophers and chemists be left behind?

Perhaps it is improper to include Atlan's name in the list of abolitionists. Atlan is not making a case for the legalisation of drugs; what he seeks to do is expose the intellectual hypocrisy on the subject. For example the following statement was read out at a serious seminar on drug addiction, 'All heroin addicts smoked hashish before graduating to heroin. So hashish leads to heroin.' These are some of the absurd syllogisms that dominate any discussion on drugs. Atlan wonders why when it comes to drugs there is so much intellectual dishonesty. He is of the view that drug use leads to a form of knowledge which destroys order as we know it. Liberalising drugs is striking at the roots of modernity and replacing it with a different order. This becomes clear when Atlan traces the origins of modern thought.

In premodern societies, there were three paths to knowledge: dreams, ecstasy as a means to accede to the sacred and conscious, rational knowledge. In the eighteenth century however, modernity rejected the sacred and the subconscious and based itself entirely on reason - rational thinking was the only way to acquire true knowledge. In the age of enlightenment visionaries were repressed and confined to psychiatric hospitals. The freedom to hallucinate was only granted to artists provided they did not disturb social order; Freud was the first to upset the rational scheme of things with his rehabilitation of the subconscious. The second blow came about in 1938 with the invention of LSD and Hofmann's discovery of its psychic effects in 1941. Ever since - Atlan feels this discovery was no less revolutionary than the introduction of psychoanalysis - we know that ecstasy does exist as an objective state which can be reproduced in the laboratory. Psychedelic drugs induce psychic states which give rise to different levels of reality.

Besides, a new discipline - ethnobotany - has brought to light the relationship between drugs and religion: *plant geography coincides with the geography of myths and legends*. For example it has been confirmed that mushrooms growing in India do in fact give rise to visions described in the sacred Vedic texts. The *soma rasa* of the Vedas seems to be a product of the fly agaric amanite just as the intoxicating qualities of wine coincide with the 'intoxication of the Gods' in Mediterranean religions. The direct relationship between drugs and religious ecstasy can still be seen among archaic cults such as Siberian shamanism, and North American Indians. However, these are rare exceptions, as all religions have successfully occulted and ritualised their origins.

What the drug addict is doing under the influence of LSD, Atlan tells us, is tearing away the veil to show us the hidden face of modernity. Through psychedelic experiences and the rediscovery of ecstasy addicts destabilise the rationality of the modern world. They strip religious rituals of their significance; the clergy obviously has no desire to see these rituals being reduced to mushrooms or chemical compounds. Prohibition is the only way to counter the threat. The custodians of order in the modern world - the police, the judges and the priests - have a common interest in prohibiting all forms of experimentation with drugs. After all, asks Atlan, is there any one who really wants cities to be once again invaded by new mystics and prophecy merchants? This would mean a return to barbarism. We all prefer that the sacred remain shrouded behind the veil of ritual and that prohibition of the irrational be the norm.

This brings Atlan to Talmudic contradictions. We have just learnt that modernity is based on the denial of irrational knowledge. We know that drugs lead to different levels of consciousness and to reality which we cannot pretend to ignore. But we want to give up neither modernity nor knowledge. For Atlan, the dilemma is no different from that of the legendary rabbi of Prague: ought he to create Golan which was unreasonable or should he give up the ideal knowing that he could have created it? To put it in everyday terms, should we give up genetic manipulation because we know that it could lead to both good and evil?

For Atlan, the denial of knowledge, escapism or prohibition can never be the answer because nothing can remain suppressed forever. He therefore suggests a twin strategy: the 'substitution strategy' and the 'strategy of desire.' First the substitution strategy: the pious Hasidic of Galicia, recounts Atlan, used to get drunk on vodka on the evening of sabbath and drink to life; the awakening was always painful. So they decided to replace vodka with water to toast to life; it worked; they were just as ecstatic with water as they had been with vodka. As for knowledge, the only real knowledge is the desire for knowledge. When applied to drugs, this means that the urge for drugs is more stimulating than the drug itself.

22

THE PLAN FOR ARMISTICE

Drugs are a calamity and addicts, the wretched victims of this calamity. That drugs are perceived the world over as a barbaric threat is the invention of modern States. The war against drugs, oblivious to the real sufferings of addicts, is not a remedy but a means to give fresh legitimacy to governments which have failed abysmally be it on the economic or the social front. Unfortunately, their war is not just a symbolic one, it is gruesomely real. All the elements are there: violence abroad - remote controlled battles in Latin America, the recolonisation of the Third World - and violence at home - police files on civilians, manipulation of information, ideological brain-washing, constant lies and imprisonment for having a mind of one's own. In short, a *Brave New World* under the watchful eye of a benevolent *nomenklatura* which calls itself the State and knows how to distinguish Good from Evil much better than us ordinary mortals.

Who then is the real enemy in this crusade? Drugs? But drugs are mere plants and one can hardly fight against plants!

INVENTING THE ENEMY

The real enemy is *the alien*. Addicts come from elsewhere; worse still, they are always socially inferior. As long as the use of opium was restricted to the elite, there was no political reaction. Baudelaire, Cocteau, Malraux all used drugs; school teachers still talk of them to their students as if they were demi-gods. In the United States, the war against cocaine began in right earnest when the drug travelled from elitist Manhattan to the ghettos of Bronx. What started out as a limited operation blew into a full scale war the day slum dwellers and hippies took to drugs, and Bob Dylan fans switched over to Heavy Metal. What makes a Black who takes drugs worse than a White who takes drugs? In France, do journalists and actors make better use of drugs than Beurs? As a result of this clubbing together of Blacks, Beurs and drugs (though most visible, they are not the only addicts and dealers; they are alien, thus inferior) addiction and barbarism have become synonymous in the public perception. Addicts become all the more barbaric because they use drugs from the 'South' (opium and cocaine) rather than drugs from the 'North' such as alcohol and tobacco. States wage wars against tropical drugs, not against those from cooler climes. Northern drugs are 'cultivated', southern drugs, 'wild'.

All in all, the war against drugs is more of a cultural and racial war - North versus South - and a class war - deviants versus the votaries of order. We have seen this in France, the United States, Japan and Russia. The war against drugs is above all a generational war - adults versus adolescents, old senators versus young barbarians. Italy and Spain amply illustrate this point. Tolerance towards cannabis in the seventies and eighties has now given way to repression, though it is hard to tell what is really being suppressed - drugs or a certain culture. Cannabis, a symbol of adolescent protest in a predominantly Catholic society, is being hounded out not because it is harmful but because the adult world hopes to restore the moral order of its forefathers. It is within its rights to do so. However repression does not really seem to be the most effective way to go about reconciling parents with their offspring.

ADULT ABDICATION

Young addicts are screaming out their rejection of adulthood and modernity. The war against drugs is the adults way of hitting back at this intolerable rejection. Adults support prohibition because they can hand over the charge of their children, out of their control, to the State or the psychiatrist. The responsibility of looking after the neighbours children, especially if they happen to coloured is also con-veniently shifted to the State.

Why have parents abdicated their responsibility? This has happened because we are living in a new society where culture is no longer transmitted vertically from parents to children. Children look for cultural norms and values to other children of their own age group. In the case of alcohol, parents handed down the rituals associated with drinking, not the peer group. As parents knew what to do, everything was within acceptable limits. In the case of marijuana, some parents do know what to do; having experiment-ed with the drug when they were young, they feel less insecure when their children use it occasionally. This partially explains the new tolerance for marijuana and the acculturation of the drug. However, as regards other drugs, parents just do not know what to do and say to their children about the use of substances they themselves had never tried. They have even less to say because of the scarcity of information on the subject; whatever little information there is has been jealously guarded courtesy the war against drugs. So what else can the family do but hand over its responsibility to the police, thereby allowing collective responsibility to replace whatever little authority parents may have had.

If the above analysis is valid, then the war against drugs, by transferring parental power to the community, only serves to accentuate the generational break; it strengthens peer group solidarity and weakens family ties. The war against drugs thus aggravates what it claims to cure every time parental authority is eroded by the authority of a policeman or a doctor.

THE SUPERIORITY OF SPONTANEOUS ORDER

Let us get back to the extremely enlightening example of Nicot's weed. Nobody doubts that cigarettes are part of our cultural heritage. How did we manage to assimilate such a dangerous multicultural red Indian custom as smoking tobacco? It all began with the lure for the exotic among the elite; the habit later spread among the people through mimesis. Tobacco became ours because we began to grow it. It became national because the state taxed it and earned revenue. What is truly remarkable in this story is how society, once all prohibition had been lifted, spontaneously found a set of rules to 'cope' with the drug. The legalisation experiments in the case of hashish also illustrate the superiority of spontaneous order over decreed order, to use an expression dear to Hayek.

Conversely, prohibition stops any kind of social codes from evolving: not capable of eradicating the drug, prohibition only serves to encourage its savage proliferation. So if prohibition continues, we will be running the risk of increased uncontrolled use of cocaine, opium drugs and chemical drugs as well as social instability. This 'savagely organised' pro-liferation of new drugs is to be feared as long as we remain in the war paradigm. The war is the dealers joy and the addicts sorrow. Both are part of the same dynamic.

AT THE ROOT OF THE PROBLEM

Out of all the ideological arguments put forth by the anti-drug combatants, the weakest, though it is projected as being the most logical, is the supply reduction argument. Saying that if only Peruvian peasants would stop growing coca and Laotian peasants would put an end to poppy cultivation for addiction to stop is totally absurd, however reasonable such arguments may seem on the surface. First, because Peruvian or Laotian peasants, like all peasants the world over, are perfectly rational beings. They sell whatever people are willing to buy and obviously grow crops for which they expect maximum returns. Now what could be easier to grow on a large scale when one has no water, fertilizers or equipment than coca, poppy or cannabis? As the outlay is almost nil these countries can produce drugs in unlimited quantities. Why should Peruvian or Laotian peasants die of hunger or poverty just to stop cocaine and heroin from reaching New York and Paris? Which code of ethics, which economic principle says they should starve to protect addicts in the West?

Why would Southern peasants be unwilling to grow other crops just as remunerative but less harmful?

For the simple reason that currently nothing is more profitable than coca, poppy or cannabis. And nothing is more profitable because the war against drugs has made prices sky rocket; tomatoes and pineapples are nowhere near as lucrative as drugs. So it is the war against drugs which is creating economic conditions conducive to the cultivation of drugs. It is also creating drug friendly political conditions; we know that many governments in the producer countries and their armed forces, often allies of the United States, stand to gain directly from drugs. Things could not be otherwise, given the poverty of these countries, the huge profit margins and their condescension towards the West, which is as quick to condemn as to consume. Unless all drug producing countries, from Bolivia to Morocco, Nigeria to Lebanon, Pakistan to Russia, are wiped off the map, the war against drugs in the South will be nothing but a charade, even more futile in the South than in the North.

Suppose for the sake of argument we accept that the drugs will eventually be eradicated from the South. Will this put an end to drug addiction in the North? The answer is no, because it is obvious that the North will start growing its own poppy and cannabis. At present, neither cannabis nor poppy are grown in the North not because of an unfavourable climate but because it much cheaper to import from the South. All this makes sound economic sense; something those waging the war against drugs refuse to take into account. Once again for the sake of argument, however absurd it may seem, let us assume that every poppy and cannabis field in the world were destroyed, what is there to stop people from switching over to synthetic drugs? As long as there are consumers there will be producers: demand creates its own supply. Supplies can only be curtailed if demand were to fall or prices crashed. The criminalisation of drugs, by continually pushing up the risk premium and swelling profit margins, acts as an incentive to produce more not less. The war against drugs is a self-defeating war; it increases supply while claiming to reduce it and traps producer countries in an economic and political relationship of drug dependence. No one ever talks about this because governments engaged in the war against drugs are using it to regain political legitimacy - their own survival is more important than the truth.

TO LEGALISE OR NOT TO LEGALISE?

The time has come to take stock of all the arguments put forth. First, it is clear that the criminalisation of drugs is much more perverse than the drugs themselves. When drugs cannot be taken freely, it takes its toll on public health as addicts are forced to use dirty syringes or take spurious drugs. More drug addicts die of AIDS than of overdose; the ones who live on cannot be treated properly as society treats them as criminals. The tragedy of the anti-drug war is that it makes criminals out of innocent drug users and millionaires out of dealers; it encourages the Mafia, it helps drug traffickers get rich and it subverts the entire state apparatus be it the police, the customs or the judiciary.

What can be said in favour of the war against drugs? Till date there hasn't been a single long term gain. This is not to say that legalisation will guarantee instant success. It simply means legalisation is likely to do less harm than prohibition.

In the first place, legalisation will ensure better use of public money. The money allocated to the war could be used instead to educate people, carry out research and provide better treatment. The anti-smoking campaign and to a lesser extent the anti-alcohol campaign amply illustrate that governments can bring down consumption without having to flex their muscles. The success of the anti-smoking drive - smokers were not made out to be criminals- is all the more remarkable given the fact that the government made only a half-hearted attempt, what with the tremendous pressure put by the tobacco lobby and its own appetite for tax money. The drop in the number of smokers was not due to prohibition; had any restriction been imposed, the results of the anti-smoking campaign would have probably been as disastrous as in the case of cocaine and hashish. In fact if governments go too far in their anti-smoking crusade, it could well degenerate into another futile war.

When the prices of drugs fall, and this is bound to happen if they are legalised, drug trafficking will cease to be profitable. Drug cartels would not disappear overnight, but it would take them some time to recover from this blow. Our cities would be safer to live in and many Third World governments would no longer have to submit to drug traffickers. The administration and police would become less corrupt, and peasants would switch over to other crops. We would also do well to take note of the fact that all the so called 'revolutionary' or 'liberation' movements - be they in Lebanon, India, Peru or Ireland - are financed by drug money. The legalisation of drugs would help to dismantle all these terrorist outfits.

When all is said and done, the only people who stand to loose are terrorists, corrupt leaders, Mafioso, dishonest police officers, dealers, illegal immigrants, dispensers of cheap morality, state financed researchers and votaries of a totalitarian state.

Common sense dictates that drugs should be legalised. They ought to be legalised, but is legalisation feasible?

BREAKING THE UNHOLY ALLIANCE BETWEEN SPECIALISTS AND THE STATE

On the one hand, we agree that it makes sense to legalise drugs; on the other, we know this is virtually impossible. Impossible because the social and political forces opposing such a move are far more powerful and much better organised than a handful of disparate abolitionist thinkers. Liberals go unheard because the State and specialists have got together to make any debate on drugs impossible. It is not easy to fight against this alliance which goes as far back as the 'war against madmen'; even then, the war was backed by lawyers and experts.

Robert Castel, a psychiatrist and research scholar at the *Ecole des hautes études en sciences sociales* in Paris, traced the origin of this alliance in France. It began in 1838 when it was decided that madness was a disease which had to be contained. At the time, millions of French lived in abject poverty, two million children had been abandoned and there was no social security of any kind. These however were minor issues for the deputies; their main concern was to combat madness. The deputies spent weeks debating before adopting what was to be the first 'social law' of the Old Regime:-the automatic confinement of the insane.

The success of this first collaboration between the State, represented by the prefect, and medical power, in the person of Esquirol, a specialist in mental health, marked the beginning of a long, uninterrupted partnership between the two. In 1838, there were not more than ten thousand insane people in the whole of France, but they disturbed bourgeois order just as addicts are threatening modernity today. Nothing has changed, all that has happened is that the straight jacket has replaced the night shirt. Anyone who disturbs order has to be locked up, be it the madman or the addict; both are barbarians whom society neither wants to see nor hear.

In 1838, says Robert Castel, it so happened that conservatives and liberals found themselves on the same side, as both were opposed to this alliance of the State and experts. The conservatives were against it because they felt the State could not replace the family, the liberals because they refused to accept automatic confinement, which in their view was an attack on the right to freedom. The same sharp division exists today on the subject of drug addiction. Unfortunately, those who uphold the family are dwindling in numbers and liberals these days are not quite clear about what they stand for. One can hardly call this an alliance.

DEFINING, DISCUSSING AND EDUCATING

Stopping the war altogether is difficult but the least we can do is to work for an armistice. This could be achieved on the basis of a few simple principles as they emerged from my discussions, in particular with Robert Castel and Claude Olievenstein.

Robert Castel suggests the term addict be applied only to 'visible' drug users, in other words a tiny minority. Most users - whether they take drugs

occasionally, for kicks, or because they are depen-dent
- remain invisible. They are able to manage their
addiction on their own and live a normal life for the
most. Drugs are just a part of their lives not the be
all and end all; most of them will eventually give up
the habit of their own accord without any kind of
outside intervention. Branding such users criminals, as
in America, is an aggressive intrusion into people's
privacy. 'Let us leave these private, invisible users in
peace and reserve the medico-police treatment for only
those addicts who constitute a public menace' is
Castel's sane advice. In this way, while the war against
drugs will be scaled down the State's political prestige
will remain intact. There will still be need for the
medical establishment repression, and the public will
be kept happy. Such a redefinition of addiction will
elicit a milder reaction than the libertarian programme
which calls for a total withdrawal of the State. It also
demands that addicts who break the law be punished
for the crimes they have committed, like any other
criminal- whether the crime was committed under the
influence of drugs is irrelevant.

Robert Castel has not dealt however with the
marketing of the drugs. From where are the 'invisible'
drug addicts going to get their supplies, from the
black market or from a public office, as is being
suggested by the abolitionist jurist Francis Caballero?
Caballero advocates a neutral state marketing system
in which no brand names or advertising would be
allowed. It is a question of finding the least harmful
solution, and this can only emerge from a sustained
debate of the kind Claude Olievenstein has been
pressing for but which has yet to take place.

Olievenstein prefers medicalisation to crimi- nalisation
but has reservations about liberalisation- all this would

do is to lead to an increase in teenage drug addicts. In any case, introducing liberalisation or even supporting it vocally is unthinkable at this stage, as public opinion is completely against it. Any attempt to liberalise, warns Olievenstein, could be a bonanza for populist movements who would exploit it to the hilt. We can well do without anti-drug hysteria, we have enough on our plate with anti-immigrant hysteria.

This leads us to the third part of our plan for armistice: education. Curiously enough, when it comes to drugs, reliable information is hard to come by. What we have instead are lavish publicity campaigns, totally ineffective and sometimes even counterproductive. If we are serious about preventing addiction, then people have to be educated about the 'nuisance value', as Olievenstein put it, of all drugs, from alcohol to heroin. Drug education should be intended not only for teachers and students but also for the medical corps (in France, alcoholism is not considered to be a separate discipline). But this is a thankless, long term project, one not likely to yield any immediate political returns.

These three modest proposals - a reductionist definition of drug addiction, open debate and education - may just take shape, as the war against drugs notwithstanding, it is obvious that addiction is on the rise. Drugs are no longer confined to the other, to the socially inferior, now we are all affected.

Just how affected we are was brought home to me when I went to visit Claude Olievenstein at the Marmottan Centre he has been heading for the last twenty years. It was the 16th of August, 1991. The waiting room was empty. Olievenstein couldn't get over the fact; this was the first time such a thing happened in the last twenty years. No one waiting to

get themselves deaddicted when usually every morning
the room was crowded with at least twenty to thirty
patients. 'The patients seem to have taken a long
weekend!'exclaimed Olievenstein. I thought that was
a healthy development - addicts were getting back into
the mainstream. And wasn't taking a long weekend
a sign that the barbarians were becoming modern?
Olievenstein reacted differently; drug addiction, he
concluded, was no longer confined to marginals, it had
begun to affect the middle classes, those that went on
long weekends. So it is barbarism which is colonising
modernity, not the other way round.

How does one counter barbarism? Through war or
reflection?

FOR A SOBER STATE

All this while, one has attempted to establish how self-
defeating prohibition is; the intent however has not
been to suggest an apologia for legalisation. First,
because it would not serve any purpose, and second
because legalisation is not some kind of a magic
solution that would, in one stroke, eradicate drugs, the
desire to take drugs and drug trafficking. What is
important is that the debate on legalisation take place,
for it is only through free debate that pressure can
be brought to bear on all those who favour repression.
If French judges have started making a distinction
between hard and soft drugs, between small dealers
and drug barons, it is because they have been listening
to the legalisation debate and abolitionist arguments,
not because the law required them to do so; the judges
themselves acknowledge this. Similarly, we do not
advocate legalising drugs but social experiments of the
kind carried out in Switzerland, Austria, Holland and

Great Britain. We are convinced there is no single solution to drug addiction; only through experimentation can we learn how to cope with the problem, either privately or through the State. What we are asking for at the end of our enquiry is the right to discuss the issue freely minus the usual exaggeration and hyperbole.

Which are the fora where such a discussion could be taken up. We had asked the same question in the case of immigration. Today in France, between media showmanship and political polarisation, there are hardly any fora for debate. And what should we discuss? The suppression of liberticidal laws which give the police, the customs and the magistrates powers far beyond their jurisdiction. The laws make no distinction between the different kinds of drugs; this is left to the discretion of public servants. They decide who is guilty and who is not. Their decision is influenced by personal opinion or the general mood; the offense committed has little to do with it. The war against drugs must restore the rule of law and the law should allow social experiments which help make drug addiction a personal rather than a public issue. By normalising drugs, we would be able to reallocate the money spent on the war to more peaceful operations such as deaddiction centres, sorely lacking in funds. It is also time that we have a sensible drug education programme for the affected groups and educators alike instead of populist slogans.

However, all these measures - it would require no less than attitudinal revolution for them to be implemented in France - would not be enough to attack the root of the problem, namely why the need for drugs in the first place?

THERE ARE TWO DIFFERENT SETS OF REASONS

The first category has to do with personal reasons; an individual may decide that drugs are the way to overcome stress or to self-discovery. There is little public authorities can do in these cases and it is important that things remain as such. The responsibility for such addicts should fall either on their families or on the individual.

Then there are the social and community reasons-uprooting of immigrants and their children, unemployment, welfare dependency, ghettos. Here, society can act by mitigating the objective causes for addiction. A couple of football matches or a boxing club are certainly not the answer. We have to put an end to the ghetto culture, and this can only happen with the economic integration of unskilled youth, particularly unskilled immigrant youth. Immigration and drugs are but two sides of the same coin: we find the same cause and effect at work, the same problems. In the first part of the book, realistic, achievable solutions had been suggested to deal with immigration. The same is possible for addiction; removing ghettos through integration into companies would be striking at the root of drug trafficking and drug use in France.

This leaves us with the question of breaking the objective alliance between the police and drug traffickers; it is in the 'interest' of both that the drug trade be criminalised and prices remain high, both 'profit' from such a situation. The only thing abolitionists can do to break this alliance is to fearlessly go on repeating their arguments: yes, there are better ways than war to contain drug addiction and they deserve to be studied, not rejected out of hand as state propaganda is doing. If only the State ceased to be intoxicated by the war against drugs and devoted itself to more socially productive work instead...

In this phantasmagoric war, the abdicator is the State, not the pacifists.

We wish to protest strongly against this political and intellectual terrorism which brands any attempt to think abdication. The modest legalisation we are suggesting is not abdication; it would certainly be far more efficient than criminalisation in bringing down drug use and checking the Mafioso. Legalisation does not mean eliminating the government all together; the government will have a role to play, only its role will change: it is the State which will regulate the drug market. Otherwise, the functions of the State will remain unchanged. It will continue to fight against traffickers, the black market, sale of drugs to minors in the same way as it has been doing for legal drugs. The oft repeated argument that the State can never be allowed to become a merchant of death is unacceptable to us. Drugs do not claim as many victims as arms do; they do not kill those who do not use them. And no one is under any compulsion to use drugs.

EPILOGUE

OLD BOURGEOIS, YOUNG BARBARIANS

Unless one is a sociologist or an economist, it is hard to see things as they really are; on the other hand, a solely economic or sociological view, though extremely useful, is bound to deform one's perspective. In 1840 when a new social class emerged, Pierre Joseph Proudhon and Marx were obliged to invent new concepts to give the proletariat its place and suggest alternative utopias to the bourgeois society of the times. The instruments they used though far from being perfect could not be dispensed with. It is thus with extreme caution that we are suggesting the following new terms even though they are rather approximate: barbarian and bourgeois order.

A NEW CLASS STRUGGLE

Like Marx, who was not always wrong, I do believe that bourgeois and barbarian attitudes are to a certain extent determined by economic circumstances. The bourgeois has material possessions or hopes to acquire them in the near future; the barbarian, in true proletarian fashion, has nothing or rejects possession. Economic factors apart, barbarian attachment to their community or tribe distinguishes them from the bourgeois who adhere to the principle of personal responsibility. Karl Popper wrote, ' I call a society closed when it is a magic or tribal society. The open society is one in which individuals are confronted with personal decisions.' The distinction that Popper has made between what he calls the open society and its enemies is valid for our own society. However, even if some religions or drugs do induce tribal or barbaric behaviour, they can only have a decisive influence when coupled with economic deprivation. It is the coming together of both these factors that make the barbarian. If we accept barbarian and bourgeois order as valid categories, then it is also true that modern societies are disturbed by cultural, economic and geographic confrontations just as in the past society was disturbed by the confrontation between the proletariat and the bourgeoisie. We are witnessing violent times and the resurgence of alternative utopias which are both pro and anti barbarian. They are anchored in new myths which are in fact today's social realities.

Who are the barbarians? Today immigrants and drug addicts are perceived as such, but are they really as barbaric as they are made out to be? It does seem like it, because they are strange and foreign to bourgeois order; however, bourgeois order has a tendency to exclude or repress them and makes no effort to understand them. By denying them access to the bourgeois order, we are creating the conditions to make all our dire prophecies come true. Bourgeois societies are engendering barbarism precisely because they fear barbarism. Repression and marginalisation as a response to a hypothetical threat leads to the very real threat of the creation of a new social class. Though one wonders, is it so much a new class as a new 'age group'.

THE YOUTHFUL DRIFT

Who is barbarian, if not a child? Till the twentieth century, there is no doubt about it, children were considered savages, and education alone could civilise them. It is only fairly recently that youth has been idealised to such an extent that even the old want to stay forever young. Media, showbiz and advertising just heighten this perception. Sexuality has been given the status of a culture, and the body beautiful exalted to such a point that it has become more important than knowledge and understanding. These are the new norms of our times in which elders are exchanging their authority for youthfulness. In a modern society, adults play at being children. For them, everything has become a game. Even war has become a game at which grown children play. Western soldiers enjoy themselves in front of their video screens without having to lose a single drop of blood (not their own at least) and then return home to the kind of welcome reserved for sports heroes.

Such infantilism in the West becomes all the more disquieting when we shift to the Third World. For the first time in the history of humankind, some countries have a child population which is in excess of their adult population; this is true in Africa, the Maghreb and Latin America. All hope of development is doomed in advance by the very youthfulness of these populations. What is even more worrying is that adults are hopelessly inadequate and incapable of doing their duty, for it is they who have not only to feed their children but give them their culture. In terms of sheer numbers, it has become impossible to bring up so many. In a demographically balanced society, children learnt from their parents and not from the street. Such societies were not modern but archaic. When we say that Africa and Latin America are in the process of becoming barbaric what we mean is that cultural transmission is not occurring because adults have abdicated. Young Algerians or young Moroccans become barbaric the minute they cease to be Algerian or Moroccan and become only young. In this way infantilism is ruining both the economies of the Third World and its civilisation. It is corroding the norms that provide the bulwark for stability and continuity. Barbarians are nomads without any attachment: it is but natural that they migrate to the North.

A BLACK IDEOLOGY

In our societies, counter societies are in the making; marginalism, the black market, unemployment and teenage violence are the bonds that hold them together. Try visiting Argenteuil, Brixton or Los Angeles and you will see. The new classes are products of modern society, just as the proletariat was involuntarily born out of the industrial revolution. It is creating its own system of values and claims. It has its own language and will eventually find its ideologists to justify its rebellion. This is the significance of what we have called the Black Revolution with the Black becoming the archtypal dissident who rejects adult bourgeois order as radically as communism did in its time.

However, the threat to bourgeois order coming from barbarians seems paradoxical as the bourgeois is strong and the barbarian is weak. The threat perceived by the bourgeois and the middle classes is for the most part unfounded, but not entirely so. The corrosion of bourgeois cultural norms under the impact of barbarism is happening here and now. An uneasy bourgeois conscience is contributing to the process of self destruction, what with the media devoting more space to barbaric shows than to the classics and schools following suit. All in all, barbarians are dangerous because they confer legitimacy to populism. Neither immigrants nor drug addicts are powerful enough to pose a real threat to bourgeois order. However, their constant interface is a very real threat indeed.

TO PAY, TO REPRESS OR TO INTEGRATE

These conclusions are bound to be questioned thus making it possible to address the real issues even if basic solutions do not necessarily emerge.

The simplest solution is the one suggested by populist movements. It calls upon us to give up our bourgeois values, advocates recourse to the repression and exclusion of the barbarian using barbaric methods: deportation of immigrants and repression of drug addicts. But for how long can a police State in our cities and on our borders remain bourgeois? It will ultimately become what it seeks to protect us from. Were we to blindly follow the populists, bourgeois order would come to resemble the enemy it is inventing just as the fascists in the past landed up being no different from their communist enemies. Should we wish to avoid this, then the merit of bourgeois order shall be to manage the 'social question' without violence.

What strategic options does the bourgeois order have to defend itself? It can pay, repress or integrate. The French government has opted for the pay and repress strategy: by providing social allowances to appease the marginal sections of society and financing the police force to contain them. Such policies do little to temper barbarism as immigration, unemployment and drug addiction are thriving. They do nothing to incorporate immigrants and drug addicts into bourgeois society; in fact they only serve to exclude them from it. The alternative to the pay and repress strategy is the integration strategy. Unfortunately at this stage France does not have anything like an integration strategy. Integration only exists as antiquated secular cultural discourse. There is not a single concrete economic plan for integration - now the only effective means of integrating barbarians is economic integration. Which just goes to show how hollow French discourse on integration is. This may be attributed to the fact that integration is hard to sell to voters and difficult to manage: it is by no means easy to achieve, nor does it happen overnight. It would require much explaining and not yield spectacular results.

Integration would also require - and this is something that no one ever seems to mention - an effort on the part of both bourgeois and barbarian. For integration to take place, it is not enough to say that 'they' must integrate; we must give them some place in our cities, offices and schools. In Amsterdam and Vienna, we saw how when the bourgeoisie made an effort to integrate drug addiction, it became less visible. Conversely French style non integration forces addicts to the periphery or the underground metro. Are we going to finally accept the fact of drug addiction so as to be able to integrate addicts, or will we turn a blind eye even if it means allowing drug addiction and violence to escalate. Similarly, what are we going to do with immigrants from the Maghreb and Africa and their children? Are we ready to reserve places for them on the job market and in schools, as in the United

States and Canada, to facilitate economic integration, or are we going to keep legal jobs only for those of pure French stock, forcing immigrants to work on the black market?

Once we have answered all these questions, then alone can integration become a policy.

FOR A JUST STATE

A policy of integration assumes, paradoxically enough, less of the State. There is nothing doctrinal about it, the State is just objectively incapable of integrating. The State, by its very nature, restrains and controls: it knows how to close the market but does not have a clue as to how to keep it open; it knows how to bureaucratise but does not have a clue as to how to liberalise. And it is only through the liberalisation of the labour market and private initiative that integration can be achieved. The example of the integration of the work force in the past sheds light on the present situation: bourgeois capitalism integrated workers, not state socialism. Decentralisation is the way to integrate immigrant children so that we can at last have diversified schools. Decriminalisation - once again, the need for a reduced state - would be far more effective in tackling the problem of addiction than the war against drugs. Less State and more private initiative is the best way to remove the North-South imbalance, this being the main reason for the spread of barbarism, immigration and drug addiction.

Unfortunately bourgeois order seems to be succumbing to fatigue, its elite too depleted or sceptical to be effective. In that case, the barbarians will have the last word; bourgeois order will either cave in or there will be a new synthesis. We are entering a new world which will perhaps produce more prophets and artists than the bourgeois society. The barbarian world threatens nonetheless to destroy prosperity and freedom; a look at history will tell us that only bourgeois order has been able to produce both together.

In this quarrel of our century, right and left have lost all meaning, as we lost our traditional moorings. And what does it mean to be a liberal? The answer to my mind is to acknowledge things as they are, be impertinent and work towards the peaceful coexistence of the bourgeois and the barbarian as both are in fact destined to live together.

We would wish to conclude with the following lines of Constantin Cavafys poem, *'Waiting for the Barbarians'*:

Why this sudden bewilderment, this confusion?
(How serious people's faces have become.)
Why are the streets and squares emptying so rapidly, everyone going home lost in thought?
Because night has fallen and the barbarians haven't come.
And some of our men just in from the borders say there are no barbarians any more.
Now what is going to happen to us without barbarians?
They were, those people, a kind of solution.

July, 1992, Boulogne.

WAITING FOR THE BARBARIANS

What are we waiting for, assembled in the forum?

    The barbarians are due here today.

Why isn't anything going on in the senate?
Why are the senators sitting there without legislating?

    Because the barbarians are coming today.
    What's the point of senators making laws now?
    Once the barbarians are here, they'll do the
    legislating.

Why did our emperor get up so early, and
why is he sitting enthroned at the city's main gate,
in state, wearing the crown?

    Because the barbarians are coming today
    and the emperor's waiting to recieve their leader.
    He's even got a scroll to give him,
    loaded with titles, with imposing names.

Why have our consuls and praetors come out today
wearing their embroidered, their scarlet togas?
Why have they put on bracelets with so many amethysts,
rings sparkling with magnificent emeralds?
Why are they carrying elegant canes
beautifully worked in silver and gold?

Because the barbarians are coming today
and things like that dazzle the barbarians.

Why don't our distinguished orators turn up as usual
to make their speeches, say what they have to say?

Because the barbarians are coming today
and they're bored by rhetoric and public speaking.

Why this sudden bewilderment, this confusion?
(How serious people's faces have become.)
Why are the streets and squares emptying so rapidly,
everyone going home lost in thought?

Because night has falled and the barbarians
haven't come.
And some of our men just in from the border say
there are no barbarians any longer.

Now what's going to happen to us without barbarians?
They were, those people, a kind of solution.

BIBLIOGRAPHY

Chapter 1
Han ENTZINGER, *Etnishe minderheden in Nederland*, Mepel (Boom), 1990.
Maarten T'HART, *L'Echelle de Jacob, Actes Sud*, 1991.

Chapters 2 and 3
L'Allemagne d'aujourd'hui, Presses de l'Ecole normale supérieure, December, 1991.
Ernest JUNGER, *Les Falaises de marbre*, Gallimard, Paris, 1960.
Peter SCHNEIDER, *L'Allemagne dans tous ses états*, Grasset, Paris, 1991.

Chapter 4
Five Views of Multiracial Britain - Commission for racial equality, London 1978.
Harry GOULBOURNE, *Ethnicity and Nationalism in Post Imperial Britain*, Cambridge University Press, 1991.
Enoch POWELL, *Freedom and Reality*, Paperfronts Elliott right way books, Kingwood, 1969.
A. SIVANANDAN, *A Different Hunger, Writings on Black Resistance*, Pluto Press, London, 1987.

Chapters 5 and 6
Martin ANDERSON, *Imposters in the Temple*, Simon and Schuster, New York, 1992.
Martin BERNAL, *Black Athena*, Rutgers New Brunswick, 1987.

Stephen CARTER, *Reflections of an Affirmative Action Baby*, Basic Books, New York, 1991.

Cheick Anta DIOP, *Civilisation ou Barbarie*, Présence africaine, Paris, 1981.

Dinesh D'SOUZA, *Illiberal Education*, The Free Press, New York, 1991.

Gertrude EZORSKY, *The Case for Affirmative Action*, Cornell University Press, Ithaca, 1991.

Roger KIMBALL, *Tenured Radicals*, Harper and Row, New York, 1990.

David LEHMANN, *Signs of the Times*, Poseidon Press, New York, 1991.

Nicholas LEMANN, *The Promised Land*, Knopf, New York, 1990.

Ali MAZRUI, *Cultural Forces in World Politics*, James Currey, London, 1990.

Arthur SCHLESINGER, *The Disuniting of America*, Norton, New York, 1992.

Thomas SOWELL, *Preferential Policies*, William Morrow, New York, 1990.

Shelby STEELE, *The Content of Our Character*, St Martin's Press, New York, 1990.

William WILSON, *The Truly Disadvantaged*, Chicago University Press, 1987.

Richard ZWEIGENHAFT and William DOMHOFF, *Blacks in the White Establishment*, Yale University Press, 1991.

Chapter 7

Gary BECKER, *A Treatise on the Family*, Harvard University Press, Boston, 1981.

Wayne CORNELIUS, *The North American Free Trade Agreement and Mexican Migration to the United States*, US Mexican Studies University of California, San Diego, June, 1991.

Chapter 8

Yoshimi ISHIKAWA, *Strawberry Road*, Kodansho, Tokyo, 1991.
Doï TAKEO, *Le Jeu de l'indulgence*, l'Asiathèque, Paris, 1988.

Chapters 10, 11 and 13

Jean-Claude BARREAU, *De l'Islam en général et du monde moderne en particulier*, Le Pré aux Clercs, Paris, 1991.
Guy BOUDIMBOU, *Habitat et Modes de vie des immigrés africains en France*, L'Harmattan, Paris, 1992.
Jean-Claude CHESNAIS, *La Revanche du tiers-monde*, Robert Laffont, Paris, 1987.
Bruno ETIENNE, *La France et l'Islam*, Hachette, Paris, 1989.
Ernest GELLNER, *Nations et Nationalisme*, Payot, Paris, 1989.
Alain GILETTE, Abdelmalek SAYAD, *L'Immigration algérienne*, Entente, Paris, 1984.
Immigrants in two democracies: French and American Experience, edited by Donald Horowitz and Gérard Noireil, New York Univesity Press, 1992.
Christian JELEN, *Ils feront de bons français*, Robert Laffont, Paris, 1991.
Jeanne-Hélène et Pierre Patrick KALTENBACH, *La France, une chance pour l'Islam*, Editions du Félin, Paris, 1991.
Gilles KEPEL, *Les Banlieues de l'Islam*, Le Seuil, Paris, 1987.
Julia KRISTEVA, *Etrangers à nous-même*, Fayard, Paris, 1988.
Camille LACOSTE-DUJARDIN, *Yasmina et les autres de Nanterre et d'ailleurs*, La Découverte, Paris, 1992.
Georges LAPASSADE et Philippe ROUSSELOT, *Le Rap ou la Fureur de dire*, Loris Talmart, Paris, 1990.

Claude LEVI-STRAUSS, *Le Regard éloigné*, Plon, Paris, 1983.

Sami NAIR, *Le Regard des vainqueurs; les enjeux français de l'immigration*, Grasset, Paris, 1992.

Dominique SCHNAPPER, *L'Europe des immigrés*, François Bourin, Paris, 1992.

La France de l'intégration, Gallimard, Paris, 1990. Edited by Michèle TRIBALAT, *Cents Ans d'immigration, étrangers d'hier, français d'aujourd'hui*, INED, PUF, 1991.

Pierre WEIL, *La France et ses étrangers. L'aventure d'une politique d'immigration 1938-1991*, Calamann-Lévy, Paris, 1991.

Fouad, ZAKARIYA, *Laïcité ou islamisme*, La Découverte, Paris, 1991.

Slimane ZEGHIDOUR, *Le Voile et la bannière*, Hachette, Paris, 1990.

Chapter 12

Eric FOTTORINO, Christophe GUILLEMIN, Erik ORSENA, *Besoin d'Afrique*, Fayard, Paris, 1992.

Chedly AYARI, *Enjeux méditerranéens, Pour une coopération euro-arabe*, Alif, Tunis, 1992.

Chapter 14

Alain LABROUSSE, *La Drogue, l'Argent et les Armes*, Fayard, 1991.

Véronique NAHOUM-GRAPPE, *La Culture et l'Ivresse*, Quai Voltaire, Paris, 1991.

Chapter 15

Peter Dale SCOTT, Jonathan MARSHALL, *Cocaïne Politics: Drugs, Armies and the CIA in Central America*, University of California Press, Berkeley, 1991.

Arnold TREBACH, *Drug Prohibition and the Conscience of Nations*, the Drug Policy Foundation, Washington DC, 1990.

National Drug Control Strategy, The White house, Washington DC, 1991.

Chapter 17
Jean-Luc DOMENACH, *Chine: l'archipel oublié*, Fayard, Paris, 1992.
Jonathan SPENCE, *The Search for Modern China*, Hutchinson, London, 1990.

Chapter 18
Gabriel NAHAS, *La Peste blanche du vingtième siècle*, Buchet Chastel, Paris, 1992.

Chapter 19
Alain EHRENBERG, *Le Culte de la performance*, Calmann-Lévy, 1991.
Edited by Alain EHRENBERG, *Individus sous influence*, Editions Esprit, Paris, 1991.
Rapport TRAUTMAN, *Lutte contre la toxicomanie et les stupéfiants*, documentation française, 1990.

Chapter 20
Christian BACHMANN, Anne COPPEL, *Le Dragon domestique*, Albin Michel, 1989.
Peter COHEN, *Drugs as a Social Construct*, University of Amsterdam, 1990.
A.C.M. JANSEN, *Cannabis in Amsterdam*, Coutinho, 1991, Amsterdam.
Isabelle STENGERS, Olivier RALET, *Drogues, le défi hollandais*, Les empêcheurs de penser en rond, Paris, 1991.

Chapter 21
Henri ATLAN, *Tout, non, peut-être*, Le Seuil, 1991.
Francis CABALLERO, *Droit de la drogue*, Dalloz, Paris, 1989.
Thomas SZASZ, *Rituel de la drogue*, Payot, Paris, 1992.

Milton and Rose FRIEDMAN, *Tyrannie du statu quo,* J.C. Lattès, Paris, 1984.

Dealing With Drugs, edited by Ronald HAMOWY, Pacific research institute for public policy, San Francisco, 1987.

Chapter 22

Robert CASTEL, *L'Ordre psychiatrique,* Editions de Minuit, Paris, 1976.

Charles-Henri de CHOISEUL PRASLIN, *La Drogue, une économie dynamisée par la répression,* CNRS, Paris, 1991.

L'Esprit des drogues, revue Autrement, Paris, April 1989.

Claude OLIEVENSTEIN, *Il n'y a pas de drogués heureux,* Robert Laffont, Opéra Mundi, Paris, 1977.

Claude OLIEVENSTEIN, *Destin du toxicomane,* Fayard, Paris, 1983.

Konferenz: *Europaïsche Stadte im Zentrum des illegan Drogenhandels,* Stadt Francfurt-am-Main, November 20, 1990.

Epilogue

C.P. CAVAFY, *Collected Poems,* translated by Edmund Keeley and Philip Sherrand, edited by George Savidis, The Hogharth Press, London, 1984.

INDEX